SOUNDTRACKS: AN INTERNATIONAL DICTIONARY OF COMPOSERS FOR FILM

To

Juliet and Ken Cockroft

in celebration of 30 years of friendship
(1967–1997)

SOUNDTRACKS

AN INTERNATIONAL DICTIONARY
OF COMPOSERS FOR FILM

STEWART R CRAGGS

Ashgate

Aldershot • Brookfield USA • Singapore • Sydney

© Stewart R. Craggs, 1998 *DB# 1496530*

Published by
Ashgate Publishing Limited
Gower House
Croft Road
Aldershot
Hants GU11 3HR
England

Ashgate Publishing Company
Old Post Road
Brookfield
Vermont 05036–9704
USA

Ref.
ML
102
.M68
C73
1998

British Library Cataloguing-in-Publication data.

Craggs, Stewart R. (Stewart Roger)
  Soundtracks: an international dictionary of composers for film
  1. Composers – Dictionaries   2. Motion picture music
  I. Title
  781.5'42'0922

Library of Congress Cataloging-in-Publication data.

Craggs, Stewart R.
  Soundtracks: an international dictionary of composers for film / by Stewart R. Craggs.
  ISBN 1–85928–189–3 (acid-free paper)
  1. Motion picture music—Bio-bibliography—Dictionaries.
  I. Title.
  ML102.M68C73   1997
  781.5'42'0922—dc21   97–19854
  [B]   CIP
                                          MN

ISBN 1 85928 189 3

Printed on acid-free paper

Phototypeset in 10 on 12pt Sabon by Intype London Ltd and printed in Great Britain by Biddles Limited, Guildford.

Contents

Foreword

The concept of 'Moving Pictures' allied to a purpose-written music score is almost as old as the moving picture itself – one of the first examples being the collaboration between Camille Saint-Saens and the Pathé brothers in 1908. In the heyday of the silent movie, cinemas could hire, along with the reels of film, music scores and orchestral parts to be played in the pit by a theatre orchestra – a considerable improvement on the (usually inadequate) upright piano pounding away while a member of the staff banged the rear of the screen to enhance the excitement of a battle scene.

The advent in the early 1930s of the sound-track incorporated with the film itself made it possible for a music score to be completely synchronised with the action, and provided the incentive for composers in the major film-making countries to write full-length scores, thereby enriching the medium enormously and establishing the film score as we know it today.

The list of such composers must be immense and a book such as this will undoubtedly be of great value to all who are interested in the subject.

London 1997   Douglas Gamley

Preface

In the early days of the cinema, critics, the press and the industry itself gave little thought to the background music composed to accompany films. Indeed, the writing of such music was shown even less regard by the world of serious music where it was viewed as commercialisation of the art. Yet almost every modern composer made some contribution to the film.

However, a sea change in attitude occurred in the late 1960s when public perception and appreciation, of this neglected art started to grow and film/record companies issued LPs, and later CDs, of a given film, almost immediately after its release. The famous incident of Sir William Walton's highly original score for *The Battle of Britain* (1968) being rejected or 'pulled' (i.e. completely removed from the soundtrack and replaced by another, by another composer) because it would not fit onto an LP comes to mind. Composers also often felt that their music was wasted in film. Another trend, therefore, has been that suites of their film music have been prepared for concert hall use, thus helping to keep this interest alive.

The present dictionary has been compiled from a wide variety of sources. Very brief biographical details of a composer are given, together with dates, wherever possible. I have followed the practice established in Katz's *International Film Encyclopaedia* (1994) of using the heading 'FILMS' (divided into Feature and Documentary) to indicate that what follows is a complete list of the credits. A partial listing is headed 'FILMS INCLUDE'. Dates given with film titles generally indicate the year of release. Some however reflect the year of a premiere, or the year when a film was completed. Significant scores for television are also mentioned in some entries, as are commercial recordings available on compact disc. A select list of films with music wholly or partly by classical composers and an index of film titles mentioned conclude the volume.

I am most grateful to the following friends and colleagues for help and information, particularly Mrs Mary Alwyn, Christopher Bornett of the Royal College of Music Library, Douglas Gamley for writing the Foreword, Mrs Ann Jeffrey for typing the manuscript, Kevin McBeath, Maureen Murray, Mrs Margaret Reizenstein, Mrs Fiona Searle, David Sharpe, Deputy Head of

Library and Information Services at the British Film Institute, Mrs Bertha Stevens, George Wells for help with the proofs, and Dr Simon Wright.

No compilation can be wholly free from omissions or inaccuracies. I would be grateful, therefore, if readers would let the publishers know of any such defects. Corrections will be incorporated into any reprints and further revisions.

Sunderland 1997   Stewart R. Craggs

Abbreviations

AFU	Army Film Unit
AKS	Army Kinematography Services
arr.	arranged (by); arranger
BAFTA	British Association for Film and Television Arts
BBC	British Broadcasting Corporation
BC	British Council
BFI	British Film Institute
CBS	Columbia Broadcasting System
CFU	Crown Film Unit
COI	Central Office of Information
GPOFU	General Post Office Film Unit
ICI	Imperial Chemical Industries
MGM	Metro-Goldwyn-Mayer
MoI	Ministry of Information
RAF	Royal Air Force
RCM	Royal College of Music
RKO	Radio-Keith-Orpheum
UN	United Nations

ABADY, Temple (1903–1970)
British composer who originally wrote music for the theatre.
FILMS INCLUDE: *Feature*: All over the Town (1949); Both Sides of the Law (1954); Dear Mr Proback (1948); Kill Me Tomorrow (1958); Martin and Gaston (1953); Miranda (1948); The Woman in the Hall (1947). *Documentary*: Boy Builders (CFU, 1947); Hausa Village (Taurus, 1946); Railways (CFU, 1946); The Three As (CFU, 1947).

ABDEL-RAHIM, Gamal (1924–   )
Egyptian composer who studied in Germany. Has written music for the cinema, radio and television.

ADDINSELL, Richard (1904–1977)
British composer who wrote music for the theatre, including revues. Provided the score to Clemence Dane's *Adam's Opera* produced at the Old Vic., London in 1928. Between 1929 and 1932 Addinsell lived in Berlin and Vienna. He returned to England in 1932 and visited America the following year where he signed a six-month contract to write background film music for RKO. He entered films in 1936 with the score to Alexander Korda's film *The Amateur Gentleman*, starring Douglas Fairbanks, Jun. Wrote the popular 'Warsaw Concerto' in the style of Rachmaninov (played by Louis Kentner on the soundtrack) which featured in the 1941 film *Dangerous Moonlight*. Also many songs for Joyce Grenfell.
FILMS INCLUDE: *Feature*: The Amateur Gentleman (1936); Beau Brummel (1954); The Big Blockade (1941); The Black Rose (1950); Blithe Spirit (1945); Contraband (1940); Dangerous Moonlight (1941); Dark Journey (1937); Encore (1952); Farewell Again (1937); Fire over England (1937); Gaslight (1940); Goodbye Mr Chips (1939); The Greengage Summer (1961); Highly Dangerous (1951); Life at the Top (1965); The Lion has Wings (1939); Love on the Dole (1941); Macbeth (1961); Out of the Clouds (1955); Passionate Friends (1949); The Prince and The Showgirl (1957 – his song 'I Found a Dream' was sung by Marilyn Monroe); The Roman Spring of Mrs Stone (1961); Scrooge (1951); Sea Devils (1953); South Riding (1937); A Tale of Two Cities (1958); Tom Brown's Schooldays (1951); Under Capricorn (1949); Vessel of Wrath (1938); Waltz of the Toreadors (1962); The War Lover (1962). *Documentary*: ATS (AFU, 1942); Britain at Bay (MoI, 1940); Camouflage (AFU, 1941); The Day will Dawn (CFU, 1942); A Diary for Timothy (CFU, 1946); The Green Belt (BC, 1941); Men of the Lightship (CFU, 1940); The New Lot (AFU, 1942); The Siege of Tobruk (AFU, 1942); Special Despatch (AFU, 1941); This England (1941); This is Colour (ICI, 1941); Troopship (AFU, 1942); Ulster (MoI, 1940); W.R.N.S. (MoI, 1941); We Sail at Midnight (CFU, 1942).
RECORDINGS: Film Music. Marco Polo 8.223732; ASV CD WHL 2108.

1

ADDISON, John (1920–)
British composer. Since 1948 has written many scores for films and, from the mid-1980s, TV films. Won an Oscar in 1963 for *Tom Jones*.
FILMS INCLUDE: The Amorous Adventures of Moll Flanders (1965); Barnacle Bill (1957); The Black Knight (1954); Brandy for the Parson (1951); A Bridge Too Far (1977); Carlton-Browne of the F.O. (1958); Centennial (TV, 1978); The Charge of the Light Brigade (1968); Cockleshell Heroes (1955); Code Name Emerald (1985); Country Dance (1969); Dead Cert (1974); The Entertainer (1960); A Fine Madness (1966); A French Mistress (1960); Girl in the Headlines (1963); Girl with Green Eyes (1963); Go to Blazes (1962); The Guinea Pig (1949); Guns at Batasi (1964); High and Dry (1954); High Treason (1951); His and Hers (1960); The Honey Pot (1966); The Hour of Thirteen (1952); I was Happy Here (1965); I was Monty's Double (1958); It's Great to be Young (1956); Joseph Andrews (1976); Josephine and Men (1955); The Loneliness of the Long Distance Runner (1962); Look Back in Anger (1959); The Loved One (1965); Lucky Jim (1957); Luther (1973); Make Me an Offer! (1954); The Man Between (1953); Mr Forbrush and the Penguins (1971); One Good Turn (1954); Operation Hurricane (1952); The Peaches (1964); Pearl (TV, 1980); Phantom of the Opera (TV, 1988); Pool of London (1950); Private's Progress (1956); Reach for the Sky (1956); The Red Beret (1953); Ride a Wild Pony (1975); School for Scoundrels or How to Win Without Actually Cheating (1959); Seven Days to Noon (1950); The Seven-per-cent Solution (1976); The Shiralee (1957); Sleuth (1972); Smashing Time (1967); Start the Revolution Without Me (1969); Strange Invaders (1983); Swashbuckler (1976); A Taste of Honey (1961); That Lady (1955); Three Men in a Boat (1956); Time Bomb (1952); To Die For (1989); Tom Jones (1963); Torn Curtain (1966); Touch and Go (1955); The Ultimate Solution of Grace Quigley (1984).
RECORDINGS: A Bridge Too Far. Silva Screen FILMCD151; The Man Between. EMI CDGO2059; Torn Curtain. Silva Screen FILMCD159.

ADLER, Larry (1914–)
American harmonica player and composer. Famous for his score for *Genevieve*.
FILMS INCLUDE: Calling All Stars (1937); A Cry from the Streets (1958); Genevieve (1953); The Hellions (1961); A High Wind in Jamaica (1965); The Hook (1962); Jumping for Joy (1955); King and Country (1964); Many Happy Returns (1934); Playing the Thing (1972); They Found a Cave (1962); Time of the Heathen (1961).

ADLER, Richard (1921–)
American composer and lyricist. Wrote *The Pajama Game* (1957) and *Damn Yankees* (1958) with Jerry Ross (1926–1955).

RECORDINGS: Pajama Game. Koch Schwann 310089.

AGER, Milton (1893–1979)
American composer and vaudeville accompanist. With Jack Yellen, wrote the score for Sophie Tucker's first film, *Honky Tonk* (1929) which included the famous song 'Happy Days are Here Again'.

AKHRON, Joseph (1886–1943)
American violinist and composer of Lithuanian birth. Settled in Russia in 1913 and served in the Russian Army from 1916 to 1918. Toured extensively and in 1925 went to live in America, settling in New York. Wrote many scores including *Spring Night* (*A Night with Pan*), a ballet for the screen (1935).

ALEXANDER, Jeff (1910–1989)
American composer. Wrote scores for many Westerns.
FILMS INCLUDE: The Affairs of Dobie Gillis (1953); All the Fine Young Cannibals (1960); Ask Any Girl (1959); Clambake (1967); Day of the Evil Gun (1968); Dirty Dingus Magee (1970); Double Trouble (1966); Escape from Fort Bravo (1953); The Gazebo (1960); The George Raft Story (1961); Gun Glory (1957); The High Cost of Loving (1957); It Started with a Kiss (1959); Jailhouse Rock (1957); Kate Bliss and the Tickertape Kid (TV, 1978); Kid Galahad (1962); Kismet (1955); The Mating Game (1958); The Murder Men (1962); Party Girl (1958); Prisoner of War (1954); Ransom! (1955); Remains to be Seen (1953); Rogue Cop (1954); The Rounders (1964); Saddle the Wind (1958); The Sea Gypsies (1978); The Sex Symbol (TV, 1974); The Sheepman (1958); Slander (1956); Speedway (1968); Support your Local Sheriff! (1968); The Tender Trap (1955); These Wilder Years (1956); Westward the Women (1951); The Wings of Eagles (1956).

ALEXANDER, Van (1915–   )
American composer, author and arranger.
FILMS INCLUDE: Andy Hardy Comes Home (1958); The Atomic Kid (1954); Baby Face Nelson (1957); The Big Operator (1959); I Saw What You Did (1965); Jaguar (1955); The Last Mile (1959); Platinum High School (1960); Senior Prom (1958); Strait-Jacket (1963); Strange Holiday (1969); Tarzan and the Valley of Gold (1965); Twinkle in God's Eye (1955); When Gangland Strikes (1956).

ALNAR, Hasan Ferid (1906–1978)
Turkish composer and conductor. Famous, at the age of 12, as a player of the Turkish psaltery. At 16 he composed an operetta. Later conductor of the

Presidential Philharmonic Orchestra and professor of composition at the State Conservatory.

FILMS INCLUDE: Halici Kiz (1952); Namik Kamal (1949); Streets of Istanbul (1931).

ALWYN, William (1905–1985)

British composer. Also a conductor and flautist, painter and poet. Wrote five symphonies. Began composing for documentary films in 1936 and entered the field of feature films in 1941, scoring many films, notably for Carol Reed.

FILMS INCLUDE: *Feature*: Bedevilled (1955); The Black Tent (1956); Captain Boycott (1943); The Card (1952); Carve Her Name with Pride (1958); The City Speaker (1947); The Crimson Pirate (1952); The Cure for Love (1950); Devil's Bait (1959); Escape (1948); Escape to Danger (1943); The Fallen Idol (1948); Fortune is a Woman (1957); Geordie (1955); Golden Salamander (1950); Great Day (1945); Green for Danger (1946); The History of Mr Polly (1949); The House in the Square (1951); I Accuse! (1958); I Saw a Dark Stranger (1946); In Search of the Castaways (1962); Killers of Kilimanjaro (1959); Lady Godiva Rides Again (1951); Madeleine (1950); The Magic Box (1951); The Magnet (1950); Mandy (1952); Manuela (1957); The Master of Ballantrae (1953); Medal for the General (1944); The Million Pound Note (1954); The Naked Edge (1961); Night of the Eagle (1962); A Night to Remember (1958); Night Without Stars (1951); The October Man (1947); Odd Man Out (1947); On Approval (1944); Penn of Pennsylvania (1941); The Rake's Progress (1945); The Rocking Horse Winner (1949); The Running Man (1963); Safari (1956); Saturday Island (1952); The Seekers (Land of Fury) (1954); Shake Hands with the Devil (1959); The Ship that Died of Shame (1955); The Silent Enemy (1958); The Smallest Show on Earth (1957); Smiley (1956); Squadron Leader X (1942); State Secret (1950); Svengali (1954); Swiss Family Robinson (1961); Take My Life (1947); They Flew Alone (1942); Third Man on the Mountain (1959); Wings over Empire (1939); The Winslow Boy (1948). *Documentary*: Air Outpost (1937); The Birth of the Year (1938); A City Speaks (1947 – music played by the Hallé Orchestra, conducted by John Barbirolli); Daybreak in UDI (1949); Desert Victory (1943); Festival in London (1951); Fires were Started (CFU, 1942); The Future's in the Air (1936); The Harvest Shall Come (1941); HMS Minelayer (1941); A Letter for Ulster (1943); Lifeboats (1937); Mites and Monsters (1938); New Worlds for Old (1937); Peace Thanksgiving (1945); Powered Flight (1953); Royal Heritage (1951); Royal River (1951); Spring at the Zoo (1938); Tunisian Victory (1944); Wales (1942); The Way Ahead (1944); Welcome to Britain (MoI for the US Army, 1944); Winter on the Farm (1942); The Zoo and You (1938).

RECORDINGS: Film Music. Chandos CHAN9243.

AMFITHEATROF, Daniele (1901–1983)
Russian composer and arranger. Educated in Rome. In 1934, while still in Rome, he wrote the score for Max Ophüls's film *La Signora di Tutti*. Emigrated to the USA in 1937, and for two years conducted the Minneapolis and the Boston Symphony Orchestras. In 1939 he went to Hollywood and was appointed by MGM as a composer and conductor.
FILMS INCLUDE: An Act of Murder (1948); Another Part of the Forest (1948); The Big Heat (1953); The Desert Fox (1951); Dr Gillespie's Criminal Case (1943); Dr Gillespie's New Assistant (1942); Edge of Eternity (1959); The Fan (1949); Fraülein (1958); From Hell to Texas (1958); The Get-Away (1941); Guest Wife (1945); Heller in Pink Tights (1960); House of Strangers (1949); Human Desire (1954); I'll Be Seeing You (1943); Lassie Come Home (1943); The Last Hunt (1955); Letter from an Unknown Woman (1948); The Lost Moment (1947); Major Dundee (1965); The Mountain (1956); The Naked Jungle (1954); Northwest Passage (1940); O.S.S. (1946); Salome (1953); La Signora di Tutti (1934); Suspense (1946); That Kind of Woman (1958); Trial (1955); The Unholy Wife (1957); The Virginian (1946).

AMRAN, David (1930–   )
American composer.
FILMS INCLUDE: The Arrangement (1969); The Beat Generation – An American Dream (1987); The Manchurian Candidate (1962); Pull My Daisy (1959); Splendour in the Grass (1961); This Song for Jack (1982); The Young Savages (1961).

ANTHEIL, George (1900–1959)
American composer and pianist of German descent. Studied composition with Ernest Bloch. Moved to Europe in 1922 to pursue a career as a concert pianist. His playing of piano pieces at the Champs Elysées in October 1923 caused a riot which ensured his notoriety. In 1924 Antheil began working with Léger and with the film-maker Dudley Murphy on the *Ballet Mécanique*. Léger and Murphy created one of the first abstract films which was to be accompanied by Antheil's music for 16 player-pianos controlled from a switchboard. However synchronisation of the pianos with one another and with the film proved impossible and the film and the music became autonomous works. He returned to the USA and began composing for Hollywood films in 1935 while continuing his work in the concert hall.
FILMS INCLUDE: Angels over Broadway (1940); Ballet Mécanique (1924); The Buccaneer (1938); Dementia (1953); The Fighting Kentuckian (1949); Harlem Picture (1934); House by the River (1950); In a Lonely Place (1950); The Juggler (1953); Knock on any Door (1949); Make Way for Tomorrow (1937); Millions in the Air (1935); Not as a Stranger (1955); Once in a Blue Moon (1935); The Plainsman (1936); The Pride and The Passion (1957); Repeat

Performance (1947); The Scoundrel (1935); The Spectre of the Rose (1946); Union Pacific (1939); The Young Don't Cry (1957).

Also wrote music for CBS TV documentaries including Hunters of the Deep (1954).

RECORDINGS: Ballet Mécanique. MusicMasters 67094–2; The Pride and The Passion. Cloud Nine Records CNS5001; The Spectre of the Rose. Varèse-Sarabande VSD5207.

APPLEBAUM, Louis (1918–)

Canadian composer and conductor. Studied in New York with Roy Harris, and with Healey Willan. Became staff composer and later music director of the National Film Board of Canada, for which he wrote scores for 42 documentaries including *Action Stations* (1942), *Fortress Japan* (1944), *Ordeal by Ice* (1945) and *New Faces Come Back* (1946). Also worked in New York and Hollywood – his score for *The Story of GI Joe* was nominated for an Academy Award in 1947.

FILMS INCLUDE: Around is Around (1952); Dreams That Money Can Buy (1946 – with Bowles, Cage, Diamond and Milhaud); Farewell to Yesterday (1950 – a documentary with McBride and Mohaupt); Lost Boundaries (1949); The Mask (1961); The Story of GI Joe (1945); Stratford Adventure (1954 – documentary); Teresa (1951); Tomorrow the World (1944); Walk East on Beacon (1952); The Whistle at Eaton Falls (1951).

ARLEN, Harold (1905–1986)

American composer, famous for songs such as 'Over the Rainbow', 'That Old Black Magic', and 'Stormy Weather'. From 1934 turned to composing musicals and films with lyrics by E.Y. Harburg, Johnny Mercer and Ira Gershwin. Many of Arlen's films are musical plays, the most enduring of which is *The Wizard of Oz*.

FILMS INCLUDE: At The Circus (1939); Cabin in the Sky (1943); The Country Girl (1954); Down Among The Sheltering Palms (1952); The Farmer Takes A Wife (1953); Gay Purr-ee (1962); Gold Diggers of 1937 (1936); Here Come The Waves (1944); I Could Go On Singing (1963); Love Affair (1939); Mr Imperium (1950); My Blue Heaven (1950); The Petty Girl (1950); The Singing Kid (1936); The Sky's The Limit (1943); A Star Is Born (1954); Strike Me Pink (1936); Summer Stock (1950); Take a Chance (1933); That Certain Feeling (1956); The Wizard of Oz (1939 – Academy Award for 'Over The Rainbow').

RECORDINGS: Take A Chance. Collins Classic Coll 1137–2; The Wizard of Oz. Phillips Classics 432 109–2PH.

ARNAUD, Léon (1904–   )
French composer and conductor who went to Hollywood.
FILMS INCLUDE: Babes in Arms (1939); The Big Store (1941); Dubarry was a Lady (1943); Easter Parade (1948); Seven Brides for Seven Brothers (1954); Sombrero (1953); Three Little Words (1950); The Thrill of Brazil (1946).

ARNELL, Richard (1917–   )
British composer and conductor. Studied at the Royal College of Music (1933–39) with John Ireland. Lived in and visited the USA for long periods. Music consultant to the London International Film School.
FILMS INCLUDE: *Feature*: The Black Panther (1977); The Third Secret (1964); The Visit (1964). *Documentary*: The Antagonist; Astronaut One (1973); Combat Zone (1969); Farm Front (US Department of Agriculture, 1942); The Land (US Department of Agriculture, 1941); Masters of Animation (with David Hewson, electronics).

ARNOLD, David (1962–   )
British composer. Began by scoring many of Danny Cannon's student films. Unlike Cannon, Arnold was turned down when he applied to the National Film and Television School. The breakthrough came when the director, Roland Emmerick, heard his score for Cannon's film *The Young Americans* (1993). Arnold has also collaborated in writing pop songs for Björk and Shara Nelson. His music for *Stargate* (1994), was conceived on a grand scale, the epic quality of which was continued in *Independence Day* (1996).
FILMS INCLUDE: Independence Day (1996); Last of the Dogmen (1995); Stargate (1994); Trapped in Paradise (1994); The Young Americans (1993).
RECORDINGS: Independence Day. RCA Victor 09026 68564–2; Last of the Dogmen. EastWest 0630 11991–2; Stargate. Milan 74321 24901–2.

ARNOLD, Malcolm (Sir Malcolm Arnold) (1921–   )
British composer, conductor and trumpeter. Has composed nine symphonies and was a member of the London Philharmonic Orchestra (1942–48). His most famous work was for David Lean: *The Sound Barrier* (1952); *Hobson's Choice* (1954) and *The Bridge on The River Kwai* (1957). He and Sir William Walton turned down Lean's request for music to *Lawrence of Arabia* (subsequently composed by Maurice Jarre); Arnold also refused to write the score for *The Blue Max* (taken up by Jerry Goldsmith).
FILMS INCLUDE: *Feature*: Africa – Texas Style (1967); The Angry Silence (1960); Battle of Britain (1969 – orchestrated several sections of Walton's score); Beautiful Stranger (1954); Blind Date (1959); Blue Murder at St Trinian's (1957); The Boy and The Bridge (1959); The Bridge on The River Kwai (1957: Academy Award); The Captain's Paradise (1953); The Chalk Garden (1964); The Constant Husband (1954); David Copperfield (1970); The Deep

Blue Sea (1955); Dunkirk (1958); Four Sided Triangle (1953); The Great St Trinian's Train Robbery (1966); The Heroes of Telemark (1965); A Hill in Korea (1956); Hobson's Choice (1953); Home at Seven (1951); I am a Camera (1955); The Inn of the Sixth Happiness (1958); The Inspector (1962); Island in the Sun (1957); It Started in Paradise (1952); The Key (1958); The Lion (1962); Man of Africa (1953); The Night My Number Came Up (1955); Nine Hours to Rama (1962); No Love for Johnnie (1961); On the Fiddle (1961); Port Afrique (1956); A Prize of Gold (1955); The Pure Hell of St Trinian's (1960); The Reckoning (1969); The Roots of Heaven (1958); The Sea Shall Not Have Them (1954); Sky West and Crooked (1965); The Sleeping Tiger (1954); Suddenly, Last Summer (1959); Tamahine (1962); The Thin Red Line (1964); Tiger in the Smoke (1956); Trapeze (1956); Tunes of Glory (1960); Value for Money (1955); Whistle Down the Wind (1961); The Woman for Joe (1955); You Know What Sailors Are (1954); *Documentary*: Airways (1950); The Beautiful Country of Ayr (1949); Channel Islands (1952); Hawick, Queen of the Border (1948); North Sea Strike (1967); Report on Steel (1948); The Royal Tour – New Zealand (1954); The Struggle for Oil (1948); Women in our Time (1948).

RECORDINGS: The Bridge on the River Kwai. Columbia mono CK66131; Film Music Chandos CHAN9100.

ARTEMYEV, Eduard (1937–)

Russian composer.

FILMS INCLUDE: At Home Among Strangers (1974); Platanov (1977); A Slave of Love (1976); Solaris (1972); Stalker (1979).

ARUNDEL, Denis (1898–1988)

English actor, producer, author and composer. Read music at Cambridge with Cyril Rootham and C.V. Stanford. Became a professional actor and producer about 1926, appearing on the stage, the radio (famous as radio's Dr Morelle) and television, and occasionally in films. Wrote two operas, a ballet and much incidental music.

FILMS INCLUDE: Lumber (a documentary); A Simple Case (1932 – directed by Vsevolod Pudovkin).

AURIC, Georges (1899–1983)

French composer who studied with Vincent d'Indy. A member of the music group 'Les Six'. In 1924, he was among the Paris intellectuals who appeared in René Clair's avant-garde film *Entr'acte*. Auric's first film score was for Jean Cocteau's experimental *Le Sang d'un Poete* (1930). He wrote about 100 film scores, working with other directors such as Clair, Ophüls, Pascal, Huston, Delannay, Wyler, Cavalacanti and Clouzot.

FILMS INCLUDE: A Nous la Liberté (1931 – directed by René Clair); Abdulla

The Great (1954); Aimez-vous Brahms? (1961); L'arbre de Noel (1969); La Belle et la Bête (1946 – Cocteau); Les Bijoutiers du Clair de Lune (1958); Bonjour Tristesse (1957); Caesar and Cleopatra (1945 – having been rejected by Arthur Bliss); Celui qui doit mourir (1957); La Chambre Ardente (1961); Corridor of Mirrors (1948); Danger Grows Wild (1966); Dangerous Exile (1957); Dead of Night (Ealing, 1945 – his first score for an English film); The Divided Heart (1954); Du Rififi Chez Les Hommes (1955); Father Brown (1954); L'esclave (1953); Gervaise (1956); The Good Die Young (1954); La Grande Vadrouille (1966); Heaven Knows, Mr Allison (1957); Hue and Cry (1946); The Innocents (1961); It Always Rains on Sunday (1947); The Journey (1958); The Lavender Hill Mob (1951); Lola Montes (1955); The Mind Benders (1963); Moulin Rouge (1952); Le Mystère Picasso (1956); Noces de Sable (1948); Notre-Dame de Paris (1956); The Open Window (1952); La P . . . Respectueuse (1952); Passport to Pimlico (1949); Le Rendez-vous de Minuit (1961); Roman Holiday (1953); Ruy Blas (1948); Le Sang d'un Poete (1930); Les Sorcières de Salem (1957); The Spider and the Fly (1949); The Story of Esther Costello (1957); Le Testament D'Orphe ou Ne Me Demandez pas Pourquoi (1959); Thomas L'Imposteur (1964); The Titfield Thunderbolt (1952); Torrents (1946); The Wages of Fear (1953); Walk into Paradise (1956). RECORDINGS: La Belle et la Bête. Marco Polo 8.223765; Moulin Rouge. EMI CZS7 67875–2; The Lavender Hill Mob; Passport to Pimlico; The Titfield Thunderbolt. Silva Screen FILMCD 177.

AXT, William (1888–1959)
American composer who worked almost entirely for MGM in the 1930s as composer and musical director. Helped with and contributed to the music (mainly written by Honegger) for *Pygmalion* (1938).
FILMS INCLUDE: Ben Hur – A Tale of Christ (1925); The Big Parade (1925); La Boheme (1926); David Copperfield (1935); Dinner at Eight (1933); Don Juan (1926); The Flying Fleet (1929); Forsaking All Others (1934); The Kiss (1929); Libeled Lady (1936); Parnell (1937); Piccadilly Jim (1936); The Scarlet Letter (1926); Smilin' Through (1932); Stand Up and Fight (1939); Tell No Tales (1939); The Thin Man (1934); White Shadows of the South Seas (1928).

AYRES, Mark (1960–)
British composer who studied music and electronics with Peter Dickinson, Roger Marsh and Tim Souster. Has also written for television, e.g. *Casualty*, *Doctor Who* and *Rockliffe's Babies*.
FILMS INCLUDE: The Innocent Sleep (1995).

BACALOV, Luis Enriquez (1933–   )
Argentinian composer working in Italy.
FILMS INCLUDE: Il Boss (Murder Inferno) (1973); La Citta Delle Donne (1980); Colpo in Canna (Stick 'em up Darlings) (1974); Coup de Foudre (At First Sight) (1983); Django (1966); Entre Nous (1983); The Man Called Noon (1973); Milano Calibro 9 (The Contract) (1972); La Noia (The Empty Canvas) (1963); The Postman (Il Postino) (1994); Il Prezzo del Potere (The Price of Power) (1969); Quien Sabe? (A Bullet For The General) (1966); Una Rosa per Tutti (A Rose for Everyone) (1966); Seduzione (Seduction) (1973); La Strega in Amore (The Witches) (1966); Le Transfuge (1985); L'Ultima Chance (Last Chance) (1973); Il Vangelo Secondo Matteo (The Gospel According to St Matthew) (1964 – nominated for an Academy Award); Un Verano Para Matar (Summertime Killer) (1971); Una Vergine per Il Principe (A Maiden for a Prince) (1965).
RECORDINGS: Il Postino. CAM Productions COS024.

BACHARACH, Burt (1928–   )
American composer, songwriter, conductor and arranger. Studied music with Darius Milhaud in California. In 1969 he won two Oscars for scoring the film *Butch Cassidy and The Sundance Kid* and for the song 'Raindrops Keep Fallin' On My Head'. Other songs he has written with lyricist Hal David include 'Alfie', 'What the World Needs Now', 'I'll Never Fall In Love Again', 'What's New Pussycat?' and 'Do You Know The Way To San José?', some sung by Dionne Warwick.
FILMS INCLUDE: The April Fools (1969); Arthur (1981 – Academy Awards); Arthur 2: On The Rocks (1988); Best Defence (1984); The Blob (1958); The Boys in the Band (1970 – the song 'The Look of Love' was sung by Bacharach himself); Butch Cassidy and The Sundance Kid (1969 – Academy Awards); Caccia Alla Volpe (After the Fox) (1966); Casino Royale (1967 – theme tune performed by Herb Alpert and the Tijuana Brass); Country Music Holiday (1958); Forever My Love (1962); Lizzie (1957); Lost Horizon (1972); Love in a Goldfish Bowl (1961); Made in Paris (1965); The Man Who Shot Liberty Valance (1962); Night Shift (1965); Promise Her Anything (1965); Send Me No Flowers (1964); Together? (1979); What's New Pussycat? (1965 – Tom Jones had a hit with Bacharach's song); Wives and Lovers (1963).
RECORDINGS: Arthur. Telarc CD80243; Butch Cassidy and The Sundance Kid. Spectrum 551 433–2; Casino Royale. Varèse-Sarabande VSD 5265.

BADALAMENTI, Angelo (1937–   )
American composer. Created the music for TV series *Twin Peaks* with Julee Cruise.
FILMS INCLUDE: Blue Velvet (1986); The Comfort of Strangers (1990); Cousins

(1989); Gordon's War (1973); Hotel Room (TV – 1993); A Nightmare on Elm Street III (1987); Twin Peaks (TV, 1990); Weeds (1987).
RECORDINGS: Blue Velvet. Telarc CDTER1127; Cousins. Telarc CD 80243; A Nightmare on Elm Street III. Varèse-Sarabande VSD 47293.

BAKER, Buddy (1918–   )
American composer who worked for Walt Disney films.
FILMS INCLUDE: The Apple Dumpling Gang (1974); The Best of Walt Disney's True Life Adventures (1975); Charley and The Angel (1973); Escapade in Florence (1962); The Fox and The Hound (1981); Geronimo's Revenge (1960); Guns in The Heather (1968); Hot Lead and Cold Feet (1978); The Hound that thought he was a Raccoon (1960); King of the Grizzlies (1969); Menace on the Mountain (1972); The Million Dollar Duck (1971); The Misadventures of Merlin Jones (1963); The Monkey's Uncle (1964); My Dog, The Thief (1969); Napoleon and Samantha (1972 – nominated for an Academy Award); Rascal (1968); Return of the Big Cat (1974); The Shaggy D.A. (1976); Six-Gun Law (1959); Superdad (1974); Treasure of Matecumbe (1976); The Wahoo Bobcat (1963); Wicked Woman (1953); Winnie the Pooh and the Honey Tree (1965).

BAND, Richard (1957–   )
American composer and guitarist. Son of Albert Band (1924–   ), the Italian-born film director and producer who worked with John Huston, and brother of Charles Band (1952–   ), the American producer and director of low-budget horror films, with whom he has collaborated.
FILMS INCLUDE: The Alchemist (1981); Castle Freak (1995); Cinderella (1976); The Day Time Ended (1979); Dr Heckyl and Mr Hype (1980); Dracula's Dog (1977); The Dungeonmaster (1984); Eliminators (1986); End of the World (1977); Fairy Tales (1978); Ghoulies (1984); The House on Sorority Row (1982); Laserblast (1978 – co-written with Joel Goldsmith, son of Jerry); Lunch Wagon (1980); Mansion of the Doomed (1975); Metalstorm: The Destruction of Jared-Syn (1983); Night Shadows (1983); Parasite (1982); Puppet Master III Toulon's Revenge (1990); Re-animator (1985); The Resurrected (1991); Swordkill (1984); Terrorvision (1986); The Tourist Trap (1978); Troll (1985); Zone Troopers (1985).
RECORDINGS: The Alchemist. Intrada MAF7046D; Castle Freak. Intrada MAF7065D; The House on Sonority Row. Intrada MAF7046D; Re-animator. Silva Screen FILM CD082; The Resurrected. Intrada MAF7036D.

BANKS, Don (1923–1980)
Australian composer. Resident in the UK for many years but returned to Australia in 1973. Worked for Hammer films.
FILMS INCLUDE: The Brigand of Kandahar (1965); Captain Clegg (1961);

Crooks in Cloisters (1964); The Evil of Frankenstein (1964); Hysteria (1964); Jackpot (1960); Monster of Terror (1965); The Mummy's Shroud (1966); Nightmare (1963); Petticoat Pirates (1961); The Price of Silence (1960); The Punch and Judy Man (1962); Rasputin The Mad Monk (1965); The Reptile (1966); The Torture Garden (1968); Treasure of San Teresa (1959).

BARBER, Chris (1930–   )
British jazz musician and band-leader who formed his first traditional jazz band in 1949. The renewed interest in traditional jazz in the early 1960s brought wide success to Barber, his wife Ottilie Patterson (the band's singer) and the group.
FILMS INCLUDE: It's Trad, Dad! (1962); Momma Don't Allow (1955).

BARBIERI, Gato (1934–   )
Argentinian composer and jazz saxophonist.
FILMS INCLUDE: Before the Revolution (1964); Diario di un Vizio (1993); Firepower (1979); Last Tango in Paris (1973); The Pig's War (1975); Stranger's Kiss (1983).

BARRON, Bebe (1927–   ) and **Louis** (1920–   )
American composers and pioneers in the field of electro-acoustic music.
FILMS INCLUDE: Forbidden Planet (1956); Heavenly Menagerie (1951).
RECORDINGS: Forbidden Planet. Small Planet/GNP Crescendo PRD001.

BARRY, John (1933–   )
English composer. Formed his own jazz group which provided the backing for the singer Adam Faith and several of his major pop songs. Arranged Monty Norman's theme for the first James Bond film, *Dr No* in 1962, and continued his association with the Bond films until *The Living Daylights* (1987). Barry has won three Academy Awards: two for *Born Free* (1965) and one for *The Lion in Winter* (1968), and has received other Oscars for *Out of Africa* (1985) and *Dances with Wolves* (1990).
FILMS INCLUDE: Alice's Adventures in Wonderland (1972); The Amorous Prawn (1962); 'Beat' Girl (1959); The Black Hole (1979); Body Heat (1981); Born Free (1965); Chaplin (1992); The Cotton Club (1984); Dances with Wolves (1990); The Day of the Locust (1974); Deadfall (1968); The Deep (1977); Diamonds are Forever (1973); A Doll's House (1973); Dutchman (1966); First Love (1977); Follow me! (1971); Four in the Morning (1965); From Russia With Love (1963); The Golden Seal (1983); Goldfinger (1964); Hanover Street (1979); High Road to China (1983); The Ipcress File (1965); It's all Happening (1963); Jagged Edge (1985); King Kong (1976); The L-Shaped Room (1962); The Last Valley (1970); The Legend of the Lone Ranger (1981); The Lion in Winter (1968); The Living Daylights (1987); The Man with the Golden Gun

(1974); Mary, Queen of Scots (1971); Midnight Cowboy (1969); Moonraker (1979); My Life (1993); Never Let Go (1960); Night Games (1979); Octopussy (1983); On Her Majesty's Secret Service (1969); Out of Africa (1985); The Quiller Memorandum (1966); Raise the Titanic (1980); Robin and Marian (1976); Seance on a Wet Afternoon (1964); Somewhere in Time (1980); The Tamarind Seed (1974); Thunderball (1965); Touched by Love (1980); A View To A Kill (1985); Walkabout (1970); The Whisperers (1966); The White Buffalo (1977); The Wrong Box (1966); You Only Live Twice (1967); Zulu (1963).
RECORDINGS: Chaplin. Epic 472602–2; Dances With Wolves. Epic 467591–2; From Russia With Love. EMI CDP795344–2; Goldfinger. EMI CDP795345–2; The Lion in Winter. Columbia CK66133; Midnight Cowboy. EMI CDP748409–2; Moonraker. EMI CDP790620–2; Thunderball. EMI CDP790628–2; A View To A Kill. EMI CDP746159–2; You Only Live Twice. EMI CDP790626–2; Zulu etc. Silva Screen FILM CD022.

BART, Lionel (1930–)
British composer and lyricist. First gained attention during the 1950s with songs and film scores for Tommy Steele. Also had great success with West End musicals such as 'Fings Aint' What They Used To Be' (1959).
FILMS INCLUDE: The Alternative Miss World (1980); Black Beauty (1971); The Duke Wore Jeans (1958); In The Nick (1959); Lock Up Your Daughters! (1969); Man In The Middle (1963); Oliver! (1968); Sparrows Can't Sing (1962); Tommy The Toreador (1959).

BART, Una
British composer who acted as assistant to Ernest Irving in the music department of Ealing Studios.
FILMS INCLUDE: Champagne Charlie (1944).

BARTON, Dee
American composer. Worked with Clint Eastwood as director.
FILMS INCLUDE: High Plains Drifter (1973); Play Misty For Me (1971); Thunderbolt and Lightfoot (1974).

BARTOŠ, František (1905–1973)
Czech composer and writer. Wrote much chamber music and incidental music for plays and films. In later life he gave more of his attention to musicology.

BASKIN, Richard
American composer.
FILMS INCLUDE: The Best Little Whorehouse in Texas (1982); Buffalo Bill and

The Indians or Sitting Bull's History Lesson (1976); Honeysuckle Rose (1980); Nashville (1975); Sing (1989); Welcome to Los Angeles (1976).

BASNER, Veniamen (1924–1996)
Russian composer. Composed much classical music, musicals and 50 film scores. Friend of Shostakovich.

BASSMAN, George (1914–   )
American composer and orchestrator who worked for MGM in the 1930s and 1940s.
FILMS INCLUDE: *Feature*: Babes in Arms (1939); Cabin in the Sky (1943); Go West (1940); Mail Order Bride (1963); Middle of the Night (1959); The Postman Always Rings Twice (1946); Ride The High Country (1962); Too Many Girls (1940 – orchestrations); The Wizard of Oz (1939 – orchestrations). *Documentary*: Japan And The World Today (US Government, 1950).

BATE, Stanley (1911–1959)
British composer. Studied composition with Ralph Vaughan Williams at the Royal College of Music. Won many prizes. Also had tuition from Hindemith in Berlin and Nadia Boulanger in Paris (1936). Wrote works in many genres including four symphonies and four piano concertos.
FILMS INCLUDE: *Feature*: Jean Helion (1946); The Pleasure Garden (1952 – sponsored by the British Film Institute and produced by James Broughton, the film won an award at Cannes in 1953 and starred Hattie Jacques and her husband, John Le Mesurier). *Documentary*: The Fifth Year (1945); Light Through the Ages (1953).

BATH, Hubert (1883–1945)
British composer and conductor. Wrote comic operas, popular cantatas and orchestral works. A pioneer of British film music, Bath raised the standards of film background music from the very beginning and wrote music for the first sound films made in the UK including *Blackmail*, the first British all-talking picture, directed by Alfred Hitchcock for Gaumont-British. In 1933, Bath joined the permanent staff of Louis Levy's music department at the Lime Grove Studios, Shepherd's Bush, working there for almost ten years. He had great success with his 'Cornish Rhapsody' which featured in the score of *Love Story* (1944), but died while working on a new score for *The Wicked Lady* in April 1945.
FILMS INCLUDE: *Feature*: Blackmail (1929); Dear Octopus (1943); The Great Barrier (1937); Kitty (1929 – half sound, half silent); Love Story (1944); Rhodes of Africa (1936 – from which came the march 'Empire Builders'); They Were Sisters (1945); The Thirty-Nine Steps (1935); Under The Green-

wood Tree (1929); Waltzes from Vienna (1934); A Yank at Oxford (1937); Yellow Sands (1938); *Documentary*: The Air Plan (RAF Unit); Operational Height (RAF Unit, 1943).
RECORDINGS: Cornish Rhapsody. Classics for Pleasure CD-CFP9020.

BATH, John (1916–)
British Composer and conductor. Son of Hubert Bath. He served in the Army during World War II, at the War Office film section; editing, composing and conducting music for Army training films.
FILMS INCLUDE: *Feature*: The Voice Within (1946). *Documentary*: According To Our Records (AKS, 1944); A Day In The Line (AKS, 1945); New Hobbies (Shell, 1946); Pool of Contentment (CoI, 1946); Read All About It (AKS, 1945); The Story of D.D.T. (AFU, 1944); Techniques of Instruction (AKS, 1944).

BATT, Mike (1950–)
British composer and producer.
FILMS INCLUDE: Caravans (1978); Watership Down (1978 – theme); Wombling Free (1977).

BANDRIER, Yves (1906–)
French composer and writer. Founded the Institut des Hautes Études Cinématographiques with Marcel L'Herbier in 1945. In 1947 he toured the USA lecturing on the problems of music and film.
FILMS INCLUDE: La Bataille du Rail (1945); Le Château de Verre (1950); Le Lycée sur La Colline (1954); Le Maudit (1947); Le Monde du Silence (1956); Les Sept Péchés Capitaux (1952); Le Tempestaire (1943); Voilà Nous! (1952).

BAX, Arnold (Sir Arnold Bax) (1883–1953)
British composer and pianist. Master of the King's Music (1942–1953). Wrote works in many genres including seven symphonies.
FILMS INCLUDE: *Feature*: Oliver Twist (1948). *Documentary*: Journey into History (1952); Malta G.C. (Crown and RAF/Army Film Units, 1942).
RECORDINGS: Malta G.C. Cloud Nine Recordings ACN7012; Oliver Twist. Cloud Nine Recordings ACN7012.

BAXTER, Les (1922–)
American composer.
FILMS INCLUDE: Beach Party (1963); Bikini Beach (1964); Bop Girl (1957); The Bride and The Beast (1958); The Comedy of Terrors (1963); The Dalton Girls (1957); The Dunwich Horror (1969); Escape from Red Rock (1957); The Fall Of The House Of Usher (1960); Flareup (1969); Fort Bowie (1957); Frogs (1972); Hell's Belles (1969); Hot Blood (1956); House of Sand (1962); How

To Make It (1969); I Escaped From Devil's Island (1973); The Invisible Boy (1957); Macabre (1957); Master Of The World (1961); The Mini-Skirt Mob (1968); Muscle Beach Party (1964); Outlaw's Son (1956); Pajama Party (1964); Panic in Year Zero! (1962); The Pit and The Pendulum (1961); The Raven (1963); Rebel in Town (1956); Revolt At Fort Laramie (1956); Sergeant Deadhead (1965); The Storm Rider (1957); Tales of Terror (1962); Untamed Youth (1957); Wild In The Streets (1968); A Woman's Devotion (1956); The Yellow Tomahawk (1953); The Young Racers (1963).

BAZELON, Irwin (1922–1996)
American composer who studied with Milhaud. Wrote much music for the theatre and television, and author of a book on film music.
FILMS INCLUDE: *Documentary*: Rice (1962).

BEATLES, The
The British pop group from Liverpool which achieved great popularity in the 1960s. It consisted of John Lennon (1940–1980), Paul McCartney (1942–), George Harrison (1943–) and Ringo Starr (Richard Starkey) (1940–). Lennon and McCartney composed hundreds of songs, and the group starred in several films before its dissolution in 1970. Individual members also appeared separately in other films.
FILMS INCLUDE: (as a group): A Hard Day's Night (1964); Help! (1965); Let it Be (1970); Yellow Submarine (1968 – music and images). Paul McCartney wrote the score for The Family Way (1966) and the title song for Live and Let Die (1973).

BEAVER, Jack (1900–1963)
British composer and music director. Associated with music for the silent cinema, and later worked for the BBC scoring radio adaptations of films. Also worked with Louis Levy and the music department at Shepherd's Bush collaborating with Hubert Bath on many early films. In 1934 he became resident composer for the Gaumont-British series *Secrets of Life* and *Secrets of Nature*, and in 1939, in addition to writing music, he conducted the recording sessions.
FILMS INCLUDE: Atlantic Ferry (1941); The Case of the Frightened Lady (1940); The Dark Tower (1942); Flying Fortress (1942); The Night Invader (1942); The Peterville Diamond (1942); The Prime Minister (1940); Showtime (1947); This Was Paris (1941); The Thirty-Nine Steps (1935); The Wife of General Ling (1937).
RECORDINGS: The Thirty-Nine Steps (with Louis Levy). Silva Screen FILM CD159.

BECAUD, Gilbert (1927–)
French composer.
FILMS INCLUDE: Babette Goes To War (1959); Casino de Paris (1957); Croquem-itoufle (1959); Un Homme Libre (1973); La Maison sous les Arbres (1971); Le Pays d'où Je Viens (1956); Les Petits Matins (1962); Toute une Vie (1974).

BECCE, Guiseppe (1877–1973)
Italian composer who originated the 'Kinothek' in Berlin, a catalogued library of music used for the musical accompaniment to silent films (1919).
FILMS INCLUDE: Condottieri (Knights of The Black Eagle) (1937); Hänsel und Gretel (1954); Der Rebell (1932); Tartuffe (1926).

BENJAMIN, Arthur (1893–1960)
Anglo-Australian composer. Wrote operas, chamber music and numerous other pieces which include the popular 'Jamaican Rumba' (1938).
FILMS INCLUDE: *Feature*: Above Us The Waves (1956); The Clairvoyant (1934); Fire Down Below (1957); An Ideal Husband (1947); The Man Who Knew Too Much (1934); The Master of Bankdam (1947); The Return of the Scarlet Pimpernel (1937); The Scarlet Pimpernel (1934); The Turn of the Tide (1935); Under The Red Robe (1937); Wings of the Morning (1936 – the first British Technicolour feature film). *Documentary*: The Conquest of Everest (1953); The Cumberland Story (1947); Lobsters (1936); Steps of the Ballet (1948); Under the Caribbean (1954); Wharves and Strays (1935).

BENNETT, Richard Rodney (1936–)
British composer. Has written works in many genres including operas and three symphonies. His interest in jazz emerges in his film scores from time to time e.g. *Blind Date* (1959).
FILMS INCLUDE: The Angry Hills (1959); Billion Dollar Brain (1967); Billy Liar (1963); Blind Date (1959 – the musical director was Malcolm Arnold); The Brink's Job (1978); The Buttercup Chain (1970); The Devil Never Sleeps (1962); The Devil's Disciple (1959); Equus (1977); Face in the Night (1956); Far From The Madding Crowd (1967); Figures in a Landscape (1970); Four Weddings and a Funeral (1994); Hamlet at Elsinore (1963); Heavens Above! (1963); Indiscreet (1958); Interpol (1957); Lady Caroline Lamb (1972); The Man Inside (1958); The Mark (1961); Murder on the Orient Express (1974 – nominated for an Academy Award); The Nanny (1965); Nicholas and Alexandra (1971 – nominated for an Academy Award); One Way Pendulum (1964); Only Two Can Play (1961); Permission to Kill (1975); The Return of the Soldier (1982); The Safecracker (1957); Secret Ceremony (1968); Song of The Clouds (1957); Voices (1973); The Witches (1966); The Wrong Arm of the Law (1962); Yanks (1979).
RECORDINGS: Murder on the Orient Express. Cloud Nine Records CNS5007.

BENNETT, Robert Russell (1894–1981)
American composer, orchestrator and conductor. Wrote works in many genres including several symphonies, concertos and overtures. From the 1920s to 1960s he was the leading orchestrator for Broadway musicals and scored some 300 among them *Rose Marie* (Friml) (1924); *Showboat* (Kern) (1927), *Oklahoma!* (Rodgers) (1943), *Annie Get Your Gun* (Berlin) (1946), *Kiss Me Kate* (Porter) (1948), *The Sound of Music* (Rodgers) (1959) and *Camelot* (Loewe) (1960). From 1930 he worked in Hollywood film studios.
FILMS INCLUDE: Annabel takes a Tour (1937); Carlot (1938); Fifth Avenue Girl (1938); Fugitives for a Night (1937); Pacific Liner (1938).

BERGMAN, Alan (1925–) and **Marilyn** (1929–)
American songwriters and lyricists. Have several Academy Awards to their credit.
FILMS INCLUDE: Any Wednesday (1966); Harry and Walter go to New York (1976); Le Mans (1971); The Life and Times of Judge Roy Bean (1971 – nominated for an Academy Award); Pieces of Dreams (1970 – nominated for an Academy Award); Shirley Valentine (1989 – nominated for an Academy Award); Stolen Hours (1963); The Thomas Crown Affair (1968 – Academy Award); Tootsie (1982); The Way We Were (1973 – Academy Award); Welcome Home (1989); Yentl (1983 – Academy Award).

BERGSMA, William (1921–)
American composer who studied with Howard Hanson.
FILMS INCLUDE: Titian – The Boy Painter (1945).

BERKELEY, Lennox (1903–1989)
British composer. Studied in Paris from 1926–32. Wrote four symphonies and much vocal music.
FILMS INCLUDE: *Feature*: The First Gentleman (1947–8); Hotel Reserve (1944). *Documentary*: Out of Chaos (1944); The Sword of the Spirit (1942 – for the Catholic Film Society); Youth in Britain (1957).

BERLIN, Irving (1888–1989)
American composer and lyricist. His first big success was the song 'Alexander's Ragtime Band' in 1911. Wrote about 1500 songs and received the Medal of Merit for his patriotic musical *This is the Army* (1943) and the Congressional Gold Medal for his song 'God Bless America'. He also won an Oscar for the song 'White Christmas' which he wrote for the film *Holiday Inn* (1942).
FILMS INCLUDE: Alexander's Ragtime Band (1938 – nominated for an Academy Award); Annie Get Your Gun (1950); The Awakening (1928); Call Me Madam (1953); The Cocoanuts (1929); Coquette (1929); Easter Parade (1948); Follow the Fleet (1936); Glorifying the American Girl (1929); Holiday Inn (1942);

The Jazz Singer (1927); Lady of the Pavements (1929); Mammy (1929); On the Avenue (1937); Sayonara (1957); There's No Business Like Show Business (1954); This is The Army (1943); Top Hat (1935); White Christmas (1954). RECORDINGS: Annie Get Your Gun. EMI CDC7 54206–2; Easter Parade. Philips Classics 446 406–2PH; Follow The Fleet. Philips Classics 446 406–2PH; Top Hat. Philips Classics 446 406–2PH; White Christmas. Philips Classics 446 406–2PH.

BERNARD, Armand
French composer.
FILMS INCLUDE: Adventures du Roi Pausole (1933); Blonde des Tropiques (1957); Coquin D'Anatole (1952); Les Quintuplets au Pensionnat (1953); Les Disparus de St Agil (1938); La Femme en Homme (1931); Le Joueur D'Échecs (1927); The Merry Monarch (1933); Le Million (1931); La Mome aux Boutons (1958); Raphael Le Tatoue (1938); Sous Les Toits de Paris (1930); Trois Jours de Bringue à Paris (1954).

BERNARD, Guy
French composer.
FILMS INCLUDE: Le Chaudronnier (1949); Colette (1951); La Maison de Molière (1956); The Naked Heart (1955); Paris 1900 (1948); La Route des Epices (1953); Le Sel de la Terre (1951); Trois Victoires d'Enfants (1962).

BERNARD, James (1925–)
British composer associated with Hammer horror films.
FILMS INCLUDE: Across the Bridge (1957); The Curse of Frankenstein (1957); The Damned (1961); The Devil Rides Out (1967); Dracula (1958); Dracula Has Risen From The Grave (1968); Dracula – Prince of Darkness (1965); Frankenstein and the Monster from Hell (1973); Frankenstein Created Woman (1966); Frankenstein Must Be Destroyed (1969); The Gorgon (1964); Greece the Immortal Land (1958); The Horror of Frankenstein (1970); The Hound of the Baskervilles (1959); Kiss of The Vampire (1962); The Legend of the 7 Golden Vampires (1974); Nor The Moon By Night (1958); Pacific Destiny (1956); A Place For Gold (1960); The Plague of The Zombies (1966); Quatermass 2 (1957); The Scars of Dracula (1970); The Secret of Blood Island (1964); She (1965); Taste The Blood of Dracula (1969); The Terror of The Tongs (1960); Windom's Way (1957); X The Unknown (1956).
RECORDINGS: Dracula Has Risen From The Grave. Silva Screen FILM CD714; Taste The Blood of Dracula. Silva Screen FILM CD714.

BERNERS, Gerald (Lord) (1883–1950)
British composer and painter. Self taught but had some lessons from Stravinsky.

FILMS INCLUDE: Champagne Charlie (1945 – contributed 2 songs); Halfway House (1944); Nicholas Nickleby (1947).
RECORDINGS: Nicholas Nickleby. EMI CDM5 65098–2.

BERNSTEIN, Charles (1943–)
American composer, mostly for television.
FILMS INCLUDE: Coast to Coast (1980); Cujo (1983); The Entity (1981); Gator (1976); A Green Journey (1990); Hex (1973); The Hunter (1980); Independence Day (1982); Love at First Bite (1979); Love, Lies and Murder (1991); Mr Majestyk (1974); A Nightmare on Elm Street (1984); Outlaw Blues (1977); The Sea Wolf (1993); A Small Town in Texas (1976); Surabaya Conspiracy (1975); Sweet Kill (1971); That Man Bolt (1973); Trackdown (1976); Viva Knievel! (1977); White Lightning (1973).
RECORDINGS: A Nightmare on Elm Street. Varèse-Sarabande VSD47255.

BERNSTEIN, Elmer (1922–)
American composer and conductor. Composed music for US Armed Forces radio shows before entering films. Won an Emmy for scoring television's *The Making of a President* and an Oscar for the original score of the film *Thoroughly Modern Millie* (1967).
FILMS INCLUDE: The Age of Innocence (1993 – nominated for an Academy Award); Airplane! (1980); Airplane II The Sequel (1982); The Amazing Mr Blunden (1972); An American Werewolf in London (1981); Baby The Rain Must Fall (1964); Big Jake (1971); Birdman of Alcatraz (1962); The Black Cauldron (1985); Blind Terror (1971); Bloodbrothers (1978); The Blues Brothers (1980); Bolero (1984); Boots Malone (1951); The Bridge at Remagen (1969); The Buccaneer (1958); By Love Possessed (1961); Cape Fear (1991); The Caretakers (1963); The Carpetbaggers (1963); Cast a Giant Shadow (1966); The Chosen (1981); The Comancheros (1961); Desire Under The Elms (1957); Doctors' Wives (1970); Drango (1956); The Eternal Sea (1955); Fear Strikes Out (1956); Five Days One Summer (1982); From Noon Until Three (1975); Genocide (1981); Ghost Busters (1984); A Girl Named Tamiko (1962); God's Little Acre (1958); Gold (1974); The Good Mother (1988); The Good Son (1993); The Great Escape (1962); Guns of The Magnificent Seven (1968); The Gypsy Moths (1969); The Hallelujah Trail (1964); Hawaii (1966 – nominated for an Academy Award); Heavy Metal (1981); Honky Tonk Freeway (1981); Hud (1962); I Love You, Alice B. Toklas! (1968); The Incredible Sarah (1976); It's A Dog's Life (1955); Kings of The Sun (1963); Legal Eagles (1986); The Liberation of L.B. Jones (1969); Love With The Proper Stranger (1963); The Magnificent Seven (1960); The Magnificent Seven Ride! (1972); The Man With The Golden Arm (1955 – nominated for an Academy Award); Meatballs (1979); Men in War (1957); The Miracle (1959); Nightmare Honeymoon (1972); Rampage (1962); The Rat Race (1960);

Return of The Seven (1966 – nominated for an Academy Award); The Reward (1965); Saddle the Wind (1958); Saturn 3 (1980); The Scalphunters (1967); The Shootist (1976); The Silencers (1966); Slap Shot (1977); Slipstream (1989); Some Came Running (1958); The Sons of Katie Elder (1965); Spacehunter: Adventures in The Forbidden Zone (1983); Spies Like Us (1985); The Story on Page One (1959); Summer and Smoke (1961 – nominated for an Academy Award); Sweet Smell of Success (1957); The Ten Commandments (1956 – offered the commission following the sudden death of original choice Victor Young); Thoroughly Modern Millie (1967); To Kill A Mockingbird (1962 – nominated for an Academy Award); Trading Places (1983); True Grit (1969); The View From Pompey's Head (1955); A Walk in The Spring Rain (1969); Walk on The Wild Side (1962); Where's Jack? (1969); The World of Henry Orient (1963); The Young Doctors (1961); Zulu Dawn (1979).
RECORDINGS: The Age of Innocence. Epic EK 57151; The Comancheros/True Grit. Varèse-Sarabande VCD47236; Genocide. Intrada FMT8007D; The Great Escape. Intrada MAF7025D; The Magnificent Seven/The Hallelujah Trail. Koch International 37222–2; The Ten Commandments. MCA MCAD42320.

BERNSTEIN, Leonard (1918–1990)
American composer, conductor and pianist. Principal conductor of the New York Philharmonic Orchestra from 1957 to 1970.
FILMS INCLUDE: On The Town (1949); On The Waterfront (1954); West Side Story (1961).
RECORDINGS: On The Town. TER CDTER2 1217; On The Waterfront. Philips 432 109–2PH; West Side Story. Sony SK48211.

BEST, Peter
Australian composer.
FILMS INCLUDE: Abracadabra (1982); The Adventures of Barry McKenzie (1972); Barry McKenzie Holds His Own (1974); Crocodile Dundee (1986); Heroes (TV, 1990); Heroes II (TV, 1991); Libido (1973); Petersen (1974); The Picture Show Man (1977); Rebel (1985); We Of The Never Never (1982).
RECORDINGS: Crocodile Dundee. Silva Screen FILM CD009; Heroes I and II. Silva Screen FILM CD112.

BETTS, Harry
American composer.
FILMS INCLUDE: At Long Last Love (1975); The Big Mouth (1967); Black Mama, White Mama (1973); The End (1978); Nighthawks (1981); Richard Pryor Live on The Sunset Strip (1982); A Swingin' Summer (1965); Thank God It's Friday (1978); Winter A-Go-Go (1965).

BIDGOOD, Harry (1898–   )
British composer, music director and dance-band leader. Associated with British musical films, including the George Formby pictures *Bell-Bottom George* (1943); *He Snoops to Conquer* (1944); *I Didn't Do It* (1945); *Let George Do It* (1940); and *George in Civvy Street* (1946). Bidgood was also music director to the Vera Lynn film *One Exciting Night* (1945), and for the Butchers musical *I'll Turn to You*, in which he conducted the London Symphony Orchestra.

BINET, Jean (1893–1960)
Swiss composer who lived in the USA from 1919 to 1923, and in Brussels from 1923 to 1929 when he returned to Switzerland. Wrote ballets and incidental music for the radio and stage.
FILMS INCLUDE: *Feature*: Alice in Switzerland (1940); Château de Chillon (1944); Jim et Jo, détectives (1943); La Kermesse Blanche; L'Oasis dans la Tourmente (1941); La Suisse Musicienne (1939). *Documentary*: Ciné Journal Suisse (1940, 1941 and 1944); Pigeons Voyageurs (Army documentary, 1944).

BINGE, Ronald (1910–1979)
British composer, arranger and organist for a silent cinema that had a small orchestra. Later became an arranger for Mantovani, before and after World War II, when he reorganised the Mantovani Orchestra and created its distinctive sound. His 'Elizabethan Serenade', written for the Mantovani Orchestra in 1952 became very popular worldwide.
FILMS INCLUDE: The Adventures of Sadie (1955); Dance Little Lady (1955); Desperate Moment (1953).

BIRTWISTLE, Harrison (1934–   )
British composer who has written works in many genres including opera, ballet and brass band. Has written one score; for Sidney Lumet's (1973) film *The Offence*.

BLACK, Stanley (1913–   )
British composer and band leader. Scored almost 200 films.
FILMS INCLUDE: An Alligator Named Daisy (1955); As Long As They're Happy (1955); Ballad in Blue (1964); The Battle of The Sexes (1959); Behind the Headlines (1956); Blood of the Vampire (1958); Bond of Fear (1956); Bottoms Up (1959); Boyd's Shop (1960); Breakaway (1956); Broth of a Boy (1959); The City Under The Sea (1965); Come Dance With Me (1950); The Cracksman (1963); Crooks in Cloisters (1964); The Day The Earth Caught Fire (1961); Double Bunk (1960); The Double Man (1967); Five Golden Hours (1961); Follow That Horse! (1960); The Full Treatment (1960); Further Up The Creek (1958); Hand in Hand (1960); Hell is a City (1959); House of

Mystery (1961); Impulse (1954); Lili Marlene (1951); The Long and The Short and The Tall (1960); Make Mine a Million (1959); The Man in the Back Seat (1961); The Man Who Wouldn't Talk (1957); Mrs Fitzherbert (1947); My Teenage Daughter (1956); The Naked Truth (1957); Now and Forever (1955); Operation Cupid (1959); Passport to Treason (1956); Petticoat Pirates (1961); The Pot Carriers (1962); The Punch and Judy Man (1962); Rattle of a Simple Man (1964); The Rebel (1960); Rhythm Racketeers (1936); Sands of The Desert (1960); Sparrows can't Sing (1962); Summer Holiday (1962); That Woman Opposite (1957); These Dangerous Years (1957); Tiger By The Tail (1955); Time Lock (1957); Tommy The Toreador (1959); Too Many Crooks (1959); Valentino (1977); The Vicious Circle (1957); Violent Moment (1958); West 11 (1963); What A Crazy World (1963); The Wicked Lady (1983); Wonderful Life (1964); Wonderful Things (1957); A Yank in Ermine (1955); The Young Ones (1961).

BLAIN, Kenneth
British composer. Contributed the song 'The Seaside Band' to the film *The Ghost Train* (1941).

BLAKE, Howard (1938–   )
British composer who has written for the theatre and television as well as the cinema. Had great success with *The Snowman* which includes the classic 'Walking in the Air'.
FILMS INCLUDE: Agatha (1978 – but not used); All The Way Up (1970); Amityville II: The Possession (1982); Amityville 3-D (1983); Blood Relatives (1977); The Changeling (1979); The Duellists (1977); An Elephant called Slowly (1971); Endless Night (1972); Flash Gordon (1980); Granpa (1989); The Hunger (1983); The Lords of Discipline (1982); A Month in the Country (1987 – for which he received the Anthony Asquith award for an outstanding film score); The Odd Job (1978); Riddle of the Sands (1979); Ride of the Valkyrie (1967); Scream for Help (1984); The Snowman (1982); Some Will – Some Won't (1969); Victor/Victoria (1982).
RECORDINGS: Flash Gordon. Silva Screen FILMCD146; A Month in the Country. ASV CDDCA905; The Snowman. ASV CDDCA910.

BLANCHARD, Terence (1962–   )
American composer, jazz trumpeter who has scored four of Spike Lee's films. Played with Art Blakey's Jazz Messengers in the 1980s before leading his own band.
FILMS INCLUDE: Crooklyn (1994); Do The Right Thing (1989); The Inkwell (1994); Jungle Fever (1991); Malcolm X (1992); School Daze (1987); Sugar Hill (1994); Trial by Jury (1994).

BLANE, Ralph (1914–)
American composer who, with Hugh Martin (1914–) as lyricist, wrote 'Best Foot Forward' (1943) and 'Meet Me in St Louis' (1944).

BLISS, Arthur (Sir Arthur Bliss) (1891–1975)
British composer of American descent. Knighted in 1950 and appointed Master of the Queen's Music in succession to Sir Arnold Bax in 1953. His first score to Korda's *Things to Come* (1935) was a landmark in the art of film music composition as much of it was written before the film was shot, and in collaboration with the author, H.G. Wells. He withdrew his score for Bernard Shaw's *Caesar and Cleopatra* (1945) because he was unable to work with the film's producer, Gabriel Pascal. As a result a completely new score had to be written by George Auric. For *Men of Two Worlds* (1945), Bliss used indigenous Tanganyikan rhythms and motifs, particularly in the three-movement piano concerto, 'Baraza', which was played by Eileen Joyce on the original soundtrack.
FILMS: The Beggar's Opera (1952/3 – musical additions and arrangements realised from the original airs by John Gay. Produced by Herbert Wilcox and Laurence Olivier who also played and sang the part of McHeath); Caesar and Cleopatra (1944); Christopher Columbus (1949); Conquest of the Air (1936/7 – much of the score had been cut by the time the film was released in 1940); Men of Two Worlds (1945); Presence au Combat (1945); Seven Waves Away (1956 – the film starred Tyrone Power and the music score included a mouth organ); Things To Come (1934/5); Welcome The Queen (1954 – written in the form of a march which formed the last section and the end titles of this film which celebrated the return of Queen Elizabeth II and Prince Philip from their Royal Tour).
RECORDINGS: Christopher Columbus. Marco Polo 8 223315; Conquest of The Air. Classics for Pleasure CD-CFP4666; Men of Two Worlds. Marco Polo 8 223315; Seven Waves Away. Marco Polo 8 223315; Things To Come. Philips 446 403–2PH.

BLITZSTEIN, Marc (1905–1964)
American composer and pianist. Studied in New York, Philadelphia, Paris (with Nadia Boulanger) and Berlin (with Arnold Schoenberg). Much experimentation in his early works, especially in his theatre music.
FILMS INCLUDE: *Documentary*: Chesapeake Bay Retriever (1936); Hands (1927); Native Land (1941); Night Shift (1942); Spanish Earth (1937 – collaborated with Virgil Thompson); Surf and Seaweed (1931); The True Glory (1945 – jointly produced for the UK's MoI (with music by William Alwyn) and the US Office of War Information (with music by Blitzstein). The film received an Academy Award for best documentary); War Department Manual (1935).

RECORDINGS: Native Land. RCA 09026 62568–2

BLOOD, Dennis
Irish composer who wrote scores for documentary films.
FILMS INCLUDE: *Documentary*: Crofters (1944); Farmer's Boy (1945); The Gen (RAF Newsreel); Power in the Land (1947); The True Story of Lili Marlene (CFU, 1944).

BLORE, John
British composer.
FILMS INCLUDE: The Butler's Dilemma (1944); Welcome Mr Washington (1944).

BLUM, Robert(1900–)
Swiss composer.
FILMS INCLUDE: Der Arzt Stellt Fest (1966); Heidi (1952); Heidi und Peter (Heidi and Peter) (1954); Die Schatten Werden Langer (The Shadows Grow Longer) (1961); The Search (1948); Swiss Tour (1949); Unser Dorf (The Village) (1953); Die Veer im Jeep (Four in a Jeep) (1951).

BLYTON, Carey (1932–)
British composer, and nephew of Enid Blyton, the famous children's writer. Studied in London and Copenhagen. Visiting professor in composition for films, television and radio at the Guildhall School of Music. Has collaborated with the Royal Society for the Protection of Birds by composing music for the Society's films.
FILMS INCLUDE: The Goshawk (1968); Kites are Flying.

BOARDMAN, Chris
American composer.
FILMS INCLUDE: The Color Purple (1985 – nominated for an Academy Award); Johnny Ryan (TV, 1990).

BOCK, Jerry (1928–)
American song composer who wrote *Fiddler on the Roof* (1971) with lyricist Sheldon Harnick (1924–).
RECORDINGS: Fiddler on the Roof. EMI CDP7 46091–2.

BOER, Lodewijk de
Dutch composer.
FILMS INCLUDE: Broken Mirrors (1984); The Family (1973); A Question of Silence (1982).

BOLLING, Claude (1930–   )
French composer and jazz pianist.
FILMS INCLUDE: An Einem Frietag um halb Zwölf (On Friday at Eleven) (1961); Bay Boy (1984); Borsalino (1970); Borsalino and Co (1974); California Suite (1978); Catch Me A Spy (1971); The Hands of Orlac (1961); Ladies Man (1960); Lucky Luke (1971); Le Magnifique (How To Destroy The Reputation Of The Greatest Secret Agent) (1973); Les Mains D'Orlac (1961); On Ne Meurt Que Deux Fois (He Died With His Eyes Open) (1985); Les Passagers (The Passengers) (1976); Silver Bears (1977); Willie and Phil (1980); World in My Pocket (1962).

BONFA, Luiz (1922–   )
Brazilian composer. His interest in Brazilian music was responsible for the worldwide following in the bossa nova, via the score for *Black Orphans* (1958).
FILMS INCLUDE: Black Orphans (1958); The Gentle Rain (1965); The Hours of Love (1965).
RECORDINGS: Black Orphans. Erato 4509–96385–2.

BOTKIN, Perry (1933–   )
American composer.
FILMS INCLUDE: Dance of the Dwarves (1983); Lady Ice (1972); Ordinary Heroes (1986); Silent Night, Deadly Night (1984); Skyjacker (1972); Tarzan The Ape Man (1981); Weekend Warriors (1986); Windmill of The Gods (TV, 1988); Your Three Minutes Are Up (1972).

BOUGHTON, Rutland (1878–1960)
British composer and writer. Composed many operas including *The Immortal Hour* (1912–13). Contributed music to one film: *Lorna Doone* (1934).

BOWIE, David (1947–   )
British pop singer and actor.
FILMS INCLUDE: Absolute Beginners (1986); Cat People (1982 – theme, lyrics, written and performed only); Labyrinth (1986 – songs); When The Wind Blows (1980 – collaborated in composition of the songs).

BOWLES, Paul (1910–   )
American composer and author. Studied composition with Aaron Copland and Virgil Thomson. In 1942 he joined the staff of the *New York Herald and Tribune* as music critic. Wrote much incidental music for the theatre in New York including some for Orson Welles' productions.
FILMS INCLUDE: *Feature*: Bride of Samoa (1933); Dreams That Money Can Buy (1946 – with Applebaum, Cage, Diamond and Milhaud); Senso (The Wanton

Countess) (1954); The Sheltering Sky (1990); Venus and Adonis (1935): *Documentary*: America's Disinherited (1937 – for the Southern Tenant Farmers' Union); Congo (1944 – for the Belgian Government in exile); Roots in the Earth (US Department of Agriculture, 1940). Also composed music for cartoons produced by MGM and Harman-Ising (who originated the *Merrie Melodies* and *Loonie Tunes* cartoon series).

BRADLEY, Scott
American composer and musical director. Scored many cartoons, especially 'Tom and Jerry', after joining MGM in 1934.
FILMS INCLUDE: Courage of Lassie (1946); The First Bad Man (1955); The Yellow Cab Man (1949).

BRAHAM, Philip (died 1934)
British composer and music director who wrote scores for early English talking pictures.
FILMS INCLUDE: City of Song (1930); Dark Red Roses (1929); First Mrs Fraser (1932); Nell Gwynn (1934 – remake starring Anna Neagle); Wedding Rehearsal (1932).

BRANT, Henry D. (1913–)
American composer.
FILMS INCLUDE: *Documentary*: Capital Story (US Office of War Information, 1945); The Pale Horseman (US Office of War Information, 1945).

BRAV, Ludwig
British composer and musical arranger, of German origin who wrote and arranged music for a number of documentary films.
FILMS INCLUDE: *Documentary*: Jerusalem; Petra; Temples of India; Wanderers of the Desert; (Technicolor films from the *World Window* series), together with The House We Live In (CFU); War Front (1941).

BREMNER, Tony (1939–)
Australian composer and orchestrator. Member of the Glyndbourne opera chorus for ten years. Reconstructed Hugo Friedhofer's score of *The Best Years of Our Lives* (1946) for the 1978 re-recording. Has also orchestrated film scores for other composers including Carl Davis, Elmer Bernstein and Maurice Jarre.
FILMS INCLUDE: The Everlasting Secret Family (1988); A Halo for Athuan (1986); Kindred Spirit (1984).
RECORDINGS: Film Music. Southern Cross SCCD1020.

BRICUSSE, Leslie (1931–)
British composer and lyricist. Has worked for the British stage and screen since the mid 1950s and acquired prominence in the late 1960s with several large-budget British and American musical productions. Bricusse won Academy Awards for the song 'Talk to the Animals' from the film *Doctor Dolittle* (1967) and lyrics for *Victor/Victoria* (1982). Also nominated for Oscars for the music and lyrics *Goodbye Mr Chips* (1969), *Scrooge* (1970), and *Willy Wonka and the Chocolate Factory* (1971).
FILMS INCLUDE: Bachelor of Hearts (1958); Bullseye! (1990); Charley Moon (1956); Doctor Doolittle (1967); Goldfinger (1964); Goodbye Mr Chips (1969); Hook (1991); The Iron Maiden (1963); Penelope (1966); Scrooge (1970); Stop The World (1966); Three Hats for Lisa (1965); Tom and Jerry – The Movie (1992); The Very Edge (1962); Victor/Victoria (1982); We Joined The Navy (1962); Willy Wonka and the Chocolate Factory (1971).
RECORDINGS: Scrooge, TER Classics CDTER1194; Stop the World. TER CDTER 1226.

BRIDGEWATER, Leslie (1893–1975)
British composer and music director. Also well known as a conductor and leader of his own orchestra. Wrote much incidental music for the theatre.
FILMS INCLUDE: *Feature*: Train of Events (1949); Walk a Crooked Path (1969). *Documentary*: Down to Earth; Looking Through; Progress; The Village That Found Itself.

BRIEL, Joseph Carl (1870–1926)
American composer who wrote and arranged music to accompany silent films including several by D.W. Griffith (1875–1948).
FILMS INCLUDE: America (1924); The Birth of a Nation (1915); The Dramatic Life of Abraham Lincoln (1923); Intolerance (1916); The Lily and the Rose (1915); Lincoln (1923); The Prisoner of Zenda (1913); Queen Elizabeth (1911); The White Rose (1923).

BRILL, Charles
British composer and conductor. Worked with the Boulting brothers on their early films.
FILMS INCLUDE: *Feature*: Pastor Hall (1940). *Documentary*: Battle of the Books (1941).

BRITTEN, Benjamin (1913–1976)
British composer and pianist. Created a life peer in 1976. Wrote much for radio and the stage, together with twelve operas. Wrote music for one feature film and many documentaries, the first of which was *The King's Stamp* written in April–May 1935.

FILMS: *Feature*: Love From A Stranger (1937 – music conducted by Boyd Neel). *Documentary*: Advance Democracy (Realistic Film Unit, 1938); Around The Village Green (Travel and Industrial Development Association, 1936); Book Bargain (GPOFU, 1937); Calendar of the Year (GPOFU, 1936); Coal Face (GPOFU, 1935); Conquering Space – The Story of Modern Communication (GPOFU, 1935); C.T.O. – The Story of The Central Telegraph Office (GPOFU, 1935); Dinner Hour (British Commercial Gas Association, 1935); Four Barriers (GPOFU/Pro Telephon, Zurich, 1936 – also included music by John Foulds); Gas Abstract (British Commercial Gas Association, 1935 – but not used); God's Chillun (GPOFU, 1935 – but not used until about 1937); How The Dial Works (GPOFU, 1935); The Instruments of the Orchestra (CFU, 1945 – script by Montague Slater. Production for the Ministry of Education); The King's Stamp (GPOFU, 1935); Line to the Tschierva Hut (GPOFU/Pro Telephon, Zurich, 1936); Men Behind The Meters (British Commercial Gas Assocation, 1935); Men of the Alps (GPOFU/Pro Telephon, Zurich, 1936 – includes music by Rossini, arranged by Britten and Walter Leigh); Message from Geneva (GPOFU, 1936); Money a Pickle (GPOFU, 1938 – also includes music by John Foulds and Victor Yates); The New Operator (Empire Marketing Board Film Unit/GPOFU, 1935 – but not used); Night Mail (GPOFU, 1935/36 – includes verse by W.H. Auden); Peace of Britain (Strand Films, 1936); The Savings Bank (GPOFU, 1935); The Savings of Bill Blewitt (GPOFU, 1936); Sorting Office (GPOFU, 1935 – but not used); Telegrams (GPOFU, 1935 – but not used); The Tocher (GPOFU, 1935 – arrangements of Rossini's music); The Way to the Sea (Strand Films, 1936 – includes verse by W.H. Auden).
RECORDINGS: The Instruments of the Orchestra. Beulah IPD13.

BRODSZKY, Nicholas (1905–1958)
Russian composer who lived in Britain and the USA. Studied in Rome, Vienna and Budapest. Wrote his first film music in Vienna in 1930 for a picture featuring Richard Tauber and Gitta Alpar. His first film score in England was for *French Without Tears* (1938).
FILMS INCLUDE: Because You're Mine (1952); Beware of Pity (1946); Carnival (1946); The Demi-Paradise (1944); English Without Tears (1944); Flame and The Flesh (1954); French Without Tears (1938); Latin Lovers (1953); Let's Be Happy (1956); A Man About The House (1947); Meet Me In Las Vegas (1956); The Opposite Sex (1956); Quiet Wedding (1940); Rich, Young and Pretty (1951); Serenade (1956); Small Town Girl (1952); Spy For A Day (1940); The Student Prince (1954); The Toast of New Orleans (1950); Tomorrow We Live (1944); The Turners of Prospect Road (1947); Unpublished Story (1944); The Way To The Stars (1945); While the Sun Shines (1946).
RECORDINGS: Because You're Mine. RCA GD60889; Carnival. EMI

CDG02059; Rich, Young and Pretty. RCA GD60889; The Student Prince (song). RCA 74321 18574–2; The Toast of Orleans. RCA GD60889; The Way To The Stars. EMI CDG02059.

BROEKMAN, David (1902–1958)
American composer who worked on early films at Universal Studios.
FILMS INCLUDE: All Quiet on the Western Front (1930); Frankenstein (1931); Gimme my Quarterback (1934); Mississippi Gambler (1929); The Phantom of the Opera (1925).

BROUGHTON, Bruce (1945–)
American composer whose career started at CBS Television working on series including *Hawaii Five-O*, *Quincy*, *How The West Was Won* and *Dallas*. His first major film score was the unconventional western *Silverado* (1985) for which he received an Academy Award nomination. Broughton returned to the Western with *Tombstone* in 1993.
FILMS INCLUDE: Big Shouts (1987); For Love or Money (1993); Harry and the Hendersons (1987); Honey, I Blew Up The Kids (1992); The Ice Pirates (1984); O Pioneers! (1991); The Prodigal (1984); Silverado (1985); Square Dance (1987); Sweet Liberty (1985); Tombstone (1993); Young Sherlock Holmes (1985).
RECORDINGS: For Love or Money. Big Screen Records 15511–2; Honey, I Blew up the Kid. Intrada MAF7030D; O Pioneers! Intrada MAF7023D; Silverado. Intrada MAF7035 D; Tombstone. Intrada MAF7038D.

BROUWER, Leo (1939–)
Cuban composer.
FILMS INCLUDE: Cantata of Chile (1976); Cuban Fight Against Demons (1972); The Days of Water (1971); Death of a Bureaucrat (1966); The First Charge of the Machete (1968); The Last Supper (1976); Lucia (1969); Vaqueros del Cauto (1965).

BRUNNER, Robert F. (1938–)
American composer who worked for Disney films.
FILMS INCLUDE: The Barefoot Executive (1970); The Biscuit Eater (1972); Blackbeard's Ghost (1967); The Boatniks (1970); The Castaway Cowboy (1974); The Computer Wore Tennis Shoes (1969); Lt Robin Crusoe USN (1966); Monkeys Go Home (1966); Never A Dull Moment (1967); North Avenue Irregulars (1978); Now You See Him, Now You Don't (1972); Smith (1968); Smoke (1970); Snowball Express (1972); The Strongest Man in The World (1975); That Darn Cat (1965); The Wild Country (1970).

BRUNS, George (1914–1983)
American composer whose film scores were almost entirely for Disney Productions.
FILMS INCLUDE: The Absent Minded Professor (1960); The Adventures of Bullwhip Griffin (1965); The Aristocats (1970); Babes in Toyland (1961 – nominated for an Academy Award); Dad, Can I Borrow The Car? (1970); Daring Game (1967); Davy Crockett and The River Pirates (1955); Davy Crockett, King of the Wild Frontier (1954); The Fighting Prince of Donegal (1966); Follow Me, Boys! (1966); Herbie Rides Again (1974); The Horse in The Gray Flannel Suit (1968); How Now Boing Boing (1955); It's Tough To Be A Bird (1969); The Jungle Book (1967); Little Boy Blew (1953); The Love Bug (1968); The Mooncussers (1962); One Hundred and One Dalmatians (1960); Pablo and The Dancing Chihuahua (1972); Ride A Northbound Horse (1969); Robin Hood (1973); Sleeping Beauty (1958 – nominated for an Academy Award); Son of Flubber (1962); The Sword in The Stone (1963 – nominated for an Academy Award); The Tenderfoot (1964); Tonka (1958); The Ugly Dachshund (1965); Westward Ho The Wagons (1956).

BRYARS, Gavin (1943–)
British composer and jazz musician. A member of the group of leading experimental English composers who were influenced by Cage, Satie etc. Has written string quartets and operas.
FILMS INCLUDE: Dynamo (1972); Necropolis (1970).

BUDD, Roy (1947–1993)
British composer and jazz pianist.
FILMS INCLUDE: The Black Windmill (1974); The Carey Treatment (1972); Catlow (1971); Diamonds (1975); Extremes (1971); Fear is the Key (1972); Field of Honour (1986); Flight of the Doves (1971); Get Carter (1971); The Internecine Project (1974); Kidnapped (1971); The Magnificent Seven Deadly Sins (1971); The Marseille Contract (1974); Paper Tiger (1974); Pulp (1972); The Sea Wolves (1980); Sinbad and The Eye of The Tiger (1977); Soldier Blue (1970); Something To Hide (1971); Steptoe and Son (1972); Steptoe and Son Ride Again (1973); The Stone Killer (1973); Tomorrow Never Comes (1977); Welcome to Blood City (1977); Who Dares Wins (1982); The Wild Geese (1978); Wild Geese II (1985); Zeppelin (1971).

BURGON, Geoffrey (1941–)
British composer and jazz musician. Has written much incidental music for television including Dr Who, Testament of Youth, Brideshead Revisited, A Foreign Field, Bleak House and Tinker, Tailor, Soldier, Spy (this includes the famous 'Nunc Dimittis' which entered the pop charts in 1979). His score for Sirens (1994) was 'pulled' and replaced by Rachel Portman's music.

FILMS INCLUDE: The Dogs of War (1980); The Happy Valley (1986); Marks (1982); Monty Python's Life of Brian (1979); Robin Hood (1991); Turtle Diary (1985).
RECORDINGS: The Television Music of Geoffrey Burgon. Silva Screen FILM CD117.

BURNS, Ralph (1922–)

American composer and musical director. Also a jazz pianist and arranger for bandleader Woody Herman. Won Academy Awards for the orchestrations of *Cabaret* (1972) and *All That Jazz* (1979).
FILMS INCLUDE: A Chorus Line (1985); High Anxiety (1977); History of the World Part One (1981); Jinxed! (1982); Lenny (1974); Lucky Lady (1975); Mame (1974); Movie Movie (1978); The Muppets Take Manhattan (1984); My Favourite Year (1982); National Lampoon's Vacation (1983); New York, New York (1977); Perfect (1985); Piaf (1974); Star 80 (1983); To Be Or Not To Be (1983); Urban Cowboy (1980); The World's Greatest Lover (1977); You're A Fool (1989).

BURNS, Wilfred (1917–)

British composer.
FILMS INCLUDE: Adolf Hitler – My Part In His Downfall (1972); Ambush in Leopard Street (1962); The Black Rider (1954); Booby Trap (1956); Breath of Life (1963); The Crooked Sky (1956); Dad's Army (1971); Down Boy! (1964); Enter Inspector Duval (1961); The Hand (1960); The London Nobody Knows (1967); Love Is A Splendid Illusion (1969); The Love Match (1955); Man From Tangier (1957); The Man Who Couldn't Walk (1960); Mark of The Phoenix (1957); Morning Call (1957); Murder in Eden (1961); Not So Dusty (1956); A Question of Suspense (1961); The Runaway (1964); Stock Car (1955); Them Nice Americans (1958); Till Death Us Do Part (1969); You Pay Your Money (1957).

BURWELL, Carter

American composer. Associated with the films of the Coen brothers.
FILMS INCLUDE: And the Band Played On (1993); Barton Fink (1991); Beat (1988); Blood Simple (1984); Checking Out (1989); A Dangerous Woman (1993); Doc Hollywood (1991); It Could Happen To You (1993); It Takes Two (1988); Miller's Crossing (1990); Pass the Ammo (1988); Psycho III (1986); Raising Arizona (1987); Rob Roy (1994).
RECORDINGS: And The Band Played On. Varèse Sarabande VSD5549; Doc Hollywood. Varèse Sarabande VSD 5332; Miller's Crossing. Varèse Sarabande VSD 5288; Rob Roy. Virgin Records CDVMM18.

BUSBY, Bob (1901–   )
British composer and instrumentalist. Started to write for films in 1922 (for UFA in Berlin), followed by a long period of composition and arranging for orchestras in Austria, Hungary, France, Spain and Holland. Started to write for British films in 1932.
FILMS INCLUDE: Give Us the Moon (1944); I'll be Your Sweetheart (1944); King Arthur was a Gentleman (1942); Waterloo Road (1944).

BUTLER, Artie
American composer.
FILMS INCLUDE: Grease 2 (1982); The Howard Experiment (1973); It's Show-time (1976); O'Hara's Wife (1982); The Rescuers (1977).

BUTTING, Max (1888–1976)
German composer who devoted himself particularly to chamber music. Wrote ten string quartets. His Opus 23 is 'Music for a Film'.

BUTTOLPH, David (1902–   )
American composer and music director. Went to Hollywood in 1934 as a conductor and then as a composer of major films, first for Twentieth Century Fox and then for Warner Brothers. Composed scores for westerns and other action films.
FILMS INCLUDE: The Big Land (1957); Boomerang! (1947); The Bounty Hunter (1954); The Burning Hills (1956); Chad Hanna (1941); Chain Lightning (1949); A Cry in the Night (1956); The D.I. (1957); The Deep Six (1958); The Gorilla (1939); Guns of The Timberland (1959); The Horse Soldiers (1959); House of Wax (1953); The House on 92nd Street (1945); I Died a Thousand Times (1955); Jump Into Hell (1955); The Lone Ranger (1956); Lone Star (1951); Long John Silver (1954); The Man Behind The Gun (1953); The Man From Galveston (1963); Manila Calling (1942); My Favourite Blonde (1942); PT 109 (1962); Rope (1948); Santiago (1956); Secret of The Incas (1954); The Steel Jungle (1956); Swamp Water (1941); Target Zero (1955); Ten Tall Men (1951); This Gun For Hire (1942); Westbound (1959).
RECORDINGS: Rope. Silva Screen FILM CD159.

BUTTS, R. Dale (1910–1990)
American composer who worked almost entirely for Republic.
FILMS INCLUDE: Accused of Murder (1956); Affair in Reno (1956); Bal Tabarin (1952); Bells of Coronado (1949); Champ for a Day (1953); City That Never Sleeps (1953); Dakota Incident (1956); Deadline Alley (1955); Double Jeopardy (1955); Down Dakota Way (1949); The Far Frontier (1949); The Fighting Chance (1955); The Fighting Kentuckian (1949); Geraldine (1953); Hell's Half Acre (1954); Hell's Outpost (1954); Hit Parade of 1951 (1950); I Cover

The Underworld (1955); In Old Amirillo (1951); The Last Bandit (1949); The Man Is Armed (1956); Night Time in Nevada (1948); No Man's Woman (1955); North of The Great Divide (1950); Oh, Susanna (1951); The Outcast (1954); Road To Denver (1955); Rock Island Trail (1950); San Antone (1952); Santa Fe Passage (1955); The Savage Horde (1949); The Sea Hornet (1951); Sea of Lost Ships (1953); The Shanghai Story (1954); A Strange Adventure (1956); Stranger at my Door (1956); Sunset in the West (1950); Terror at Midnight (1956); Thunder over Arizona (1956); Too Late for Tears (1949); Toughest Man in Arizona (1952); Trigger, Jr (1950); The Vanishing American (1955); The WAC from Walla Walla (1952); Woman of the North Country (1952).

BYRD, Bretton (1904–)
British composer and music director. Composed music for travelling revues and pantomimes, played in dance bands and conducted for many variety acts. Introduced to Louis Levy in 1930 and joined the music staff at the Gainsborough Studios. Provided incidental music, orchestrations, songs and musical direction for an extensive list of films. Collaborated closely with Yehudi Menuhin during the recording work for the film *The Magic Bow* (1946).
FILMS INCLUDE: Bad Sister (1948); Caravan (1946); The Goose Steps Out (1942); It's Love Again (1936); Look Before You (1948); Love on Wheels (1932); Tony Draws a Horse (1948); A Window in London (1939).

CACAVAS, John (1930–)
American composer. Well known for his work on horror film soundtracks and, more recently, television work e.g. *Kojak* for which he wrote the theme.
FILMS INCLUDE: Airport '75 (1974); Airport '77 (1977); Hangar 18 (1980); Horror Express (1972); Redneck (1972); The Return of Ironside (1993); The Satanic Rites of Dracula (1973); Senza Ragione (1972); Separate Ways (1981); A Time To Die (1983).

CADMAN, Charles W. (1881–1946)
American composer.
FILMS INCLUDE: Captain of The Guard (1930); Double Cross Roads (1930); Drums of Love (1928); The Rubaiyat of Omar Khayyam (1922).

CAILLIET, Lucien (1891–1985)
American composer who wrote for films between 1945 and 1953.
FILMS INCLUDE: The Enchanted Valley (1948); The Fugitive (1947); Fun on a Weekend (1947); Harpoon (1948); Red Stallion in the Rockies (1949); The Secret of my Success (1965); She Wore a Yellow Ribbon (1949); Special Agent

(1949); State Department File 649 (1949); Thunder in the Pines (1949); Tropic Zone (1953); The Winner's Circle (1948).

CALKER, Darrell (1905–1964)
American composer who wrote for films between 1946 and 1960.
FILMS INCLUDE: Adventure Island (1947); Beyond the Time Barrier (1959); Big Town (1947); Case of the Baby Sitter (1947); Chartroose Caboose (1960); Dangerous Millions (1946); A Date with Death (1959); The Fighting Redhead (1949); The Fighting Stallion (1950); From Hell It Came (1957); The Hat Box Mystery (1947); Jewels of Brandenburg (1947); The Marshal's Daughter (1953); My World Dies Screaming (1958); Shoot to Kill (1947); Slaughter Trail (1951); Speed to Spare (1948); Tucson (1949).

CALVI, Gérard (1922–)
French composer.
FILMS INCLUDE: Ah! Les Belles Bacchantes! (1954); Allez France (1964); Astérix et Cléopatre (1968); Barbe-Bleue (1951); La Belle Americaine (1961); Les Compagnons de la Marguerite (1966); Deux Billets pour Mexico (1967); Les Douze Travaux d'Astérix (1975); En Compagnie de Max Linder (1963); La Tulipe Noire (1963).

CAMERON, John (1944–)
British composer.
FILMS INCLUDE: All The Right Noises (1969); The Bermuda Triangle (1978); Black Beauty (1971); Charley-One-Eye (1973); Every Home Should Have One (1969); The Great Scout and Cathouse Thursday (1976); I Will . . . I Will . . . For Now (1975); Kes (1969); The London Connection (1979); Lost and Found (1979); Made (1972); The Man From Nowhere (1976); The Mirror Crack'd (1980); Moments (1973); Moontrap (1989); Morons from Outer Space (1985); Nasty Habits (1976); Night Watch (1973); Out of Season (1975); Poor Cow (1967); The Rise and Rise of Michael Rimmer (1970); The Ruling Class (1971); Scalawag (1973); Sex Play (1974); Silver Dream Racer (1980); The Strange Vengeance of Rosalie (1971); The Stud (1978); Sunburn (1979); The Thief of Bagdad (1978); A Touch of Class (1972 – nominated for an Academy Award); Whiffs (1975); Who? (1974).

CARBONARA, Gerald (1886–1959)
American composer who wrote music for early westerns.
FILMS INCLUDE: Ambush (1939); Arrest Bulldog Drummond (1939); Big Brown Eyes (1936); The Case Against Mrs Ames (1936); The General Died at Dawn (1936); Geronimo (1940); The Gracie Allen Murder Case (1939); Henry Aldrich Haunts a House (1943); The Kansan (1943); The Patriot (1928); Poppy (1936); Sawdust Paradise (1928); Spendthrift (1936); Tombstone – The

Town Too Tough To Die (1942); Trail of the Lonesome Pine (1936); Warming Up (1928).

CARLOS, Wendy (1941–)
American composer. A former engineer and born Walter Carlos. A pioneer in the use of synthesizers.
FILMS INCLUDE: A Clockwork Orange (1971); The Shining (1980); Tron (1982).

CARMICHAEL, Hoagy (1899–1981)
American song composer and lyricist. Gave up the law profession to become a bandleader, arranger and songwriter; 'Stardust' (1931) is one of his most popular songs. Composed songs for many films, starting in 1936. The song 'In The Cool Cool Cool of the Evening', written for the film *Here Comes The Groom*, won an Academy Award in 1951.
FILMS INCLUDE: Anything Goes (1936); Belles on Their Toes (1952); The Best Years of our Lives (1946); College Swing (1938); Gentlemen Prefer Blondes (1953); Here Comes The Groom (1951); Johnny Angel (1945); Johnny Holiday (1949); The Las Vegas Story (1952); Night Song (1947); Road Show (1941); Thanks for the Memory (1938); Timberjack (1954); To Have and Have Not (1944); Topper (1937); Young Man With a Horn (1950).

CARPENTER, John (1948–)
American composer. Also well known as a director of horror films, including the *Halloween* series. Has scored many of his own films, often in collaboration with Alan Howarth, a synthesizer expert. Acknowledges that Herrmann and Morricone are important influences.
FILMS INCLUDE: Assault on Precinct 13 (1976); Big Trouble in Little China (1986); Black Moon Rising (1985); Dark Star (1974); El Diablo (1983); Escape from New York (1981); Eyes of Laura Mars (1978); The Fog (1979); Halloween (1978); Halloween II (1981); Halloween III: Season of The Witch (1983); The Philadelphia Experiment (1984); Silence of the Hams (1994); They Live (1988); Village of The Damned (1995).
RECORDINGS: Dark Star. Varèse Sarabande VSD5327; Escape from New York. Varèse Sarabande VSD47224; Halloween. Varèse Sarabande VSD47230; Village of The Damned. Varèse Sarabande VSD5629.

CARPI, Fiorenzo (1918–)
Italian composer.
FILMS INCLUDE: The Cry (1970); An Eel Worth 300 Million (1971); Giacomo Casanova: Childhood and Adolescence (1969); Italian Secret Service (1968); Out of Frame (1969); Salon Kitty (1976); The Vacation (1971); A Very Private Affair (1962); Without Family (1972).

CARTER, Benny (1907–)
American composer, arranger and jazz alto saxophonist. Has also written music for television features.
FILMS INCLUDE: Buck and The Preacher (1971); A Man Called Adam (1966); Red Sky at Morning (1970).

CARWITHEN, Doreen (1922–)
British composer. Wife (and former pupil) of William Alwyn.
FILMS INCLUDE: *Feature*: The Boys in Brown (1949); The Break in The Circle (1955); On The Twelfth Day (1956 – chosen for the Royal Command Performance); The Stranger Left No Card (1952); Three Cases of Murder (1954). Also worked with Arthur Bliss on Christopher Columbus (1949) and with John Greenwood on Broken Journey (1948). *Documentary*: Britain Now, Can Europe Unite?; Elizabeth is Queen (1953 – official film of the Coronation of HM Queen Elizabeth II); Gun Dogs; Mine's a Miner; Northern Frontier; This Modern Age (a series which included 'Fisheries', 'Gambling', 'Harvest from the Wilderness' and 'Hong Kong'); The Tower; Travel Royal (Pathé); Way of a Ship. Also worked with Ralph Vaughan Williams on Dim Little Island (MoI).

CARY, Tristram (1925–)
British composer, third son of the novelist, Joyce Cary. Became interested in electronic music while serving as a radio operator in the Navy during World War II. Founded the electronic studio at the Royal College of Music. Has written both conventional and electronic music for films and television.
FILMS INCLUDE: Blood from the Mummy's Tomb (1971); The Boy Who Stole A Million (1960); The Ladykillers (1955); A Lecture on Man (1962); Time Without Pity (1957); Town on Trial (1957); A Twist of Sand (1968).
RECORDINGS: The Lady Killers. Silva Screen FILMCD 177.

CASTELNUOVO-TEDESCO, Mario (1895–1968)
Italian composer who wrote music for films in America (where he had settled) between 1941 and 1957. Studied composition with Pizzetti.
FILMS INCLUDE: And Then There Were None (1945); The Black Parachute (1944); Brigand (1952); The Day of The Fox (1957); Everybody Does It (1949); Mark of the Avenger (1951); Night Editor (1946); The Return of The Vampire (1943); Strictly Dishonorable (1951); Time Out of Mind (1947 – with Miklos Rozsa).

CHAGRIN, Francis (1905–1972)
Rumanian-born composer who wrote music for over 200 films (mostly British) from 1934. Pupil of Dukas and Nadia Boulanger in Paris where he scored French films including *Ce Colle* (with Fernandel), *La Lutte pour le Vie*, *La*

Grande Croisière and *David et Goliath*. Settled permanently in London in 1938 and in 1944–46 further studied with Seiber. Organised the music for the BBC Service to the French Resistance movement during World War II.
FILMS INCLUDE: *Feature*: The Beachcomber (1954); Charley Moon (1956); Clue of the Twisted Candle (1960); The Colditz Story (1954); Danger Within (1958); Greyfriars Bobby (1961); In the Cool of the Day (1963); An Inspector Calls (1954); Last Holiday (1950); Law and Disorder (1940); The Man Who Was Nobody (1960); Marriage of Convenience (1960); The Monster of Highgate Ponds (1960); No Time For Tears (1957); The Scamp (1957); Silent Battle (1939); Simba (1955); The Snorkel (1958). *Documentary*: Animal Legends (1938); Behind The Guns (Merton Park, 1940); Behind the Maginot Line (1938); The Bridge (Data Films, 1946); Britain's Youth (Strand, 1939); Canteen on Wheels (Verity, 1941); Castings (Merton Park, 1944); Five Faces (Strand, 1937); Homes for the People (Basic Films, 1945); Near Home (Basic Films, 1945); Picture Paper (Verity, 1946); Telefootlers (Verity, 1941).

CHAPLIN, Charles (Sir Charles S. Chaplin) (1889–1977)
Actor, director, producer, screenwriter and composer. Went to the USA in 1910 with Fred Karno's troupe and was invited to join the Keystone Company. Also worked for Essanay and Mutual. Returned to the USA in 1972 to accept a second special Academy Award for 'the incalculative effect he has had on making motion pictures the art form of this century'.
FILMS INCLUDE: (with music by Chaplin): City Lights (1931); A Countess From Hong Kong (1966); The Gold Rush (1925 – reissued in 1942 with music and commentary by Chaplin); The Great Dictator (1940); A King in New York (1957); Limelight (1952); Modern Times (1936); Monseiur Verdoux (1947).
RECORDINGS: City Lights. Silva Screen FILMCD078; A Countess for Hong Kong. Javo JARO4167–2; Modern Times. Erato 4509–96385–2.

CHAPLIN, Saul (1912–   )
American composer, arranger and musical director. Has composed for vaudeville and the Broadway stage. Entered films in the late 1930s. Has also produced since the early 1960s.
FILMS INCLUDE: An American in Paris (arr. 1951 – Academy Award); Argentine Nights (1940); Give a Girl a Break (1953); High Society (1956); I Could Go On Singing (1963); Interrupted Melody (1955); The Jolson Story (1946); Kiss Me Kate (1953); The Last Time I Saw Paris (1954); Les Girls (1957); Lovely To Look At (1952); Man of La Mancha (1972); Manhattan Merry-Go-Round (1937); Merry Andrew (1957); Seven Brides for Seven Brothers (arr. 1954 – Academy Award); Summer Stock (1950); The Teahouse of The August Moon (1956).

CHATTAWAY, Jay (1946–)
American composer who has written music for action and horror films. Also for television e.g. *Star Trek Voyager* (1994).
FILMS INCLUDE: Bar Sinister (1990); The Big Score (1983); Invasion USA (1985); Maniac (1981); Maniac Cop (1987); Maniac Cop II (1990); Missing in Action (1984); Red Scorpion (1989); Relentless (1989); Rich Girl (1991); Vigilante (1983).

CHÁVEZ, Carlos (1899–1978)
Mexican composer and conductor. Wrote seven symphonies between 1938 and 1960, together with five ballets and an opera.

CHERWIN, Richard
American composer who wrote scores for many westerns.
FILMS INCLUDE: Bandits of the Badlands (1945); The Cherokee Flash (1948); Colorado Pioneers (1945); Conquest of Cheyenne (1946); Days of Buffalo Bill (1946); The Fatal Witness (1945); A Guy Could Change (1946); The Lone Texas Ranger (1945); Marshal of Loredo (1945); Oregon Trail (1945); Rough Riders of Cheyenne (1945); Sheriff of Redwood Valley (1946); The Tiger Woman (1945); Valley of The Zombies (1946); Wagon Wheels Westward (1945).

CHESNEY, Arthur
British composer.
FILMS INCLUDE: The Fortunate Fool (1933); I Know Where I'm Going! (1945); The Lodger: A Story of The London Fog (1926); The Lure of Crooning Water (1920).

CHIHARA, Paul (1938–)
American composer who has also written scores for many television films.
FILMS INCLUDE: Crackers (1983); Crossing Delancy (1988); Dandy, The All-American Girl (1976); Death Race 2000 (1975); Get Killed (1989); I Never Promised You A Rose Garden (1977); The Legend of Walks For Woman (1982); Prince of The City (1981); The Survivors (1983); Sweet Revenge (1976).
RECORDINGS: Crossing Delancy. Varèse-Sarabande VSD5208.

CHRISTOU, Jani (1926–1970)
Greek composer who died in a car accident on his 44th birthday. Lived in Egypt and was educated mainly in England. Settled later in Greece (1960). Wrote a film score for *Oedipus Rex* (1967–68).

CHUDNOW, David

American composer.

FILMS INCLUDE: Adventures of Don Coyote (1947); The Big Show-Off (1945); Dangerous Venture (1947); Happy's Holiday (1947); The Kid Sister (1945); Nabonga (1945); Red Planet Mars (1952); A Song for Miss Julie (1945); Trouble Preferred (1946); Unexpected Guests (1946).

CHURCHILL, Frank (1901–1942)

American composer who worked exclusively for Walt Disney, and was the composer of several popular songs e.g. 'Who's Afraid of the Big Bad Wolf?' (1933).

FILMS INCLUDE: Bambi (1942); Dumbo (1941); Snow White and The Seven Dwarfs (1937); The Three Little Pigs (1933).

RECORDINGS: Bambi. Delos DE3186; Snow White and the Seven Dwarfs. Sony MDK48294/Delos DE3186; The Three Little Pigs. Delos DE3186.

CICOGNINI, Alessandra (1906–)

Italian composer who began writing for films in 1936. Many are written for chamber-size groups, and Cicognini has won recognition for his scores. Composed for De Sica's films of the neo-realist period.

FILMS INCLUDE: Anna Di Brooklyn (1958); The Black Orchid (1958); A Breath of Scandal (1960); La Corona di Ferro (The Iron Crown) (1940); La Fortuna di Essere Donna (Lucky To Be A Woman) (1955); Guardie e Ladri (Cops and Robbers) (1951); It Started in Naples (1960); Il Corsare nero (1936); Il Ladro di Venezia (Thief of Venice) (1949); Loser Takes All (1956); I Miserabili (Les Miserables) (1947); L'Oro di Napoli (Every Day's a Holiday) (1954); Peccato che sia una Canaglia (Too Bad She's Bad) (1955); Quattro Passi fra le Nuvole (Four Steps in the Clouds) (1942); The Pigeon That Took Rome (1962); Summer Madness (1955); Tempi Nostri (A Slice of Life) (1953); Il Tetto (The Roof) (1956); Ulisse (Ulysses) (1953).

CIPRIANI, Stelvio

Italian composer.

FILMS INCLUDE: La Belva (1970); Blandy (1975); City of the Walking Dead (1980); La Classe (1984); Frankenstein – Italian Style (1976); Piranha II: The Spawning (1983); La Polizia Ringrazia (1972); Rage (1984); Rage of Honour (1987); The Stranger Returns (1966); Sweet Sins (1981); La Voce (1982); Vudu Baby (1979).

CLAPTON, Eric (1945–)

British singer, rock guitarist and composer who has written for television e.g. *Edge of Darkness* as well as the cinema. A member of The Yardbirds and Cream in the 1960s.

FILMS INCLUDE: Communion (1989); The Hit (1984); Homeboy (1988); Lethal Weapon (1987); Lethal Weapon 2 (1989); Lethal Weapon 3 (1992); Rush (1991); The Secret Policeman's Other Ball (1982); Water (1985).

CLARKE, Stanley (1951–)
American composer and bass player. Member of the 1970s jazz group Return to Forever and Animal Logic.
FILMS INCLUDE: Book of Love (1991); Boyz 'N' The Hood (1991); Cool as Ice (1991); The Five Heartbeats (1991); Little Big League (1994); Poetic Justice (1993); Watch It (1993); What's Love Got To Do With It? (1993).

CLEAVE, Van
American composer.
FILMS INCLUDE: Blueprint for Robbery (1960); Cinerama Holiday (1954); The Colossus of New York (1958); Conquest of Space (1954); The Devil's Hairpin (1957); Fancy Pants (1950); The Lonely Man (1956); Lucy Gallant (1955); Project X (1967); Quebec (1950); Red, Hot and Blue (1949); Robinson Crusoe on Mars (1964); The Space Children (1958).

CLIFFE, Frederick E.
British composer and song writer. Wrote songs for a number of George Formby films including *Come On George* (1939) and *Let George Do It* (1940).

CLIFFORD, Hubert (1904–1954)
Australian/British composer who was educated in Melbourne and then came to England. Studied at The Royal College of Music under Ralph Vaughan Williams. Worked for the BBC (1941–45). Appointed in 1946 as Music Director to Alexandra Korda's London Film Productions, going in 1947 to Hollywood to study American film music and sound recording methods on behalf of the Korda Group.
FILMS INCLUDE: *Documentary*: Battle of Britain (MoI, 1944); General Election (BC, 1945); Left of The Line (AFU, 1944); Letter from Britain (Merton Park, 1945); Power on the Land (Verity, 1943); Road to Moscow (MoI, 1944); The Second Freedom (Verity, 1943); Shakespeare's Country (Verity, 1945); Steel (Technique, 1944); Their Invisible Inheritance (Merton Park, 1945).

CLOEREC, René (1911–)
French composer.
FILMS INCLUDE: Les Aristocrates (1955); L'Auberge Rouge (Red Inn) (1951); La Blé en Herbe (1953); Le Bois des Amants (Between Love and Duty) (1960); Le Comte de Monte-Cristo (The Story of The Count of Monte Cristo) (1961); Le Diable au Corps (1946); Douce (1943); En Cas de Malheur (Love

is My Profession) (1958); Jeannot L'Intrepide (Johnny Lion-Heart) (1949); La Jument Verte (The Green Mare) (1959); Mademoiselle Strip-Tease (1957); Marguerite de la Nuit (1956); La Neige Etait Sale (The Stain on The Snow) (1954); Occupe-Toi d'Amélia (1951); Parade du Temps Perdu (1948); Le Rouge et le Noir (Scarlet and Black) (1954); La Traversée de Paris (Four Bags Full) (1956).

COATES, Eric (1886–1957)
British composer and viola player. Played in various orchestras. Composed much light music and about 100 songs.
FILMS INCLUDE: The Dam Busters (1954); High Flight (1957); Nine Men (1942 – which included his '8th Army March'); The Old Curiosity Shop (1935).
RECORDINGS: The Dam Busters. Music for Pleasure CC211; Nine Men: The Eighth Army March. Music for Pleasure CC211.

COBERT, Robert (1924–)
American composer who has also written music for television films e.g. *The Wings of War* (1983).
FILMS INCLUDE: Burnt Offerings (1976); House of Dark Shadows (1970); Ladybug, Ladybug (1963); Night of Dark Shadows (1971); Scalpel (1976).

COHN, Arthur (1910–)
American composer whose Opus 38, written in 1941, is 'Bet It's a Boy' for lantern slides and piano quintet.

COLEMAN, Cy (1929–)
American composer usually associated with the lyricist Carolyn Leigh (1926–1983).
FILMS INCLUDE: The Art of Love (1965); Blame It on Rio (song: 1984); Family Business (1989); Father Goose (1964); Garbo Talks (1984); The Heartbreak Kid (song: 1972); Power (1986); Spartacus (1960); Sweet Charity (1968 – nominated for an Academy Award); The Troublemaker (1964).

COLLINS, Anthony (1893–1963)
British composer and musical director (who worked with Herbert Wilcox). Studied composition with Gustav Holst. An orchestral player in the Covent Garden and London Symphony Orchestras. Entered films as a composer and conductor in 1937. Went to the USA in 1939 and settled in Hollywood where he wrote music for many famous films and composed and conducted for the Orson Wells radio programme. Returned to the UK in 1945, and then back to the USA and Hollywood to continue his work for RKO Radio Pictures.
FILMS INCLUDE: The Adventures of Robinson Crusoe (1953); The Countess of Curzon Street (1947); Derby Day (1952); Destroyer (1943); Forever and A

Day (1945); I Live in Grosvenor Square (1945); Irene (1940); Laughing Ann (1953); Nurse Edith Cavell (1940); Odette (1950); Piccadilly Incident (1946); The Rat (1937); A Royal Divorce (1938); Sixty Glorious Years (1938); Sunny (1941); Swiss Family Robinson (1940); Tom Brown's Schooldays (1940); Victoria the Great (1937).

COLLINS, Phil (1951–)
British singer, songwriter and actor. Member of the rock band Genesis.
FILMS INCLUDE: Against All Odds (1984 – song nominated for an Academy Award); And The Band Played On (TV, 1993); Buster (1988 – nominated for an Academy Award); Calamity the Cow (1967); Frauds (1993); Hook (1991); The Secret Policeman's Other Ball (1982).

COLOMBIER, Michel (1939–)
French composer who has written scores for mainly American films.
FILMS INCLUDE: Against All Odds (1984); L'Arme a Gauche (Guns for the Dictator) (1964); The Couch Trip (1988); Un Flic (Dirty Money) (1972); The Forbin Project (1970); The Golden Child (1986); L'Heritier (The Inheritor) (1972); Major League II (1994); The Money Pit (1985); Onze Mille Vierges (Bisexual) (1975); Paul et Michelle (1974); Purple Rain (1984); Ruthless People (1986); Satisfaction (1988); Steel (1979); White Nights (1985); Who's Harry Crumb? (1989).

COLOMBO, Alberto (1888–1954)
Italian composer and musical director who also worked in America.
FILMS INCLUDE: All That I Have (1951); Annie Oakley (1936); Big Leaguer (1953); Chatterbox (1936); Hot Tip (1935); Powdersmoke Range (1935); The Return of Peter Grimm (1935); Seven Keys to Baldplate (1935); The Sickle or The Cross (1949); The Silver Streak (1934); South of Panama (1941); Two in Revolt (1936); Village Tale (1935); You for Me (1952); Zorro Rides Again (1937 – serial).

CONDE, Antonio Diaz (1915–)
FILMS INCLUDE: The Pearl (1948); Plunder of the Sea (1953); Rosanna (1956); The Torch (1950); The White Orchid (1954).

CONSTANTIN, Jean (1925–)
French composer.
FILMS INCLUDE: Candide (1960); Explosion (1972); Love and the Frenchwoman (1960); The Man We Need (1979); Revenge (1978); Shoot the Pianist (1960).

CONSTANTINESCU, Paul (1909–1963)

Romanian composer. Studied at the Bucharest Conservatory and then in Vienna with Schmidt.

FILMS INCLUDE: Drăgus (1944); A Lost Letter (1952); The Mill of Luck and Plenty (1956); Resounding Valley (1949); A Stormy Night (1942); An Unforgettable Night (1940).

CONTI, Bill (1942–)

American composer who had great success with the Rocky films starring Sylvester Stallone. Has also worked with director John G. Alvidgen for whom he has scored over a dozen films including The Karate Kid trilogy. Has also written themes for television series including Dynasty and Cagney and Lacey.

FILMS INCLUDE: The Adventures of Huck Finn (1993); Bad Boys (1983); Betrayed (1988); The Big Fix (1978); Blood In Blood Out (1993); Carbon Copy (1981); Citizens Band (1977); F.I.S.T. (1978); F/X (1985); For Your Eyes Only (1981); The Formula (1980); The Fourth War (1990); Gloria (1980); Goldengirl (1979); Gotcha! (1985); Harry and Tonto (1974); I, The Jury (1981); The Karate Kid (1984); Karate Kid Part II (1986); The Karate Kid III (1989); Lean on Me (1989); A Man, A Woman and A Bank (1979); Mass Appeal (1984); Masters of The Universe (1987); Nails (1991); The Next Karate Kid (1994); Next Stop, Greenwich Village (1975); North and South (1985); Paradise Alley (1978); Private Benjamin (1980); The Right Stuff (1983 – Academy Award); Rocky (1976); Rocky II (1979); Rocky III (1982); Rocky IV (1985); Rocky V (1990); Seconds (1994); The Seduction of Joe Tynan (1979); Slow Dancing in the Big City (1978); That Championship Season (1982); Unfaithfully Yours (1983); An Unmarried Woman (1978); Victory (1981); Year of The Gun (1991).

RECORDINGS: The Adventures of Huck Finn. Varèse Sarabande VSD5418; North and South/The Right Stuff. Varèse Sarabande VSD47250; Rocky. Silva Screen FILMCD139; Rocky II. Silva Screen FILMCD139; Rocky III. Silva Screen FILMCD139; Year of The Gun. Milan 873 025.

CONVERSE, Frederick S. (1871–1940)

American composer. His opera The Pipe of Desire was the first American work to be performed in the New York Opera House. Also wrote five symphonies. Wrote a score for the film Puritan Passions in about 1923–24.

CONVERTINO, Michael

American composer.

FILMS INCLUDE: Aspen Extreme (1993); Bodies Rest and Motion (1993); Bull Durham (1988); Children of a Lesser God (1986); The End of Innocence (1990); The Hidden (1987); Home of Our Own (1993); Queen of Hearts (1989); Wrestling Ernest Hemingway (1993).

RECORDINGS: Children of A Lesser God. GNP Crescendo Records GNPD8007.

COODER, Ry (1947–)

American guitarist, singer and composer of folk and blues music.

FILMS INCLUDE: Alamo Bay (1985); An American Legend (1994); Blue City (1985); Blue Collar (1978); The Border (1981); Candy (1968); Crossroads (1986); Geronimo: An American Legend (1993); Johnny Handsome (1990); The Long Riders (1980); Motion and Emotion: The Films of Wim Wenders (1989); Paris, Texas (1984); Performance (1970); Southern Comfort (1981); Streets of Fire (1984); Trespass (1993).

RECORDINGS: An American Legend. Columbia 745645–2; Geronimo. Columbia 475645–2; Paris, Texas. Warner Brothers 7599–25270–2; Trespass. Sire 9362–45220–2.

COPELAND, Stewart (1952–)

American composer who was formerly the drummer in the group The Police. Has written for both stage and film.

FILMS INCLUDE: Highlander II – The Quickening (1991); Rapa Nui (1994); Rumble Fish (1983); Talk Radio (1988); Wall Street (1987).

COPLAND, Aaron (1900–1990)

American composer who studied in New York and Paris with Nadia Boulanger. Famous for his ballets *Billy The Kid* (1938), *Rodeo* (1942) and *Appalachian Spring* (1944).

FILMS: *Feature*: The Heiress (1949 – Academy Award); The North Star (1943); Of Mice and Men (1940 – nominated for an Academy Award); Our Town (1940); The Red Pony (1949); Something Wild (1961); *Documentary*: The City (1939); The Cummington Story (1945).

RECORDINGS: Music for Films. RCA 09026 61699–2.

COPPOLA, Carmine (1916–1991)

American composer and conductor. Father of Francis Ford Coppola and Talia Shire, and grandfather of Nicholas Cage.

FILMS INCLUDE: Apocalypse Now (1979); The Black Stallion (1979); Blood Red (1986); The Godfather Part II (1974); The Godfather Part III (1990 – song nominated for an Academy Award); Mustang . . . The House That Joe Built (1975); One From The Heart (1982); The Outsiders (1983); The Rain People (1969); Tonight for Sure (1961).

RECORDINGS: The Outsiders. Silva Screen FILMCD152.

CORDELL, Frank (1918–1986)

British composer.

FILMS INCLUDE: The Bargee (1964); The Captain's Table (1958); A Choice of

Weapons (1976); Cromwell (1970); Flight from Ashiya (1963); God Told Me To (1976); Hell Boats (1969); Khartoum (1966); Mosquito Squadron (1968); Never Put it in Writing (1963); Project Z (1968); The Rebel (1960); Ring of Bright Water (1969); Trial by Combat (1976); The Voice of Merrill (1952).

CORIGLIANO, John (1938–)
American composer who studied privately with Paul Creston. Worked for CBS Television (1961–72) and was music director for the Morris Theatre in New Jersey (1962–64).
FILMS INCLUDE: Altered States (1980 – nominated for an Academy Award); Revolution (1985 – won the BFI's Anthony Asquith Award).
RECORDINGS: Altered States. RCA Victor 3983–2.

COSMA, Vladimir (1940–)
Romanian born composer who has worked in France since the 1960s.
FILMS INCLUDE: Alexandre le Bien-Heureux (1967); Appelez-moi Mathilde (1969); Astérix vs Caesar (1985); Les Aventures de Rabbi Jacob (1973); Le Bal (1982); Bonsoir! (1993); Cache Cash (1994); Catherine et Cie (1975); Courage Fuyons (1979); Cuisine et Dépendances (1993); La Dérobade (1979); Diva (1981); Dracula and Son (1976); Un Eléphant ça Trompe Enormément (1976); Les Félines (1972); Le Mari de Léon (1993); Le Moutarde me Monte au Nez (1974); Neither by Day nor by Night (1972); Nous Irons Tous au Paradis (1977); Le Prix du Danger (1983); Le Retour du Grand Blond (1974); Rue Saint-Sulpice (1991); Salut L'Artiste (1973); La Soif de L'Or (1993); Le Souper (1992); Le Téléphone Rose (1975).

COURAGE, Alexander (1919–)
American composer, arranger and orchestrator who worked for CBS Radio as well as collaborating with André Previn and Adolph Deutsch as an arranger for MGM. Has also scored music for television e.g. *Lost in Space*, *The Waltons* and *Voyage to the Bottom of the Sea*. Also well known for his work on the original *Star Trek* series, and as an orchestrator for both John Williams (*Jurassic Park*) and Jerry Goldsmith (*Bad Girls* etc.).
FILMS INCLUDE: Day of The Outlaw (1959); Doctor Dolittle (1967); Follow the Boys (1963); Handle with Care (1958); Heart like a Wheel (1983); Hot Rod Rumble (1957); The Island of Dr Moreau (1977); The Left Handed Gun (1957); Legend (1985); My Fair Lady (1964); The Poseidon Adventure (1972); Shake, Rattle and Rock! (1956); Sierra Stranger (1956); Tokyo after Dark (1958); Undersea Girl (1957); The Unsinkable Molly Brown (1964).

COWARD, Noel (Sir Noel Coward) (1899–1973)
British actor, writer and composer. First appeared on the stage in 1910. Associated with the great successes like *Bitter Sweet*, *Cavalcade* and *Private*

Lives. He composed music themes for his films *Cavalcade* (1933); *In Which We Serve* (1942) and *This Happy Breed* (1944).

COWELL, Henry D. (1897–1965)
American composer and pianist who in 1912 devised the piano technique known as 'clusters'. A friend and biographer of Charles Ives, and teacher of Gershwin and Cage. Wrote 21 symphonies.
FILMS INCLUDE: Mr Flagmaker (1942).

CRESTON, Paul (1906–1985)
American composer and organist of Italian origin. Wrote six symphonies.
FILMS INCLUDE: *Documentary*: Brought into Action (US Navy, 1945).

CURB, Michael
American composer.
FILMS INCLUDE: The Big Bounce (1968); The Born Losers (1967); Devil's Angels (1967); The Devil's Eight (1969); Five the Hard Way (1969); Hot Rod Action (1969); Killers Three (1968); Skaterdater (1965); Teenage Rebellion (1967); . . .Tick . . .Tick . . .Tick (1969); The Wild Angels (1966).

CURTIN, Hoyt
American composer who has succcessfully written for television as well as the cinema. Television hits include *The Adventures of Johnny Quest*, *The Banana Splits*, *Dastardly and Mutley in their Flying Machines*, *The Flintstones*, *Huckleberry Hound*, *Scooby Doo, Where Are You?* and *The Smurfs*.
FILMS INCLUDE: Champs (1979); Cyrano (1974); Heidi's Song (1982).

CURZON, Frederick (1899–1973)
British composer and organist. At the age of 20 he was conducting and composing accompaniments for silent films. Later progressed to more ambitious sound picture scores, especially music to documentaries. Also famous for his contribution to British light music.

DALE, Jim (1935–   )
British pop singer, actor, comedian (member of the 'Carry On' team) composer (wrote the theme song of *Shalako*, 1968) and lyricist (nominated for an Oscar for writing the lyrics to the title tune for *Georgy Girl*, 1964). Has also composed music and written lyrics for several of his own stage and television productions.

DALLAPICCOLA, Luigi (1904–1975)
Italian composer, pianist and writer. Interested in, and influenced by, the music of Debussy, Monteverdi and Gesualdo. Wrote three film scores (1948 – now lost; 1948 – lost; and 1953).

DALTREY, Roger (1945–)
British rock singer, actor, composer and producer. The lead singer with The Who, he was given several dramatic roles by the director Ken Russell, including the lead in *Tommy* for which he wrote part of the score.

DANKWORTH, John (1927–)
British bandleader, jazz musician and composer. Toured widely with Cleo Laine, who began singing with his band in 1953, and who became his wife in 1960. Has written several large scale suites and *Lysistrata*, an opera-ballet.
FILMS INCLUDE: Accident (1967); All Night Long (1961); Boom (1968); The Criminal (1960); Darling (1965); The Engagement (1969); Fathom (1967); The Idol (1966); The Last Grenade (1969); The Last Safari (1967); Loser Takes All (1989); Magus (1968); Modesty Blaise (1966); Morgan: a Suitable Case for Treatment (1966); Night of 100 Stars (1977); Perfect Friday (1970); Return from the Ashes (1965); Salt and Pepper (1968); Sands of the Kalahari (1965); Saturday Night and Sunday Morning (1960); The Servant (1963); Ten Rillington Place (1970); We Are The Lambeth Boys (1959).

DARBY, Ken (1909–1992)
American composer and arranger who was involved in many musicals adapted for the screen e.g. *The King and I* (1956) and *Flower Drum Song* (1961).
FILMS INCLUDE: The Canadians (1961).

DARING, Mason (1949–)
American composer often associated with director John Sayles.
FILMS INCLUDE: The Brother from another Planet (1984); City of Hope (1991); Eight Men Out (1988); The Laserman (1988); Little Vegas (1990); Matewan (1987); Passion Fish (1992); Return of the Secaucus Seven (1980); The Secret of Roan Inish (1994); Wild Hearts Can't Be Broken (1991).

DARTON, Christian (1905–1981)
British composer. Studied with Harry Farjeon, Charles Wood and Gordon Jacob. Works include an opera and three symphonies. His first experience in film music was the composition of title music for the RAF newsreel *The Gen* in 1944.
FILMS INCLUDE: *Documentary*: The Antwerp Story (AFU, 1945); Birth Day (Data Films, 1945); The Channel Islands (CFU, 1945); Green Fields Beyond (Canadian AFU, 1946); A Harbour Goes to France (CFU, 1945); Marine

Salvage (Data Films, 1945); Muscle Menders (AFU, 1945); River Tyne (Merlin Films, 1945); Route to Moscow (MoI, 1944 – with Hubert Clifford etc); You Can't Kill a City (Canadian AFU, 1945).

DAVIE, Cedric Thorpe (1913–1983)

Scottish composer who studied at the Royal Scottish Academy of Music in Glasgow. Master of music to St Andrews University (1945), and founded the Department of Music there in 1947, becoming reader in 1956 and professor (1973–78). Has written several comic operas and his symphony won a prize in a newspaper competition in 1945.

FILMS INCLUDE: *Feature*: The Bridal Path (1959); The Brothers (1947); The Dark Avenger (1955); The Green Man (1956); The Heart is Highland (1952); Jacqueline (1956); The Kid from Canada (1957); Kidnapped (1960); Oedipus Rex (1957); Rockets Galore (1958); A Terrible Beauty (1960). *Documentary*: Scotland Speaks.

DAVIES, Hubert

British composer and arranger.

FILMS INCLUDE: *Documentary*: The Hidden Land (Visionor Educational Films, 1937).

DAVIES, Peter Maxwell (1934–   )

British composer, educated at the Royal Manchester College of Music (1952–6) with several other outstandingly gifted musicians, notably Harrison Birtwistle, Alexander Goehr and John Ogdon. Has written music in many genres including ballet and opera.

FILMS INCLUDE: The Boyfriend (1971 – after Sandy Wilson); The Devils (1971), both directed by Ken Russell.

RECORDINGS: The Boyfriend. Collins Coll 1095–2; The Devils. Collins Coll 1095–2.

DAVIS, Carl (1936–   )

American composer, living in the UK since 1961. Well known for his scores to silent films e.g. *Ben-Hur* (1925); *The Crowd* (1928); *Napoléon* (1927). Has also written music for many revues, including *That Was The Week That Was*, the stage and British television.

FILMS INCLUDE: Bedtime (1967); The Bofors Gun (1968); Champions (1983); Frankenstein Unbound (1990); The French Lieutenant's Woman (1981); Halfway Round the Circle Now (1979); I, Monster (1971); Intolerance (1916); King David (1985); The Late Great Planet Earth (1976); The Lovers! (1972); Man Friday (1975); The National Health (1973); The Other World of Winston Churchill (1966); Praise Marx and pass the Ammunition (1968); Pride and Prejudice (1995); The Rainbow (1989); Rentadick (1972); The Secret life of

Ian Fleming (1989); The Secret Policeman's Other Ball (1982); The Trial (1992); Up Pompeii (1971); Up The Chastity Belt (1971); What Next? (1974); Widow's Peak (1993); Wings (1927); A Year in Provence (1993).
RECORDINGS: Ben-Hur. Silva Screen FILMCD043; The French Lieutenant's Woman. DRG CDRG6106; Intolerance. Prometheus PCD105; Napoleon. Silva Screen FILMCD149; Pride and Prejudice. EMI CDFMC3726; The Rainbow. Silva Screen FILMCD040; The Trial. Milan 873 150; Widow's Peak. Varèse Sarabande VSD5487; A Year in Provence. Silva Screen FILMCD131.

DAVIS, Mark (1907–1994)
American composer.
FILMS INCLUDE: Bustin' Loose (1981); Cheech and Chong's Next Movie (1980); Crime of The Decade (1984); Fast Talking (1983); The Great Bank Robbery (1969); An Indecent Obsession (1985); Murderers' Row (1966); Nightmare (1981); PT 109 (1962).

DAVIS, Miles (1926–1991)
American jazz trumpeter, composer and actor.
FILMS INCLUDE: Ascenseur pour L'Echafaud (1957); Dingo (1991); Jack Johnson (1971); Listen Up: The Lives of Quincy Jones (1990); Siesta (1987).

DE ANGELIO, Guido
Italian composer who worked with Maurizio De Angelis.
FILMS INCLUDE: All the way Boys (1973); Between Miracles (1979); Blue Paradise (1982); Body Beat (1989); Charleston (1978); The Cross-Eyed Saint (1971); Great White (1982); The Immortal Batchelor (1980); Keoma (1978); Killer Fish (1978); Run, Run Joe (1974); Safari Express (1980); They Call Me Trinity (1970); Trinity is still my Name (1971); Yor, The Hunter from the Future (1983); Zorro (1975).

DE FRANCESCO, Louis (1888–1974)
American composer who worked for Twentieth Century Fox.
FILMS INCLUDE: As Husbands Go (1933); Caroline (1934); David Harum (1934); I Love You Wednesdays (1933); The Power and the Glory (1933); The Ramparts We Watch (1940); Springtime for Henry (1934); Such Women are Dangerous (1934); United We Stand (1942); The White Parade (1934).

DE SYLVA, Buddy (1895–1950)
American lyricist and composer who wrote hist for Jolson (e.g. 'April Showers' and 'California, Here I Come', both in 1921) and collaborated with George Gershwin. Also worked with Jerome Kern (e.g. 'Look for the Silver Lining', 1921). Later wrote songs for films and became a producer of musicals starring

Shirley Temple. Returned to Broadway in 1939 and Hollywood (Paramount Studios).

DE VOL, Frank (1925–   )
Italian composer.
FILMS INCLUDE: All the Marbles (1981); Attack (1956); The Ballad of Josie (1967); The Big Knife (1955); The Big Mouth (1967); Boys' Night Out (1962); Caprice (1967); Cat Ballou (1965); The Choirboys (1977); The Dirty Dozen (1967); Doc Savage . . . The Man of Bronze (1975); Emperor of the North (1973); The Flight of the Phoenix (1965); For Love or Money (1963); The Frisco Kid (1979); The Glass Bottom Boat (1966); Good Neighbour Sam (1964); Guess Who's Coming to Dinner (1967 – nominated for an Academy Award); The Happening (1966); Herbie Goes Bananas (1980); Herbie Goes to Monte Carlo (1977); Hush, Hush, Sweet Charlotte (1964 – nominated for an Academy Award); Hustle (1975); Johnny Trouble (1957); Kiss Me Deadly (1955); Krakatoa East of Java (1968); The Legend of Lylah Clare (1968); The Longest Yard (1974); Lover Come Back (1961); Pardners (1956); Pillow Talk (1959 – nominated for an Academy Award); The Ride Back (1957); Send Me No Flowers (1964); Texas Across the River (1966); The Thrill of it All (1963); Ulzana's Raid (1972); Under the Yum Yum Tree (1963); A Very Special Favour (1965); What Ever Happened to Baby Jane? (1962); What's So Bad About Feeling Good (1968); The Wheeler Dealers (1963).

DE VORZON, Barry
American composer.
FILMS INCLUDE: Exorcist III (1990); Jekyll and Hyde . . . Together Again (1982); Looker (1981); Night of the Creeps (1986); The Ninth Configuration (1980); Rolling Thunder (1977); R.P.M. (1970); Stick (1985); Tattoo (1981); Tarzan, the Ape Man (1982); The Warriors (1979); Xanadu (1980).

DELERUE, Georges (1925–1992)
French composer who studied with Milhaud. Collaborated with directors Alain Resnais, Jean-Luc Godard and Francois Truftaut.
FILMS INCLUDE: A Valparaiso (1963); Agnes of God (1985); L'Aimant de Cinq Jours (The Five-day Lover) (1961); L'Amour à Vingt Ans (Love at Twenty) (1962); L'Amour En Fuite (Love on The Run) (1978); Anne of The Thousand Days (1969); Une Aussi Longue Absence (1961); Le Bel Age (1959); Une Belle Fille Comme Moi (1972); The Black Stallion Returns (1983); Cartouche (1961); Cline (1992); Le Cerveau (The Brain) (1969); Chair de Poule (1963); Chère Louise (1972); Classe tout Risqués (The Big Risk) (1960); Il Conformista (1970); Le Corniaud (1965); Le Crime ne Paie Pas (1962); The Day of The Dolphin (1973); The Day of The Jackal (1973); Le Dernier Métro (1980); Deux Anglaises et Le Continent (1971); Dien Bien Phu (1992); Le Dimanche

de La Vie (1965); Du Cot de la Côte (1958); The Escape Artist (1982); Exposed (1983); Le Farceur (1960); La Femme D'a Cot (1981); La Française et L'Amour (Love and The Frenchwoman) (1960); French Dressing (1963); Garde à Vue (Under Suspicion) (1981); Hiroshima, Mon Amour (1959); L'Homme de Rio (1964); L'Honorable Stanislas, Agent Secret (1963); The Horsemen (1970); L'Immortelle (1962); Interlude (1968); Les Jeux de L'Amour (1960); Jules et Jim (1961); Julia (1977); A Little Romance (1979 – Academy Award); Malpertuis: Histoire D'Une Maison Maudite (1971); A Man For All Seasons (1966); Man, Woman and Child (1982); Mata Hari, Agent H-21 (1964); Maxie (1985); Un Monsieur de Compagnie (1964); Le Monte-Charge (1962); La Morte-Saison des Amours (The Season for Love) (1961); Nobody Runs Forever (1968); La Nuit Americaine (1973); Our Mother's House (1967); La Parole est au Fleuve (1960); Partners (1982); Platoon (1986); Promise at Dawn (1970); The Pumpkin Eater (1964); Rapture (1965); Rich and Famous (1981); Le Roi de Coeur (1966); Salvador (1986); Silkwood (1983); Statues d'Pouvante (1956); Steel Magnolias (1989); Tendre Poulet (1977); Les Tribulations d'un Chinois en Chine (1965); True Confessions (1981); Le Vieil Homme et L'Enfant (1966); Viva Maria! (1965); Vivement Dimanche! (1983); A Walk With Love and Death (1969); Women in Love (1969).
RECORDINGS: Agnes of God. Varèse Sarabande VSD5368; Cartouche. Prometheus PCD104; A Little Romance. Varèse Sarabande VSD5367; Platoon. Prometheus PCD136; Silkwood. DRG DRGCD6107; Steel Magnolias. Polydor 841 582–2.

DEL MAR Norman (1919–1994)
British conductor, horn player and composer who wrote two symphonies, a string quartet and a number of works for Dennis Brain. Also wrote music for Service short films including the RAF newsreel *The Gen*.

DELVINCOURT, Claude (1888–1954)
French composer who studied composition with Charles-Marie Widor. Director of the Paris Conservatoire from 1941.
FILMS INCLUDE: La Croisade Jaune (1934).

DEMUTH, Norman (1898–1968)
British composer (essentially self taught) and writer of music. Wrote operas and ballets, together with incidental music and six symphonies. Also wrote and arranged music for various short films produced by the War Office during World War II.
FILMS INCLUDE: *Feature*: Pink String and Sealing Wax (1945); *Documentary*: Fabrics of the Future (1946); The Secret Tunnel (1946).

DENISOV, Edison (1929–1996)
Russian composer who became a passionate devotee of Russian opera. Studied maths as well as harmony and counterpoint. Advised by Shostakovich. Some of his later compositions showed the influence of jazz.
FILMS INCLUDE: I Dealny Muzh (An Ideal Husband) (1981); One Night with Stalin (1990).

DÉSORMIÈRE, Roger (1898–1963)
French conductor and composer who studied with Charles Koechlin. Also an arranger and orchestrator.
FILMS INCLUDE: The Lower Depths (1936); A Quoi Rêvent Les Jeunes Filles? (1924); La Règle du Jeu (The Rules of the Game) (1939).

DEUTSCH, Adolph (1897–1980)
American composer, born in England, who went to the USA in 1910. Pupil of Walter Schumann. Associated with Warner Brothers and MGM where he was also an arranger and musical director (from 1949).
FILMS INCLUDE: Action in the North Atlantic (1943); All Through The Night (1942); The Apartment (1960); The Band Wagon (1953); The Belle of New York (1951); Deep in My Heart (1954); Father of The Bride (1950); The Fighting 69th (1940); George Washington Slept Here (1942); Go Naked in The World (1960); The Great Garrick (1937); High Sierra (1941); Indianapolis Speedway (1939); Interrupted Melody (1955) Les Girls (1957); Little Women (1948); The Maltese Falcon (1941); Manpower (1941); The Mask of Dimitrios (1944); Million Dollar Mermaid (1952); Northern Pursuit (1943); Pagan Love Song (1950); The Rack (1956); Saturday's Children (1940); Seven Brides for Seven Brothers (1954); Shadow of a Woman (1946); The Smiling Lieutenant (1931); Some Like it Hot (1959); Take me out to the Ballgame (1948); Tea and Sympathy (1956); They Drive by Night (1940); They Won't Forget (1937); Torch Song (1953).

DEVREESE, Frederic (1929–   )
Dutch composer.
FILMS INCLUDE: Benvenuta (1983); De Man die Zijn Haar Kort Liet Knippen (1965); L'Oeuvre au Noir (1988); Rendez-vous à Bray (1971); Un Soir, Un Train (1968).
RECORDINGS: Benvenuta. Marco Polo 8.223681; L'Oeuvre au Noir. Marco Polo 8–223681; Un Soir, un Train. Marco Polo 8.223681.

DIAMOND, David (1915–   )
American composer who studied with Roger Sessions and Nadia Boulanger. Has written four symphonies, ballets and incidental music.
FILMS INCLUDE: *Feature*: Behemoth The Sea Monster (1958); Dreams That

Money Can Buy (1946 – with Applebaum, Cage and Diamond). *Documentary*: A Place to Live (Philadelphia Housing Association, 1940); Strange Victory (1948).

DIKKER, Loek
Dutch composer.
FILMS INCLUDE: Body Parts (1991); Ein Mann wie Eva (1983); The Fourth Man (1983).
RECORDINGS: Body Parts. Varèse Sarabande VSD5337.

DILDINGER, Klaus
German composer.
FILMS INCLUDE: The Boat (1981); How Did A Nice Girl Like You Get Into This Business? (1970); Me and Him (1989); The Neverending Story (1984 – co-music); The Sudden Wealth of The Poor People of Kombach (1971); Die Wilden Fuenziger (1983).

DOLAN, Robert E. (1906–1972)
American composer and musical director.
FILMS INCLUDE: Anything Goes (1955); The Belles of St Mary's (1945); Duffy's Tavern (1945); Here Come The Waves (1944); The Major and The Minor (1942); The Man Who Understood Women (1959); My Favorite Brunette (1947); My Favorite Spy (1951); Road to Rio (1947); Road to Utopia (1945); Sorrowful Jones (1948); The Three Faces of Eve (1957); Welcome Stranger (1946).

DONAGGIO, Pino (1941–   )
Italian composer who worked with the conductor Claudio Abbado, early in his career. Discovered rock and roll in 1959. His song 'You Don't Have to Say You Love Me' was performed by Dusty Springfield and Elvis Presley. Wrote his first film score in 1973 for Nicolas Roeg's *Don't Look Now*.
FILMS INCLUDE: Blow Out (1981); Body Double (1984); Carrie (1976); Il Caso Moro (1986); Colpo di Coda (Twist) (1993); Così Fan Tutte (1992); Deja Vu (1984); Don't Look Now (1973); Dove Siete? Io Sono Qui (1993); Dressed to Kill (1980); Due Occhi Diabolici (1990); The Fan (1981); Giovanni Falcone (1993); Hercules (1983); Home Movies (1980); The Howling (1980); Morte in Vaticano (1982); Oblivion (1994); Over the Brooklyn Bridge (1983); La Partita (1988); Piranha (1978); Raising Cain (1992); Senza Buccia (1979); Tchin-Tchin (1991); The Tourist Trap (1978); Trauma (1993).
RECORDINGS: Colpo di Coda. CAM CO5016; Don't Look Now. TER CDTER 1007; Dressed to Kill. Varèse Sarabande VCD49148; Raising Cain. Milan 74321 10130–2.

DONALDSON, Walter (1893–1947)

American composer who wrote the score of *Makin' Whoopee!*, a musical starring Eddie Cantor (1928). Samuel Goldwyn turned it into a film with almost the same cast in 1930.

DORFF, Steve

American composer for the cinema and television.

FILMS INCLUDE: Back to the Beach (1987); Bronco Billy (1980); Cannonball Run II (1984); Every Which Way But Loose (1978); Honky Tonk Freeway (1981); Honkytonk Man (1982); My Best Friend is a Vampire (1988); Pink Cadillac (1989); Pure Country (1992); Ratboy (1986); Stick (1985).

DOUGLAS, Clive Martin (1903–1977)

Australian composer and conductor. His major works reflect an interest in aboriginal folklore. Played a pioneering role in the development of orchestral and choral broadcasts in Australia.

DOUGLAS, Johnny

British composer.

FILMS INCLUDE: The Bay of Saint Michel (1963); The Brides of Fu Manchu (1966); Circus of Fear (1966); City of Fear (1966); Code 7 Victim 5 (1963); Company of Fools (1966); Crack in the World (1964); Dateline Diamonds (1965); Dulcima (1971); The Funniest Man in The World (1967); The Guilty Party (1962); Gunfighters of Casa Grande (1964); The Hidden Face (1965); The Hi-Jackers (1963); The Invisible Asset (1963); Kid Rodelo (1965); The Material Witness (1965); The Railway Children (1970); Run Like a Thief (1967); Strictly for The Birds (1963); Touch of Death (1962); The Traitors (1962); The Undesirable Neighbour (1963); Victim Five (1964).

DOUGLAS, Roy (1907–)

British musician and composer. Member of the London Symphony Orchestra. Also has done great deal of arranging and orchestrating, particularly for ballet. Entered films in 1932, transcribing and orchestrating scores in collaboration with various composers, including Walton and Ralph Vaughan Williams.

FILMS INCLUDE: *Feature*: The Bells Go Down (1943); *Documentary*: All for Norway (Strand, 1942); Candlelight in Algeria (British Aviation Pictures, 1944); Central Front Burma (Gryphon-Verity, 1945); Night and Day (Verity, 1944); Seeds and Science (Strand, 1943); Voyage to Freedom (Strand, 1943).

DOYLE, Patrick (1953–)

Scottish composer often associated with director Kenneth Branagh. After attending the Royal Scottish Academy for Music and Drama, Doyle acted in and wrote music for several theatre productions before joining Branagh's Renaissance Theatre company as actor, composer and music director.

FILMS INCLUDE: Dead Again (1991); Exit to Eden (1994); Hamlet (1997); Henry V (1989); Indochine (1992); Into the West (1992); A Little Princess (1995); Mary Shelley's Frankenstein (1994); Much Ado About Nothing (1993); Needful Things (1993); Sense and Sensibility (1995); Shipwrecked (1990); Trapped (1981).

RECORDINGS: Dead Again. Varèse Sarabande VSD5339; Exit to Eden. Varèse Sarabande VSD5553; Henry V. EMI CDC7 49919–2; Indochine. Varèse Sarabande VSD5397; A Little Princess. Varèse Sarabande VSD5628; Mary Shelley's Frankenstein. Epic 477987–2; Much Ado About Nothing. Epic MOODCD30.

DRAGON, Carmen (1914–1984)
American composer, arranger and conductor.

FILMS INCLUDE: Career Girl (1944 – orchestrator: won an Academy Award); Dishonoured Lady (1947); Gun Point (1955); The In-Laws (1979); Invasion of The Body Snatchers (1955); Kiss Tomorrow Goodbye (1950); Mr Winkle Goes to War (1944 – in collaboration with Paul Sawton); Out of the Blue (1947); The Strange Woman (1945); The Time of Your Life (1948); When in Rome (1952); Young Widow (1945).

DRESS, Michael
British composer.

FILMS INCLUDE: The House That Dripped Blood (1970); The Mind of Mr Soames (1969); Quackser Fortune has a Cousin in The Bronx (1970); Rotten to The Core (1965); The Six Sided Triangle (1963); A Touch of Love (1969).

DUBIN, Joseph
American composer who wrote scores for westerns, and Disney productions.

FILMS INCLUDE: Bee at the Beach (1950); Call of the Rockies (1944); Cheyenne Wildcat (1944); Marshall of Reno (1944); Plutopia (1950); Silver City Kid (1944); Trail to San Antone (1947).

DUDLEY, Anne
British composer.

FILMS INCLUDE: Buster (1988); The Crying Game (1992).

DUHAMEL, Antoine (1925–   )
French composer.

FILMS INCLUDE: Belle Époque (1992); Un Conde (1970); Docteur Popaul (1972); Domicile Conjugal (1970); L'Enfant Sauvage (1969); Fugue (1966); Gala (1962); La Mort en Direct (1979); Paris Flash (1958); Pierrot le Fou (1965);

The Sailor From Gibraltar (1967); La Sirène du Mississippi (1969); Stolen Kisses (1968); Twisted Obsession (1990); Week-end (1967).

DUKE, Vernon (1903–1969)
Russian-American song composer, having fled from the Russian Revolution with his family, settled first in Constantinople (1920–21) and then in New York (1922). Became an American citizen in 1936. Developed two styles, one for his choral works, operas, ballets, orchestral and chamber works, the other for his reviews, musicals and film scores, for which he was best known.
FILMS INCLUDE: April in Paris (1952); Cabin in the Sky (1943); The Goldwyn Follies (1938); She's Working Her Way Through College (1952).

DUNAYEVSKY, Isaak (1900–1955)
Russian composer who wrote a great deal of music for the Kharkov theatre, and later for Leningrad and Moscow, where he also wrote much dance music, which led to his development as a composer of light, satirical opera. One of the first Russian composers to use jazz (1933).
FILMS INCLUDE: The Children of Captain Grant (1935); Circus (1935 – the 'Song of the Fatherland', from this score, was one of his most popular pieces); The First Platoon (1932); The Golden Lights (1934); The Happy Bride (1937); The Merry Boys (1934); Seekers of Happiness (1937); Spring (1947); Tanya (1941); Three Friends (1934); Twice Born (1933); Volga-Volga (1938); The Way of a Ship (1935).

DUNDAS, David
British composer.
FILMS INCLUDE: How to get ahead in Advertising (1989); Withnail and I (1987).

DUNING, George (1908–)
American composer and trumpet player who worked as an arranger for RKO (1939–43), an orchestrator (1944–45) and a musical director (1946–52). Many of his scores, written between 1947 and 1953 were orchestrated by Arthur Morton. Worked mainly for television since 1960.
FILMS INCLUDE: Any Wednesday (1966); Bell, Book and Candle (1958); The Corpse Came C.O.D. (1946); The Dark Past (1949); Dear Brigitte (1965); The Doolins of Oklahoma (1949 – in collaboration with Paul Sawtrell); From Here to Eternity (1953 – nominated for an Academy Award); The Last Angry Man (1959); The Man from Laramie (1955); The Man with Bogart's Face (1980); No Sad Songs for Me (1950); Paula (1952); Picnic (1935 – nominated for an Academy Award. The theme had lyrics added and became a hit song); Salome (1953 – music for the dances was written by Daniele Amfitheatrof); Terror in the Wax Museum (1973); Toys in the Attic (1963); The World of Suzie Wong (1961).

RECORDINGS: Picnic. MCA MCAD31357.

DUNLAP, Paul

American composer who wrote many scores for low budget films.

FILMS INCLUDE: The Angry Red Planet (1959); Apache Warrior (1957); Big House, U.S.A. (1955); Black Zoo (1962); Blood of Dracula (1957); The Broken Star (1955); Castle of Evil (1966); The Come-on (1956); Crime of Passion (1956); The Crowning Experience (1959); The Cruel Tower (1956); Cry Vengeance (1954); Decision at Midnight (1963); Desire in the Dust (1960); Destination Inner Space (1966); The Destructors (1966); Emergency Hospital (1956); Five Gates to Hell (1959); The Four Skulls of Jonathan Drake (1959); Frontier Gun (1958); Gang War (1958); God is my Partner (1957); Gun Fever (1957); Here Come The Jets (1959); I Was A Teenage Werewolf (1957); Last of The Desperados (1955); Lone Texan (1958); Loophole (1954); Lure of The Swamp (1957); The Money Jungle (1968); Operation CIA (1965); Oregon Passage (1958); Panic in The City (1967); Park Row (1952); Portland Expose (1957); The Quiet Gun (1956); Return From The Sea (1954); Robber's Roost (1955); Seven Women From Hell (1961); Shield for Murder (1954); Smithereens (1982); Stagecoach to Fury (1956); Strange Intruder (1956); Stranger on Horseback (1954); The Sweet and The Bitter (1962); Three Outlaws (1956); Under Fire (1957); Voice of The Hurricane (1963); The Wild Dakotas (1956); Young and Dangerous (1957); Young Fury (1964).

DuPREZ, John

British composer.

FILMS INCLUDE: Bullshot! (1983); A Chorus of Disapproval (1989); A Fish Called Wanda (1988); Monty Python's The Meaning of Life (1983); Once Bitten (1985); Personal Services (1987); A Private Function (1984); She'll be Wearing Pink Pyjamas (1984); Teenage Mutant Ninja Turtles (1990); Teenage Mutant Ninja Turtles II: The Secret of the Ooze (1991); Teenage Mutant Ninja Turtles III: The Turtles Are back . . . in Time (1992).

DZIERLATKA, Arié (1933–)

Swiss/Belgian composer.

FILMS INCLUDE: L'Amour L'Après-midi (Love in the Afternoon) (1972); Les Années Lumières (Light Years Away) (1981); Le Journal de Lady M (1993); Messidor (1978); Mon Oncle D'Amerique (1980); La Mort de Mario Ricci (The Death of Mario Ricci) (1983); La Provinciale (A Girl from Lorraine) (1980); Le Retour d'Afrique (Return from Africa) (1973).

EASDALE, Brian (1909–1995)
British composer who composed for the theatre and wrote two operas.
FILMS INCLUDE: *Feature*: The Battle of the River Plate (1956); Black Narcissus (1946); Gone to Earth (1950); The Green Scarf (1955); An Outcast of the Islands (1951); Peeping Tom (1959); The Red Shoes (1948 – Academy Award); The Small Back Room (1949). *Documentary*: Big Money (GPOFU, 1937); Ferry Pilot (CFU, 1941); Health in Industry (GPOFU, 1938); Job in a Million (GPOFU, 1937); Kew Gardens (Short Film Productions, 1937); Men in Danger (GPOFU, 1939).
RECORDINGS: The Red Shoes. Silva Screen FILMCD713.

EASTWOOD, Clint (1930–)
American actor and director who received a Fellowship of the British Film Institute in September 1993. Wrote and contributed 'Claudia's Theme' for his Academy Award winning film *Unforgiven* (1992).

EASTWOOD, Thomas (1922–)
British composer who has worked extensively in the theatre and in broadcasting. Television scores include *Mary Queen of Scots* (1969), *A Picture of Katherine Mansfield* (1973) and *Venus Brown* (1963). He composed the music-hall song for *Look Back in Anger* (1959).

EBBINGHOUSE, Bernard
British composer.
FILMS INCLUDE: Accidental Death (1963); Act of Murder (1964); Backfire! (1962); Change Partners (1965); Dead Man's Chest (1965); Death Trap (1962); Downfall (1964); Five to One (1963); Flat Two (1962); Game for Three Losers (1965); Incident at Midnight (1963); Invasion (1966); The Main Chance (1964); Man Detained (1961); Mumsy, Nanny, Sonny and Girl (1969); Naked Evil (1966); Never Back Losers (1961); Never Mention Murder (1964); Number Six (1962); On the Run (1963); Playback (1962); Prudence and the Pill (1968); Return to Sender (1963); Rocochet (1963); Solo for Sparrow (1962); Strangler's Web (1966); Time to Remember (1962); The Verdict (1964); We Shall See (1964); Which was Maddox? (1964); A Woman's Privilege (1963).

EDELMAN, Randy (1947–)
American composer and successful songwriter/arranger for artists such as Abba, Barry Manilow, Bing Crosby and Olivia Newton-John.
FILMS INCLUDE: Angels in the Outfield (1995); Beethoven (1991); Beethoven's 2nd (1993); Citizen X (1995); Come See The Paradise (1990); Dragon: The Bruce Lee Story (1993); Drop Dead Fred (1991); Executive Action (1973); Feds (1988); Gettysburg (1993); Ghostbusters II (1989); The Indian in the

Cupboard (1995); Kindergarten Cop (1990); The Last of the Mohicans (1992); The Mask (1994); My Cousin Vinny (1992); Outside In (1972); Troop Beverley Hills (1989); Twins (1988); While You Were Sleeping (1995).
RECORDINGS: Beethoven. MCA MCAD10593; Citizen X. Varèse Sarabande VSD5601; Gettysburg. Milan 17008–2; Kindergarten Cop. Varèse Sarabande VSD5305; My Cousin Vinny. Varèse Sarabande VSD5364.

EDENS, Roger (1905–1970)

American musical director and composer who influenced MGM musicals and often acted as an associate to producer Arthur Freed. Went to Hollywood in 1933 to write special material for Ethel Merman films at Paramount. Joined MGM in 1935 as a musical supervisor and occasional composer and arranger, notably for Judy Garland.
FILMS INCLUDE: Babes in Arms (1939); Broadway Melody of 1940 (1940); Cabin in the Sky (1943); Funny Face (1956); Girl Crazy (1943); Hello, Dolly! (1969); Invitation to the Dance (1954); Jumbo (1962); Lady be Good (1941); Ziegfeld Follies (1946).

EIDELMAN, Cliff (1964–   )

American composer and conductor.
FILMS INCLUDE: Christopher Columbus: The Discovery (1992); Crazy People (1990); Magdalene (1988); The Meteor Man (1993); My Girl (1994); Now and Then (1995); Picture Bride (1994); Silent Night (1988); A Simple Twist of Fate (1994); Star Trek VI: The Undiscovered Country (1992); Strike it Rich (1990); To Die For (1989), Triumph of the Spirit (1989); Untamed Heart (1993).
RECORDINGS: Christopher Columbus: The Discovery. Varèse Sarabande VSD5389; Magdalene. Intrada MAF70290; Picture Bride. Varèse Sarabande VSD5651; A Simple Twist of Fate. Varèse Sarabande VSD5538; Star Trek VI. MCA MCA10512.

EISLER, Hanns (1898–1962)

Austrian composer who collaborated with Brecht on plays and songs. Studied music with Schoenberg in Vienna, and left Germany in 1933, moving to the USA in the late 1930s to teach and work in Hollywood (for Fritz Lang, Frank Borzage and Jean Renoir, etc). Later deported and went to live and work in East Germany where he wrote that country's national anthem. Wrote 'Composing for Films' (1947).
FILMS INCLUDE: Abdul the Damned (1935); Aktion J (1961); Bel Ami (1954); China Fights (1942); The Crucible (1957); Deadline at Dawn (1946); Fidelio (1956); Forgotten Voyage (1941); Galileo (1974); Jealousy (1945); Kuhle Wampe Oder Wem Gehört die Welt? (1932); Opus III (1928); Pagliacci (1936); Der Rat Der Gotter (Council of the Gods) (1950); Song of Life (1930).

ELFMAN, Danny (1953–)
American composer, musician and singer. Well known as the composer of the theme music for the TV Series *The Simpsons*.
FILMS INCLUDE: Article 99 (1992); Back to School (1986); Batman (1989); Batman Returns (Batman II) (1992); Beetlejuice (1988); Delores Claiborne (1995); Edward Scissorhands (1990); Extreme Measures (1997); Mars Attacks (1997); The Nightmare Before Christmas (1993); Pee Wee's Big Adventure (1985); Pure Luck (1991); Sommersby (1993); Summer School (1987); Tim Burton's Nightmare Before Christmas (1993); Wisdom (1986).
RECORDINGS: Batman. Warner Bros 7599–25977.2; Beetlejuice. Geffen GED24202; Sommersby. Elektra 7559–61491–2.

ELINOR, Carli D.
Pioneer in film music.
FILMS INCLUDE: The Birth of a Nation (1915); The Bridge of San Luis Rey (1929); The Devil Dancer (1927); The Gold Rush (1925 – with Charlie Chaplin); Hearts of The World (1918); The Seventh Hour (1927 – with Bassett); What Price Glory? (1926 – with Bassett).

ELLINGTON, Duke (1899–1974)
American bandleader, composer and pianist. Generally recognised as the most important composer in jazz history, the exact number of his works is unknown but may amount to as many as 6,000.
FILMS INCLUDE: Anatomy of a Murder (1959); Assault on a Queen (1966); Black and Tan (1929); Change of Mind (1969); Check and Double Check (1930); Hit Parade (1937); Jonas (1957); New Faces (1937); Paris Blues (1961); Reveille with Beverly (1943).

ELLIS, Don (1934–1978)
American composer and jazz trumpeter.
FILMS INCLUDE: The French Connection (1971); French Connection II (1975); Moon Zero Two (1969); Ruby (1977); The Seven Ups (1973).

ELLIS, Vivian (1904–1996)
British composer and lyricist. Mostly famous for his songs which were heard on the London stage. Also contributed songs to a number of films, e.g. *Jack's The Boy* (1932), *Men are not Gods* (1936) and *Piccadilly Incident* (1946).
Other FILMS INCLUDE: Elstree Calling (1930); Out of the Blue (1931).

ELMS, Albert
British composer.
FILMS INCLUDE: Alias John Preston (1955); Bluebeard's Ten Honeymoons (1960); The Breaking Point (1961); The Depraved (1957); The Great Van

Robbery (1959); Innocent Meeting (1958); Links of Justice (1958); The Man Without a Body (1957); Manfish (1956); Moment of Indiscretion (1958); On the Run (1958); Rockets in the Dunes (1960); The Secret Man (1958); Son of a Stranger (1957); Strangers' Meeting (1957); Three Crooked Men (1958); Three Sundays to Live (1957); A Woman of Mystery (1957); A Woman Possessed (1958); The Young Jacobites (1959).

EMERSON, Keith (1944–)
British composer and keyboard player who played in the rock groups Nice, and Emerson, Lake and Palmer.
FILMS INCLUDE: Best Revenge (1983); Inferno (1980); Murderock, Uccide a Passo di Danza (1984); Nighthawks (1981).
RECORDINGS: Nighthawks. Silva Screen FILMCD139.

ENGEL, Lehman (1910–1982)
American composer of operas and ballets. Wrote scores for three documentaries commissioned by the US Navy in 1945: *The Fleet that Came to Stay*; *Fury in the Pacific*; *Well Done*.

ENO, Brian (1948–)
British composer and keyboard player. Founder member of the group Roxy Music.
FILMS INCLUDE: Dune (1984 – wrote part of the score); Land of the Minotaur (1976 – wrote part of the score).

ERDMANN, Harry (1887–1942)
German composer and conductor. Became artistic director of the Prama Film Company in 1921, where his first score was *Nosferatu* (1922). Also worked as a music critic, edited a journal devoted to film music and ran courses in film composition at the Berlin Conservatoire. Wrote a score for Fritz Lang's *Das Testament des Dr Mabuse* (1933).
RECORDINGS: Nosferatu. RCA Victor 09026 68143–2.

ERDODY, Leo (1888–1949)
American composer.
FILMS INCLUDE: Bluebeard (1944); Detour (1945); Fugitive of the Plains (1943); Larceny in Her Heart (1946); The Return of Rin Tin Tin (1947).

EVANS, David Moule (1905–1988)
British composer. Studied at the RCM with Herbert Howells. Devoted himself to teaching, and then, from 1941, entirely to composition.
FILMS INCLUDE: *Documentary*: The Gen (RAF Newsreel); London 1942

(Greenpark Films, 1942); Make Fruitful the Land (Greenpark Films, 1944); National Health (Technique).

EVANS, Ray (1915–)
American songwriter who worked in Hollywood from 1945 in partnership with Jay Livingston. Won an Academy Award for 'Buttons and Bows' in 1948 (*The Paleface*) and 'Que Sera Sera' in 1956 (*The Man Who Knew Too Much*).

FAGAN, Gideon (1904–1980)
British composer, born in South Africa who wrote and directed much music for the theatre. When James Fitzpatrick came to England to produce films in Britain for MGM in 1936, Fagan became music director to the unit. Also associated with Ernest Irving on various scores for Ealing Studio productions.
FILMS INCLUDE: *Feature*: Auld Lang Syne (1936); The Captain's Table (1936); David Livingstone (1936 – Fagan's love poem 'Ilala', written in 1941, contains themes from this film); Last Rose of Summer (1936). *Documentary*: Highlights of Capetown (music composed by Fagan); The Music Masters (music by Chopin, Liszt and Rossini, arranged by Fagan); Traveltalks: Quaint Quebec (music arranged from Canadian folk tunes).

FAIN, Sammy (1902–1989)
American composer whose songs featured in many Hollywood films.
FILMS INCLUDE: Alice in Wonderland (1951); April Love (1957); The Big Pond (1930); Calamity Jane (1953 – awarded Academy Awards); Call Me Mister (1951); A Certain Smile (1958); Dames (1934); Dangerous Nan McGrew (1930); Fashions of 1934 (1934); Follow The Leader (1930); Footlight Parade (1933); Hollywood or Bust (1956); The Incredible Mr Limpet (1963); Island of Love (1963); Joy in the Morning (1964); Love Is A Many Splendored Thing (1955 – awarded an Academy Award for the title song); Lucky Me (1954); Made in Paris (1965); Mardi Gras (1958); Myra Breckinridge (1970); Peter Pan (1952); Philbert (1963); The Rescuers (1977); Sleeping Beauty (1958); The Specialist (1975); Three Sailors and a Girl (1953).
RECORDINGS: Calamity Jane. TER CDTER2 1215; Peter Pan. Delos DE3186.

FAITH, Percy (1908–1976)
American composer and orchestral conductor.
FILMS INCLUDE: I'd Rather Be Rich (1964); Love Me or Leave Me (1955); The Oscar (1966); Tammy, Tell Me True (1961); The Third Day (1965).

FALTERMEYER, Harold
American composer.
FILMS INCLUDE: Beverley Hills Cop (1984); Beverley Hills Cop II (1987); Fatal

Beauty (1987); Fire and Ice (1982); Fletch (1985); Fletch Lives (1989); Kuffs (1992); The Running Man (1987); Tango and Cash (1989); Thief of Hearts (1984); Top Gun (1986).
RECORDINGS: Beverley Hills Cop. Telarc CD80251; The Running Man. Silva Screen SILVAD3001; Top Gun. Silva Screen FILMCD152.

FAME, Georgie (1943–)
British pop singer.
FILMS INCLUDE: The Alf Garnett Saga (1972); Entertaining Mr Sloane (1969).

FANSHAWE, David (1942–)
British composer. Devoted much time to research into African folk music, and into that of Iraq and Tonga.
FILMS INCLUDE: Arabian Fantasy; Dirty Weekend (1993); The Good Companions (TV); Requiem for a Village (1975); Tarka the Otter (1978); Three Men in a Boat (TV).
RECORDINGS: Dirty Weekend. Silva Screen FILMCD140.

FARBERMAN, Harold (1929–)
American composer and conductor. A member of the Boston Symphony Orchestra as percussionist and timpanist. Has composed operas and ballets.

FARNON, Robert (1917–)
Canadian composer who has composed for the screen and television.
FILMS INCLUDE: All for Mary (1955); Bear Island (1979); Captain Horatio Hornblower RN (1951); The Disappearance (1977); Expresso Bongo (1959); Friend or Foe (1981); Gentlemen Marry Brunettes (1955); His Majesty O'Keefe (1953); It's a Wonderful World (1956); King's Rhapsody (1955); Lilacs in the Spring (1954); The Little Hut (1956); The Road to Hong Kong (1961); Shalako (1968); The Sheriff of Fractured Jaw (1958); Spring in Park Lane (1948); Tightrope to Terror (1982); True as a Turtle (1957); The Truth about Spring (1964).
RECORDINGS: Captain Horatio Hornblower RN. Reference Recordings RRCD-47.

FENBY, Eric (1906–1997)
British composer and organist. Acted as amanuensis to the blind and paralysed Delius in France between 1928 and 1934. Wrote the score for Hitchcock's film of *Jamaica Inn* (1939).

FENTON, George (1949–)
British composer who originally wrote for television (e.g. *Bergerac, Shoestring, The Monocled Mutineer* and *The History Man*, together with music for the

BBC's *Nine O'Clock News*, *The Money Programme*, *Newsnight* and *Telly Addicts*.
FILMS INCLUDE: Adult Fun (1972); Billy the Kid and the Green Baize Vampire (1985); Bloody Kids (1979); China Moon (1994); Clockwise (1985); The Company of Wolves (1984); Cry Freedom (1987); Dangerous Liaisons (1988); The Fisher King (1991); Ghandi (1982 – nominated for an Academy Award); Hussy (1979); Interview with a Vampire (1994); The Long Walk Home (1990); A Lustful Lady (1977); The Madness of King George (1994); Memphis Belle (1990); Private Road (1971); Runners (1983); Shadowlands (1993); The Waterloo Bridge Handicap (1978); White Mischief (1987).
RECORDINGS: The Company of Wolves. TER CDTER 1094; The Madness of King George. Epic 478477–2; Shadowlands. EMI Angel CDQ5 55093–2; White Mischief. TER CDTER1153.

FERGUSON, Allyn
British composer who has written for the screen and television (e.g. *Barney Miller* and *Charlie's Angels*).
FILMS INCLUDE: The Four Feathers (1978); Get To Know Your Rabbit (1972); Little Lord Fauntleroy (1980); Support Your Local Gunfighter (1971).

FERRIS, Paul
British composer, often associated with horror films.
FILMS INCLUDE: The Blood Beast Terror (1967); Clegg (1969); The Creeping Flesh (1972); Maroc 7 (1966); Persecution (1974); The Sorcerers (1967); Witchfinder General (1968).

FEUER, Cy
American composer who wrote for films mainly between 1938 and 1942.
FILMS INCLUDE: Barnyard Follies (1940); Bowery Bow (1940); Citadel of Crime (1941); Come On, Rangers (1938); In Old Caliente (1939); Jeepers Creepers (1939); Kansas Cyclone (1941); Mercy Island (1941); Red River Valley (1941); South of Santa Fé (1942); Youth on Patrol (1942).

FIEDEL, Brad (1951–)
American composer who wrote music for modern dance classes and worked as a musician and composer whilst still at school. Wrote early scores for educational films. Later moved to Los Angeles where he got his big break with James Cameron's *Terminator* (1984).
FILMS INCLUDE: The Accused (1988); The Big Easy (1986); Compromising Positions (1985); Desert Bloom (1986); Fright Night (1985); Johnny Mnemonic (1995); Just Before Dawn (1980); Night School (1980); The Real McCoy (1993); Straight Talk (1992); The Terminator (1984); Terminator 2: Judgement Day (1991); True Lies (1994).

RECORDINGS: The Terminator/Terminator 2. Edel 0022082CIN/ Varèse Sarabande VSD5335.

FIELDING, Jerry (1922–1980)
American composer.
FILMS INCLUDE: Advise and Consent (1962); The Bad News Bears (1976); Below the Belt (1980); Beyond the Poseidon Adventure (1979); The Big Sleep (1978); The Black Bird (1975); Bring Me the Head of Alfredo Garcia (1974); Chato's Land (1971); Demon Seed (1977); The Enforcer (1976); Escape from Alcatraz (1979); For Those Who Think Young (1964); The Gambler (1974); The Gauntlet (1977); Grady Lady Down (1977); Junior Bonner (1972); The Killer Elite (1975); Lawman (1970); McHale's Navy Joins the Air Force (1965); The Mechanic (1972); Mission Impossible vs The Mob (1969); The Nightcomers (1971); The Nun and The Sergeant (1962); The Outfit (1973); The Outlaw Josey Wales (1976); Scorpio (1972); Semi-Tough (1977); Straw Dogs (1971); The Super Cops (1973); Suppose they gave a War and Nobody Came (1969); The Wild Bunch (1969 – nominated for an Academy Award).
RECORDINGS: The Outlaw Josey Wales. Silva Screen FILMCD138; The Wild Bunch. Silva Screen FILMCD136.

FIGGIS, Mike (1949–)
British director, screenwriter and jazz musician who now lives in Hollywood.
FILMS INCLUDE: The Browning Version (1994); Internal Affairs (1990); Liebestraum (1991); Mr Jones (1993); Story Monday (1987).

FILIPPI, Almedeo de (1900–)
American composer, born in Italy, who wrote orchestral and chamber works.
FILMS INCLUDE: Blockade (1930); Jazz Age (1930).

FITELBERG, Jerzy (1903–1951)
Polish composer, born in Warsaw, who lived in Paris until 1940 when he went to the USA.
FILMS INCLUDE: Poland Fight On (Polish Government, 1945); Pre-war Poland (Polish Government, 1945).

FOLK, Robert (1950–)
American composer and conductor. Has written music for *Police Academy* and all subsequent sequels.
FILMS INCLUDE: Arabian Knight (The Thief and the Cobbler) (1994); Beastmaster 2: Through the Portal of Time (1992); In The Army Now (1994); The Never Ending Story II (1990); Toy Soldiers (1991); Trapped in Paradise (1994); Tremors (1990); Troll in Central Park (1993).

RECORDINGS: In the Army Now. Intrada MAF7058D; Trapped in Paradise. Varèse Sarabande VSD5555.

FORBES, Louis (1902–)
American composer and musical director. Wrote music for documentary films produced by the Protestant Film Commission.
FILMS INCLUDE: Adventures of Tom Sawyer (1938); The Bat (1959); The Crooked Way (1949); Escape to Burman (1953); From the Earth to the Moon (1958); Hong Kong Affair (1958); Intermezzo (1939); Intrigue (1947); The Most Dangerous Man Alive (1961); Oh! Doctor (1937); Passion (1954); Pot O'Gold (1941); Second Chance (1950); The Story of G.I. Joe (1945); A Wonderful Life (1951).

FOSS, Lucas (1922–)
American composer, pianist and conductor who studied in Berlin and Paris before settling in the USA (1937). Has written operas and ballets.
FILMS INCLUDE: *Documentary*: Search into Darkness (1962).

FOX, Charles (1940–)
American composer.
FILMS INCLUDE: Barbarella (1967 – wrote part of the score); Beyond the Valley of the Dolls (1970); Bug (1975); The Corpse Grinders (1971); Crash Landing: The Rescue of Flight 232 (1992); The Duchess and The Dirtwater Fox (1976); Foul Play (1978); The Gods Must Be Crazy II (1989); Goodbye, Columbus (1969); It Had To Be You (1989); The Last American Hero (1973); The Last Married Couple in America (1979); The Laughing Policeman (1973); Little Darlings (1980); The Longshot (1985); Making It (1971); Nine to Five (1980); One on One (1977); The Other Side of the Mountain (1975); Our Winning Season (1978); Pufnstuf (1970); Two-Minute Warning (1976); Zapped! (1982).

FRANCESCO, Louis de
American composer.
FILMS INCLUDE: Adorable (1933); Berkeley Square (1937); Cavalcade (1933); State Fair (1933).

FRANKE, Christopher (1942–)
German composer and member of the group Tangerine Dream with whom he recorded over a dozen film scores from 1971 to 1988 including *Firestarter* (1984); *Legend* (1985) and *Risky Business* (1983). His solo work has concentrated on scoring television features and series including *Babylon 5* (1993–4); *The Tommyknockers* (1993) and *Walker: Texas Ranger* (1993).

FRANKEL, Benjamin (1906–1973)

British composer and musical director who studied music in Germany. Wrote music in many genres including eight symphonies, the last in 1972.

FILMS INCLUDE: *Feature*: Appointment with Venus (1951); Battle of the Bulge (1965); The Curse of the Werewolf (1960); Dear Murderer (1947); Flight from Folly (1944); A Girl in a Million (1946); Guns of Darkness (1962); Happy is the Bride (1958); He Found a Star (1943); The Importance of being Ernest (1952); A Kid for Two Farthings (1955); Libel (1959); Love in Exile (1936); The Man in the White Suit (1951); Mine Own Executioner (1947); Music Hath Charms (1937); Night of the Iguana (1964); No Monkey Business (1937); The Seventh Veil (1945); Simon and Laura (1955); The Singing Cop (1937); Sleeping Car to Trieste (1948); So Long at the Fair (1950); They met in the Dark (1944); The Years Between (1946). *Documentary*: Bon Voyage (Phoenix/MoI, 1944); The Broad Fourteens (CFU, 1945); The Fire of London (Phoenix/MoI, 1945); The Great Circle (Shell, 1944); Macbeth and Julius Caesar (British Council, 1945); Moving House (1950); The New Teacher (CFU, 1945); Public Nuisance No 1 (Cecil Films, 1936); Radio Parade of 1935 (British International Pictures, 1934).

RECORDINGS: The Battle of the Bulge. Silva Screen FILMCD151; The Curse of the Werewolf. Silva Screen FILMCD175; A Kid for Two Farthings. EMI CDGO2059; The Man in the White Suit. Silva Screen FILMCD 177.

FRICKER, Peter Racine (1920–1990)

British composer who studied with Matyas Seiber and with whom he worked closely, acting as his assistant conductor and helping with film scores. Wrote works in many genres including five symphonies.

FILMS INCLUDE: *Documentary*: Atomic Energy (1958); Das Island (1958); The Inquisitive Giant (1958); Inside the Atom (1951); Looking at Churches (1959); The Undying Heart (1952); The White Continent (1951).

FRIED, Gerald (1928–)

American composer who has written scores mainly for television e.g. *Roots* (1976) and *Testimony of Two Men* (1977), together with *The Man from U.N.C.L.E.*, *Mission Impossible* and some music for the original *Star Trek* series.

FILMS INCLUDE: The Baby (1972); The Cabinet of Caligari (1962); Cast a Long Shadow (1959); A Cold Wind in August (1960); The Cry Baby Killer (1958); Day of the Fight (1951); Dino (1957); The Grissom Gang (1971); I Mobster (1958); The Karate Killers (1967); Killer's Kiss (1955); The Killing (1956); The Killing of Sister George (1968); Nine to Five (1980); One of Our Spies is Missing (1966); One Potato Two Potato (1964); Paths of Glory (1957); The Return of Dracula (1958); The Second Time Around (1961); Soylent Green (1973); Supervientes de Los Andes (1976); Terror in a Texas Town

(1958); Too Late The Hero (1969); The Vampire (1957); Vigilante Force (1975); Whatever Happened to Aunt Alice? (1969); The Young Sinners (1958).

FRIEDHOFER, Hugo (1902–1981)

American composer and instrumentalist. In 1929, having gained valuable experience in arranging and occasionally composing music for silent films, he went to Hollywood where he worked as an arranger and composer on some of the earliest sound films. In 1935 he joined the music department of Warner Brothers as an orchestrator, working with Korngold and Steiner. His score for *The Best Years of our Lives* won an Academy Award in 1946 and was nominated a further eight times.

FILMS INCLUDE: Above and Beyond (1952); Ace in The Hole (1951); The Adventures of Marco Polo (1937); An Affair to Remember (1957); Along came Jones (1945); Angels with Dirty Faces (1938); Arsenic and Old Lace (1944); The Barbarian and The Geisha (1958); The Beast with Five Fingers (1946); The Best Years of Our Lives (1946); Between Heaven and Hell (1956); The Bishop's Wife (1947); The Blue Angel (1959); Body and Soul (1947); The Bride Came C.O.D. (1941); Broken Arrow (1950); Casablanca (1943); City for Conquest (1940); The Corn is Green (1945); Die Sister Die (1978); Geronimo (1962); The Girl in The Red Velvet Swing (1955); The Harder They Fall (1956); Homicidal (1961); In Love and War (1958); In This Our Life (1942); The Letter (1940); Lifeboat (1944); The Lodger (1944); Lydia Bailey (1952); Never so Few (1959); One-Eyed Jacks (1960); The Prisoner of Zenda (1937); Private Parts (1972); The Rains of Ranchipur (1955); The Red Baron (1971); The Revolt of Mamie Stover (1956); Santa Fe Trail (1940); The Sea Wolf (1941); The Secret Invasion (1964); Seven Cities of Gold (1955); Soldier of Fortune (1955); A Song is Born (1948); A Stolen Life (1946); The Sun Also Rises (1957); This Earth is Mine (1959); Topper Takes a Trip (1939); Vera Cruz (1954); Violent Saturday (1995); Von Richthofen and Brown (1971); White Feather (1955).

RECORDINGS: An Affair to Remember. Philips 454 647–2PH; The Best Years of Our Lives. Silva Screen SILVAD3002; Lifeboat. Silva Screen FILMCD159; Private Parts. Facet FC8105; The Sun Also Rises. RCA GD80912.

FRIZZI, Fabio

Italian composer.

FILMS INCLUDE: Amanti Miei (Cindy's Love Games) (1979); Amore Libero (Hot Dreams) (1974); . . . E Tu Vivrai nel Terrore!: L'Aldilà (And You'll Live in Terror: The Beyond) (1981); L'Occhio del Male (Manhattan Baby) (1983); Paura Nella Città dei Morti Viventi (Fear) (1980); Zombi 2 (1979).

FRONTIÈRE, Dominic (1931–   )

American composer.

FILMS INCLUDE: The Aviator (1987); Barquero (1970); Billie (1965); Brannigan (1975); Broken Sabre (1965); Cancel My Reservation (1972); Chisum (1970); Cleopatra Jones and The Casino of Gold (1975); Colour of Night (1994); Freebie and The Bean (1974); A Global Affair (1963); The Gumball Rally (1976); Hammersmith is Out (1972); Hang 'em High (1968); Hero's Island (1962); High Noon (1952); Lost Flight (1970); The Marriage-Go-Round (1960); Massacre Harbour (1968); Modern Problems (1981); On Any Sunday (1972); One Foot in Hell (1980); Popi (1969); The Right Approach (1960); Roar (1981); Seven Thieves (1960); The Stunt Man (1979); The Train Robbers (1973).

RECORDINGS: Hang 'em High. Silva Screen FILMCD138.

FRÜH, Huldreich G. (1903–1945)

Swiss composer and pianist who was a member of the well known Swiss cabaret 'Cornichon', for which he wrote several excellent song-hits.

FULTON, Norman (1909–1980)

British composer and singing teacher who worked for the BBC as supervisor of music programmes in its Latin-American service.

FILMS INCLUDE: *Documentary*: The Gen (RAF Newsreel) and Optics (an industrial film made in 1945).

FUSCO, Giovanni (1906–1968)

Italian composer, usually associated with Michelangelo Antonioni. Began composing for the Italian screen in 1936.

FILMS INCLUDE: Amore e Rabbia (Vangelo 70) (1969); L'Avventura (The Adventure) (1959); Col Ferro e Col Fuoco (With Fire and Sword) (1961); Il Deserto Rosso (Red Desert) (1964); La Donna dei Faraoni (The Pharoah's Woman) (1960); L'Eclisse (The Eclipse) (1962); La Guerra di Troia (The Wooden Horse of Troy) (1961); La Guerre est Finie (The War is Over) (1966); Hiroshima, Mon Amour (1959); La Leggenda di Enea (The War of The Trojans) (1962); Il Mare (The Sea) (1962); Sandokan, La Tigre di Mompracem (Sandokan The Great) (1963); Il Sesso Degli Angeli (Sex of Angels) (1968); La Signora Senza Camelie (The Woman Without Camelias) (1952).

GABRIEL, Peter (1950–   )

British composer and singer. Co-founder of the rock band Genesis which he left in 1975 to pursue a solo career.

FILMS INCLUDE: Birdy (1985); The Last Temptation of Christ (1988); Money Brings Happiness (1993).

RECORDINGS: Birdy. Charisma CASCD1167; The Last Temptation of Christ. Real World RWCD1.

GALLIARD, Marius-François
French composer.
FILMS INCLUDE: *Feature*: The Convict has Escaped (1947); Famille sous Les Cèdres (1939); Portrait of Innocence (1948); Les Rendez-vous du Diable (1959). *Documentary*: Forty-Million People (GPOFU).

GAMLEY, Douglas (1924–)
Australian composer, conductor and pianist resident in Britain since the early 1950s. Engaged by MGM in 1952 for the Gene Kelly film *Invitation to the Dance*, then being made at Elstree Studios, beginning as rehearsal pianist (with Geoffrey Parsons) and graduating to Assistant Music Director. In the following year he became assistant to the conductor Muir Mathison. During this period, he also played with the London Symphony, Royal Philharmonic and Philharmonia Orchestra.
FILMS INCLUDE: The Admirable Crichton (1957); And Now The Screaming Starts (1973); Another Time, Another Place (1958); Asylum (1972); The Beast Must Die (1974); Beyond This Place (1959); The Christmas Tree (1966); City of The Dead (1960); Enigma (1982); Foxhole in Cairo (1960); From Beyond The Grave (1973); Gideon's Day (1958); The Girl on a Motorcycle (1968); Land of Laughter (1957); The Land That Time Forgot (1974); Light Up The Sky (1960); The Little Prince (1974 nominated for an Academy Award for musical direction in 1975); Madhouse (1974); One Wish Too Many (1956); The Return of Mr Moto (1965); The Rough and The Smooth (1959); Spring and Port Wine (1969); Sunday, Bloody Sunday (1971); Tales from The Crypt (1972); Tarzan's Greatest Adventure (1959); Tron (1982); The Ugly Duckling (1959); The Vault of Horror (1973); Watch it Sailor! (1961).

GARCIA, Russell (1916–)
American composer who has written for the cinema and television e.g. Call My Bluff, Laredo.
FILMS INCLUDE: Atlantis The Lost Continent (1960); The Pad (1966); Radar, Secret Service (1950); The Time Machine (1960).
RECORDINGS: The Time Machine. GNP GNPD8008.

GARFUNKEL, Arthur (1941–)
American pop singer, part of Simon and Garfunkel.
FILMS INCLUDE: Acts of Love – and Other Comedies (1973); Bad Timing (1980); Boxing Helena (1993); Carnal Knowledge (1971); Catch-22 (1970); Good to Go (1986); The Graduate (1967).

GASLINI, Giorgio (1929–)
Italian composer.
FILMS INCLUDE: Bali (1971); La Notte (1960); La Notte dei Diavoli (1972);
The Pacifist (1971); Profondo Rosso (1975).

GAY, Noel (1898–1954)
British composer and song writer for the stage and screen. Closely associated
with the Arthur Askey films. His song 'Tondeleyo' which featured in the film
White Cargo (1928) was the first to be synchronised with the action in a
British talking picture.
FILMS INCLUDE: The Camels are Coming (1934); Champagne Charlie (1945);
Father Knows Best (1937); I Thank You (1941); Let's be Famous (1939); Me
and Marlborough (1935); Okay for Sound (1937); Sailors Three (1940: fea-
tured his song 'All Over The Place'); Sleepless Night (1934); Soldiers of the
Queen (1932); Time Flies (1944); White Cargo (1928).

GELMETTI, Vittoria
Italian composer.
FILMS INCLUDE: Black on White (1968); The Howl (1965); Red Desert (1964);
Under the Sign of the Scorpion (1969).

GERHARD, Roberto (1896–1970)
Spanish composer and pianist who became an English citizen. Studied with
Granados, Pedrell and Schoenberg in Vienna and Berlin (1924–28). Left his
fifth symphony incomplete when he died in Cambridge.
FILMS INCLUDE: Aboard (1958 – electronic); DNA in Reflection (1963 –
electronic); Secret People (1952); This Sporting Life (1963 – much of the
music was unused); War in the Air (1952 – five films for the BBC); Your Skin
(1958 – electronic).

GERSHWIN, George (1898–1937)
American popular composer of songs and other works, whose music was used
in films.
FILMS INCLUDE: An American in Paris (1951); Broadway Rhythms (1944); But
not for Me (1959); A Damsel in Distress (1937); Delicious (1931); Funny
Face (1956); Girl Crazy (1932 and 1943); The Goldwyn Follies (1938); Kak
Molody my Byli (1985); King of Jazz (1930); Kiss Me, Stupid (1964); Lady
be Good (1941); Porgy and Bess (1959); Rhapsody in Blue (1945); Shall We
Dance? (1937); Tea for Two (1950); That Certain Feeling (1956); When the
Boys meet The Girls (1965).
RECORDINGS: An American in Paris. EMI CDODE0N20; Goldwyn Follies.
Meridan CDE84167; Shall We Dance? EMI CDODE0N21.

GHIGLIA, Benedetto
Italian composer.
FILMS INCLUDE: Adios Gringo (1965); La Bugiarda (1964); Mattanza (1968); New York Chiama Superdrago (1966); Dimenticare Venezia (1979); Orcile (1969); A Stranger in Town (1968).
RECORDINGS: La Bugiarda. CAM CSE040.

GIANNINI, Vittorio (1903–1966)
American composer who wrote operas and orchestral works.
FILMS INCLUDE: High Over the Borders (commissioned by the New York Zoological Society with the US and Canadian governments).

GIBB, Maurice (1947–)
Australian/British pop artist and composer, member of the Bee-Gees.
FILMS INCLUDE: A Breed Apart (1984); Men, Men, Men (1973); Sargeant Pepper's Lonely Hearts Club Band (1978).

GIBBS, Michael (1937–)
South African born composer, arranger, jazz trombonist, pianist and bandleader.
FILMS INCLUDE: American Roulette (1988); Being Human (1994); Breaking In (1989); Century (1993); Close My Eyes (1991); Heat (1987); Housekeeping (1987); Iron and Silk (1991); Madame Sin (1977); Riding the Edge (1989); Twice in a Lifetime (1985); Whore (1991).
RECORDINGS: Being Human. Varèse Sarabande VSD5479.

GIBBS, Cecil Armstrong (1889–1960)
British composer who wrote a large quantity of music for choirs and amateur orchestras. Achieved immense success with his slow waltz 'Dusk' in the later 1940s. Wrote the score for Basil Dean's film of *Lorna Doone* in 1934.

GIFFORD, Harry
British composer and song writer. Wrote songs for the George Formby films including *Come on George* (1939) and *Let George Do It* (1940).

GILBERT, Herschel B. (1918–)
American composer, arranger and orchestrator.
FILMS INCLUDE: Beyond a Reasonable Doubt (1956); The Bold and The Brave (1956); Crime and Punishment U.S.A. (1959); Delay (1965); I Dismember Mama (1972); Impact (1949); Mr District Attorney (1947); Naked Dawn (1954); No Place to Hide (1955); No Time for Flowers (1952); Project Moonbase (1953); Recoil (1963); The Ring (1952); Riot in Cell Block 11 (1954); Sam Whiskey (1969); The Scarf (1951); Shamrock Hill (1949); There's a Girl

in my Heart (1949); The Thief (1952 – nominated for an Academy Award); While the City Sleeps (1956); Without Warning (1952); Witness to Murder (1954).

GILBERT, Henry F. (1868–1928)
American composer who studied composition with MacDowell (1889–92). The first to use Negro spirituals and ragtime in concert orchestral works.
FILMS INCLUDE: Down to the Sea in Ships (1922 – score now lost).

GILL, Alan
British composer.
FILMS INCLUDE: Blonde Fist (1991); A Letter to Brezhnev (1984).

GINASTERA, Alberto (1916–1983)
Argentine composer who wrote ballet and operas, together with incidental music; also wrote eleven film scores.
FILMS: Caballito Criollo (1953); El Puente (1950); Enigma de Mujer (1956); Facundo, el Tigre de Los Ilanos (1952); Hay que Bañar al Nene (1958); Los Maridos de Mamá (1956); Malambo (1942); Nace la Libertad (1949); Primavera de la Vida (1958); Rosa de América (1946); Su Segro Servidor (1954).

GLANVILLE-HICKS, Peggy (1912–1990)
Australian composer who studied at the Royal College of Music in London with Ralph Vaughan Williams, Arthur Benjamin, Constant Lanbert and Malcolm Sargent. Lived in America from 1942 and 1959, taking American citizenship in 1948.
FILMS INCLUDE: *Documentary*: The African Story (1956); Clouds (1938); Glacier (1938); The Robot (1936 – an abstract cartoon film); A Scary Time (1958); Tel (1950); Tulsa (1949).

GLANZBERG, Norbert
German composer.
FILMS INCLUDE: Il est Arrivé à Paris (It Happened in Paris) (1953); La Lumière d'en Face (The Light Across the Street) (1956); La mariée est Trop Belle (The Bride is too Beautiful) (1956); Michel Strogoff (1956); La Rage au Corps (Fire in the Blood) (1954); The Sorceress (1956).

GLASS, Paul (1934–   )
American composer.
FILMS INCLUDE: The Abductors (1957); Bunny Lake is Missing (1965); Catch my Soul (1973); Jada Goscie Jada (1962); Lady in a Cage (1963); Overlord (1975); To The Devil a Daughter (1976).

GLASS, Philip (1937–)
American composer whose minimalist style has influenced pop artists including Mike Oldfield and Brian Eno.
FILMS INCLUDE: Anima Mundi (1991); A Brief History of Time (1991); Candyman (1992); La Chiesa (1989); Closet Land (1991); Hamburger Hill (1987); Koyaanisqatsi (1982); Mishima: A Life in Four Chapters (1985); Naquoyqatsi (1991); Powaqqatsi (1988); The Thin Blue Line (1988).
RECORDINGS: Anima Mundi. Nonesuch 7559–79329–3.

GLASSER, Albert (1916–)
American composer.
FILMS INCLUDE: Air Patrol (1962); The Amazing Colossal Man (1957); The Beat Generation (1959); The Big Caper (1956); The Boy and the Pirates (1960); The Buckskin Lady (1956); Call of The Jungle (1944); The Cisco Kid in Old Mexico (1945); Confessions of an Opium Eater (1962); The Cyclops (1956); Destination 60,000 (1957); The Gay Amigo (1949); Girl in the Woods (1957); The High Powered Rifle (1960); Huk! (1956); I Shot Billy the Kid (1950); Law of the Lash (1947); Murder is my Beat (1955); Night of the Quarter Moon (1959); Oklahoma Territory (1959); Snowfire (1957); The Spider (1958); Street of Sinners (1957); Teenage Caveman (1958); Top Banana (1953); Top of the World (1955); Tormented (1960); Train to Tombstone (1950); The Treasure of Monte Cristo (1949); The Viking Women and Their Voyage to the Waters of the Sea Serpent (1957).

GLICKMAN, Mort (1898–1952)
American composer, musical director and arranger.
FILMS INCLUDE: The Blocked Trail (1943); Calling Wild Bill Elliot (1943); Days of Old Cheyenne (1943); Death Valley Manhunt (1943); Gamblers Choice (1944); Hidden Valley Outlaws (1944); The Mysterious Mr Valentine (1946); Raiders of Sunset Pass (1943).

GOEHR, Walter (1903–1960)
British composer and conductor of German birth. Involved in a great deal of film work on the continent, including a number of Julien Duvivier's early French films. Also used the name of George Walter for such films as For Freedom (1940); The Ghost Train (1941) and Spellbound (1940).
FILMS INCLUDE: Betrayed (1954); Great Expectations (1947); Lucky Nick Cain (1951); Matter of Life and Death (1946); Stop Press Girl (1949).

GOLD, Ernest (1921–)
American composer of Viennese birth who has written for both the cinema and television. Was also employed as an orchestrator and arranger.
FILMS INCLUDE: Battle of The Coral Sea (1959); A Child is Waiting (1962);

Cross of Iron (1977); The Defiant Ones (1958); Dementia (1953); Edge of Hell (1954); Exodus (1960 – awarded an Academy Award); A Fever in The Blood (1960); Fun with Dick and Jane (1976); Girl of the Limberlost (1945); Inherit the Wind (1960); It's a Mad Mad Mad Mad World (1963); Jennifer (1953); Judgement at Nuremberg (1954); The Last Sunset (1961); Man on the Prowl (1957); On the Beach (1959); The Other Woman (1954); The Runner Stumbles (1979); The Screaming Skull (1958); The Secret of Santa Vittoria (1969); Ship of Fools (1965); Tarzan's Fight for Life (1958); Tom Horn (1980); Unidentified Flying Objects (1956); Wink of an Eye (1957); Witness for the Prosecution (1957); The Young Philadelphians (1959).
RECORDINGS: Exodus. Telarc CD80168.

GOLDENBERG, Billy (1936–)
American composer who has written much for television films and series including *Kojak*, *Columbo*, *McCloud*, *Harry O* and *Executive Suite*.
FILMS INCLUDE: Busting (1973); The Domino Principle (1976); The Grasshopper (1970); Helter Skelter (1976); The Last of Sheila (1973); Play it Again, Sam (1972); Red Sky at Morning (1970); Reuben, Reuben (1982); Up the Sandbox (1972).

GOLDENTHAL, Elliot (1954–)
American composer who studied with John Corigliano and Aaron Copland.
FILMS INCLUDE: Alien 3 (1992); Batman Forever (1995); Cobb (1994); Demolition Man (1993); Drugstore Cowboy (1989); Interview with a Vampire (1994); Michael Collins (1996); Pet Semetery (1989).
RECORDINGS: Alien 3. MCA MCAD10629; Batman Forever. Varèse Sarabande VSD5671; Demolition Man. Silva Screen FILMCD156; Interview with a Vampire. GEFF GED24719; Pet Semetary. Varèse Sarabande VSD5227.

GOLDSMITH, Jerry (1929–)
American composer who studied composition with Mario Castelnuovo-Tadesco and film scoring under Miklós Rózsa. Has also written for television e.g. *Dr Kildare*, *Gunsmoke*, *The Man from U.N.C.L.E.*, *Thriller*, *The Twilight Zone* and *The Waltons*, together with chamber music and vocal works.
FILMS INCLUDE: Ace Eli and Rodger of the Skies (1973); The Agony and The Ecstasy (1965); Alien (1979); Angie (1993); Baby (1985); Bad Girls (1994); The Ballad of Cable Hogue (1970); Bandolero! (1968); Basic Instinct (1992); Black Patch (1957); The Blue Max (1966); The Boys from Brazil (1978); Breakheart Pass (1975); Breakout (1975); Capricorn One (1977); The Cassandra Crossing (1976); The Challenge (1982); Chinatown (1974); City of Fear (1958); Coma (1977); The Crimebusters (1961); The Culpepper Cattle Company (1972); Damien Omen II (1978); Damnation Alley (1977); The Detective (1968); The Don is Dead (1973); Escape from the Planet of the

Apes (1971); Face of a Fugitive (1959); Fate is the Hunter (1964); The Final Conflict (Omen III) (1981); First Blood (1982); The First Great Train Robbery (1978); The Flim-Flam Man (1967); Freud (1962); A Gathering of Eagles (1963); Gremlins (1984); Gremlins 2: The New Batch (1990); The Helicopter Spies (1967); High Velocity (1976); Hour of the Gun (1967); The Illustrated Man (1969); In Harm's Way (1965); In Like Flint (1967); Islands in the Stream (1976); Justine (1969); The Karate Killers (1967); King Solomon's Mines (1985); The Last Hard Men (1976); The Last Run (1971); Legend (1985); Lilies of the Field (1963); Link (1985); Lionheart (1987); Logan's Run (1976); Lonely are the Brave (1962); Love Field (1992); Macarthur (1977); Magic (1978); Malice (1993); The Mephisto Waltz (1971); Morituri (1965); The Most Dangerous Man in the World (1969); Night Crossing (1982); Not Without My Daughter (1991); The Omen (1976 – awarded an Academy Award); One Little Indian (1973); One of Our Spies is Missing (1966); The Other (1972); Our Man Flint (1965); Outland (1981); Papillion (1973); A Patch of Blue (1965); Patton (1969); Planet of the Apes (1967); Players (1979); Poltergeist (1982); Poltergeist II: The Other Side (1986); The Prize (1963); Psycho II (1983); Raggedy Man (1981); Rambo: First Blood, Part II (1985); Rambo III (1988); Ransom (1974); The Reincarnation of Peter Proud (1974); Rio Conchos (1964); Rio Lobo (1970); The River Wild (1994); Rudy (1993); Runaway (1984); The Russia House (1990); The Sand Pebbles (1966); The Satan Bug (1965); Sebastian (1967); Seconds (1966); The Secret of Nimh (1982); Seven Days in May (1963); Shamus (1972); Six Degrees of Separation (1993); The Spiral Road (1962); The Spy with my Face (1964); Stagecoach (1966); Star Trek The Motion Picture (1979); Star Trek V: The Final Frontier (1989); The Stripper (1963); Studs Lonigan (1960); Supergirl (1984); The Swarm (1978); Take a Hard Ride (1975); Take Her, She's Mine (1963); To Trap a Spy (1965); Tora! Tora! Tora! (1970); Total Recall (1990); The Travelling Executioner (1970); The Trouble with Angels (1966); Twilight Zone The Movie (1976); Twilight's Last Gleaming (1977); Under Fire (1983); Von Ryan's Express (1965); Warning Shot (1966); Wild Rovers (1971); The Wind and The Lion (1975).

RECORDINGS: Alien. Silva Screen FILMCD003; Angie. Varèse Sarabande VSD5469; Bad Girls. Milan 74321–22054–2; Basic Instinct. Varèse Sarabande VSD5360; First Blood. Varèse Sarabande VSD5671; Lionheart. Varèse Sarabande VSD5484; The Omen. Varèse Sarabande VSD5281; Star Trek. Columbia 983 381–2; Supergirl. Silva Screen FILMCD132.

GOODALL, Howard (1958–)

British composer who has written for television e.g. *Blackadder, Mr Bean, Red Dwarf* and *Thin Blue Line*.

GOODMAN, Alfred (1920–   )
German composer and musicologist. Emigrated to London in 1939 and New York in 1940 where he arranged music for dance bands and for the theatre.

GOODMAN, Benny (1909–1986)
American clarinettist, composer and bandleader. Provided the music for *The Benny Goodman Story* (1955).
FILMS INCLUDE: The Gang's All Here (1943); Hello Beautiful (1942); Hollywood Hotel (1938); A Song is Born (1948); Sweet and Lowdown (1944).

GOODMAN, Miles
American composer.
FILMS INCLUDE: About Last Night (1966); Footloose (1984); He Said She Said (1991); Housesitter (1992); Larger Than Life (1997); The Man Who Wasn't There (1983); The Muppet Christmas Carol (1992); Teen Wolf (1985); Zapped! (1982).

GOODWIN, Ron (1925–   )
British composer, arranger and conductor who first worked for the BBC Dance Orchestra as an arranger. In 1969, he wrote the new score for *Battle of Britain* after the music written by Sir William Walton had been rejected.
FILMS INCLUDE: The Alphabet Murders (1965); Battle of Britain (1969); Born to Run (1977); Candleshoe (1977); Children of the Damned (1963); Clash of Loyalties (1983); The Clue of the New Pin (1960); The Cracksman (1963); The Day of The Triffids (1962); Deadly Strangers (1974); Decline and Fall (1968); Diamonds on Wheels (1972); Eagle Rock (1964); The Early Bird (1965); Escape from the Dark (1976); The Executioner (1970); Follow the Boys (1963); Force 10 From Navarone (1978); Frenzy (1972); Gawain and The Green Knight (1973); Go-Kart Go (1963); I Thank a Fool (1962); I'm All Right Jack (1959); In The Nick (1959); Invasion Quartet (1961); Johnny Nobody (1960); Kill or Cure (1962); Ladies Who Do (1963); Lancelot and Guinevere (1962); The Magnificent Two (1967); Man at The Carlton Tower (1961); Man with a Gun (1958); Mister Ten Per Cent (1967); Mrs Brown, You've Got a Lovely Daughter (1968); Murder at The Gallop (1963); Murder Most Foul (1964); Murder She Said (1961); Of Human Bondage (1964); One of Our Dinosaurs is Missing (1975); Operation Crossbow (1964); Postman's Knock (1961); Quei Temerari Sulle Loro Pazze, Scatenate, Scalcinate Carriole (Monte Carlo or Bust!) (1969); Runaway Railway (1965); San Ferry Ann (1965); 633 Squadron (1963); The Spaceman and King Arthur (1979); Spanish Fly (1975); That Riviera Touch (1966); Those Magnificent Men in Their Flying Machines or How I Flew from London to Paris in 25 Hours and 11 Minutes (1965); The Trap (1966); The Trials of Oscar Wilde (1960); Valhalla

(1985); Village of Daughters (1962); Village of The Damned (1960); Where Eagles Dare (1968); Whirlpool (1959); The Witness (1959).
RECORDINGS: Battle of Britain. Silva Screen FILMCD151; Frenzy. Silva Screen FILMCD137; 633 Squadron. Silva Screen FILMCD151.

GOOSSENS, Eugene (1893–1962)
British composer and conductor, a member of the famous musical family. He was associated with the early British sound cinema, collaborating on a number of film scores including *The Constant Nymph* (1932).

GORE, Michael
American composer.
FILMS INCLUDE: The Butcher's Wife (1991); Defending Your Life (1991); Don't Tell Her It's Me (1990); Fame (1980 – Academy Award); Pretty in Pink (1986); Terms of Endearment (1993 – nominated for an Academy Award).
RECORDINGS: Terms of Endearment. Telemarc CD80168.

GOUGH, John (1903–   )
Australian composer (born in Tasmania) who came to London and studied with Ralph Vaughan-Williams at the Royal College of Music. Wrote music for short films including the RAF newsreel *The Gen*.

GOULD, Morton (1913–1996)
American composer, conductor and pianist who employed familiar jazz and folk idioms in his works. Wrote for the concert hall (four symphonies and three concerts), radio, television (including three memorable documentaries: *Verdun* (1963), *World War I* (1964–65) and *Holocaust* (1978)), films, Broadway, jazz ensembles, the ballet, theatre and school bands.
FILMS INCLUDE: *Feature*: Cinerama Holiday (1954); Delightfully Dangerous (1942); Windjammer (1958). *Documentary*: Ring of Steel (Office of War Information, 1941); San Francisco Conference (Office of War Information, 1946).

GOWERS, Patrick (1936–   )
British composer who has written for the cinema and television (e.g. *The Hound of The Baskervilles* (1988), *Smiley's People* (1982) and *Sorrel and Son* (1986)).
FILMS INCLUDE: A Bigger Splash (1975); Give God a Chance on Sunday (1970); Hamlet (1969); The Virgin and The Gypsy (1970); Whoops Apocalypse (1986).

GRAINER, Ron (1922–1981)
Australian composer, resident in Britain. Also wrote much for television e.g. *Dr Who, Edward and Mrs Simpson, Maigret, Paul Temple, The Prisoner, South Riding, Steptoe and Son* and *Tales of The Unexpected.*
FILMS INCLUDE: *Feature*: The Assassination Bureau (1968); The Bawdy Adventures of Tom Jones (1975); Before Winter Comes (1968); The Caretaker (1963); Cat and Mouse (1974); The Dock Brief (1962); The Finest Hours (1964); Hoffman (1969); I Don't Want to be Born (1975); In Search of Gregory (1969); A Kind of Loving (1962); A King's Breakfast (1963); The Legend of Young Dick Turpin (1965); Live Now, Pay Later (1962); Lock Up Your Daughters! (1969); The Moon-Spinner (1964); Mutiny on the Buses (1972); Night Must Fall (1964); Nothing but the Best (1964); The Omega Man (1971); Only When I Larf (1968); Some People (1962); Station Six Sahara (1962); Steptoe and Son (1972); Steptoe and Son Ride Again (1973); Terminus (1961); To Sir, with Love (1966); We Joined The Navy (1962); Yellow Dog (1973). *Documentary*: Giants of Steam (1963).

GRAY, Allan (1904–1973)
Polish-born composer, resident in Britain. Wrote music for the theatre and radio.
FILMS INCLUDE: The African Queen (1951); A Canterbury Tale (1944); Christmas Week-End (1946); Emil and The Detectives (1936 – Germany); I Know Where I'm Going (1945); Latin Quarter (1945); The Life and Death of Colonel Blimp (1943); Madness of The Heart (1949); A Matter of Life and Death (1946); Mr Perrin and Mr Trail (1948); The Reluctant Widow (1950); The Silver Feet (1943); This Man is Mine (1946); The Volunteer (1943).
RECORDINGS: A Matter of Life and Death. EMI CDGO 2059.

GRAY, Barry (1925–1984)
British composer and arranger. Also a freelance lyricist writing for radio and individual performers including Eartha Kitt and Hoagy Carmichael. From 1949 to 1959, he was Vera Lynn's arranger and accompanist. Associated with Gerry Anderson from 1956 and wrote music for such series as *Captain Scarlett, Stingray* and *Thunderbirds*. Also supplied electronic music for the two Dr Who films (1965 and 1966).

GREEN, John (1908–1989)
American composer, bandleader and songwriter who worked in Hollywood from 1933. From 1949 until 1958, he scored as MGM's general music director. Also active as a television composer.
FILMS INCLUDE: Alvarez Kelly (1966); Brigadoon (1954); Easter Parade (1948); The Great Caruso (1951); High Society (1956); I'll Cry Tomorrow (1955); The Inspector General (1949); Lost in a Harem (1944); Oliver! (1968); Pepe

(1960); Raintree County (1957); Rhapsody (1953); Summer Stock (1950); They Shoot Horses, Don't They? (1969); Twilight of Honour (1963).
RECORDINGS: Raintree County. RCA GD60889(1).

GREEN, Philip (1917–)
British composer.
FILMS INCLUDE: Alive and Kicking (1958); All Night Long (1961); And Women Shall Weep (1960); Bobbikins (1959); The Bulldog Breed (1960); Carry on Admiral (1957); Desert Mice (1959); The Devil's Agent (1962); The Devil's Pass (1957); Don't Panic Chaps (1959); Elstree Story (1952); The Extra Day (1956); Father's Doing Fine (1952); Flame in The Streets (1961); Follow a Star (1959); Friends and Neighbours (1959); The Girl Hunters (1963); The Golden Disc (1958); Hello London (1958); In The Doghouse (1961); Innocent Sinners (1958); The Intelligence Men (1965); It's All Happening (1963); Joey Boy (1965); John and Julie (1955); Just my Luck (1957); Landfall (1949); The League of Gentlemen (1959); Life in Emergency Ward 10 (1958); Life is a Circus (1958); Make Mine Mink (1960); Man in the Moon (1960); Man of the Moment (1955); The Man Who Finally Died (1962); The March Hare (1956); Masquerade (1965); Murder without Crime (1950); On the Beat (1962); Operation Amsterdam (1958); Piccadilly Third Stop (1960); Rooney (1958); Sapphire (1959); Sea Fury (1958); The Secret Partner (1961); The Shakedown (1959); The Singer not the Song (1960); The Square Peg (1958); A Stitch in Time (1963); Tiara Tahiti (1962); A Touch of Larceny (1959); Two Left Feet (1963); Up in the World (1956); Upstairs and Downstairs (1959); Victim (1961); The Violent Playground (1957); Who Don It? (1956); Witness in the Dark (1959); Woman and the Hunter (1957); The Yellow Hat (1966); Your Money or Your Wife (1960).

GREEN, Walter (1910–)
American composer of scores for many western films.
FILMS INCLUDE: Black Hills (1947); Cheyenne Takes Over (1947); Dead Man's Gold (1948); Frontier Revenge (1948); Hostile Country (1950); King of the Bullwhip (1951); Outlaw Women (1952); Rimfire (1949); Stage to Mesa City (1948); Wild Country (1947).

GREENBAUM, Hyam (1901–1942)
British violinst, conductor and composer. Married to the harpist Sidonie Goossens. From 1936 to 1939, he was conductor of the BBC Television Orchestra, the first musician to hold such a post. Composers such as Walton, Lambert and Rawsthorne are said to have turned to him for technical orchestral advice. Walton did confirm that his first film score Escape Me Never (1934), was actually orchestrated by Greenbaum – as were his ensuing ones until Greenbaum's death.

GREENWOOD, John (1889–1975)
British composer and conductor who studied at the RCM under Stanford and won the Arthur Sullivan prize for composition and the Grove Scholarship. Wrote scores for almost fifty films, one of which, *The Last Days of Dolwyn*, won an award at the 1948 Venice Film Festival. Also composed two symphonies, symphonic poems, chamber music, songs and a ballet.
FILMS INCLUDE: *Feature*: A.1 at Lloyd's (1940); At the Villa Rosa (1939); The Broken Boy (1937); The Drum (1937); East Meets West (1936); Elephant Boy (1937); Eureka Stockade (1948); Frieda (1947); The Gentle Gunman (1952); The Gentle Sex (1943); Hungry Hill (1946); The Lamp Still Burns (1943); The Last Days of Dolwyn (1948); Pimpernel Smith (1941); Quartet (1948); San Demetrio, London (1944); The Sleeping Cardinal (1931); Trio (1950); Twenty-One Days (1939). *Documentary*: Berth 24 (1950); The Lake District (1957); Wavell's 30,000 (CFU, 1942).
RECORDINGS: Hungry Hill. EMI CDGO 2059.

GRÉMILLON, Jean (1901–1959)
French director who studied music and was employed as a musician in the orchestra accompanying silent films. Frequently wrote his own scripts and composed the music for many of his films.
FILMS INCLUDE: Lumière d'été (1942); Maldone (1928); Pattes Blanches (1948); Le Printemps de la Liberté (1948); Le 6 Juin à l'Aube (1945); Remoques (1939); Tour au Large (1926).

GREVILLE, Ursula
British composer who wrote the music for the documentary film *The Key to Scotland* (Strand, 1935).

GRIFFITH, D.W. (1875–1948)
American film director and a very important figure in the history of American films. Collaborated in scoring two of his own films: *The Birth of the Nation* (1915) and *Intolerance* (1916).

GRIGORIU, Teodor (1926–)
Romanian composer who studied partly with Khatchaturian at the Moscow Conservatory (1954–55). Has written many incidental scores for the theatre, and has also collaborated successfully with leading Romanian film directors.
FILMS INCLUDE: Codin (1963); The Column (1968); The Danube Waves (1960); Eruption (1957); The Forest of the Hanged (1965); Lupeni '29 (1963); Our Daily Heart (1972); The Soimaru Family (1964).

GRIMM, Friedrich-Karl (1902–)
German composer, conductor and pianist. Lived in London (1929–30) where he gave a concert of his own chamber compositions at the Grotrian Hall. He was a member of the Jury for the Section of German composers in 1937–44 and began to write music for films about that time. Wrote orchestral scores for ten documentaries.

GROFÉ, Ferde (1892–1972)
American composer, conductor and arranger. Violinist in the Los Angeles Symphony Orchestra for ten years. Admired as an arranger by the bandleader Paul Whiteman who engaged him to arrange symphonic jazz which was popular at the time.
FILMS INCLUDE: Diamond Jim (1935); King of Jazz (1930); Minstrel Man (1944); Rocket Ship X-M (1950).

GROSS, Charles (1934–)
American composer who has also written music for television films. Studied with Milhand.
FILMS INCLUDE: Across the River (1965); Blue Sunshine (1977); Choices (1984); Country (1984); The Group (1966); Gunslinger (1956); Heartland (1979); In the Shadow of a Killer (1991); It Conquered the World (1956); The Long Ride (1983); My Old Man's Place (1971); Naked Paradise (1956); No Place Like Home (1989); Not of This Earth (1956); On the Yard (1978); Shake, Rattle and Rock! (1956); Sweet Dreams (1985); Valdez is Coming (1970); Whose Life is it Anyway? (1981).

GROSZ, Willhelm (1894–1939)
Austrian composer, conductor and pianist who lived in London from 1934.

GRUENBERG, Louis (1884–1964)
American composer of Russian origin who studied the piano and composition in Berlin with Busoni and Koch. Wrote opera and many orchestra works. Moved to California in the late 1930s where he became an expert in writing film music. His scores for *The Fight for Life*, *So Ends the Night* and *The Commandos Strike at Dawn* won Academy Awards.
FILMS INCLUDE: All the King's Men (1949); An American Romance (1943); Arab of Triumph (1947); The Commandos Strike at Dawn (1942); Counter Attack (1944); The Fight for Life (1938); The Gangster (1946); Quicksand (1949); Smart Woman (1947); So Ends the Night (1940); Stagecoach (1939 – part only).

GRUNENWALD, Jean-Jacques (1911–1982)

French composer and organist who wrote music for the concert hall. His scores for French films include several directed by Robert Bresson and Jacques Becker.

FILMS INCLUDE: Les Aventures D'Arsene Lupin (1957); Les Dames du Bois de Boulogne (1943); Le Défroque (The Renegade Priest) (1954); The Diary of a Country Priest (1950); Edouard et Caroline (1951); L'Étrange Désir de Monsieur Bard (1954); Monsieur Vincent (1947); Le Rideau Cramoisi (1952); La Sculpture Française Au Moyen-Age (1948); La Vérité Sur Bébé Donge (1952).

GRUSIN, Dave (1934–)

American composer and musical director who worked on the Andy Williams TV Show for several years in the 1960s.

FILMS INCLUDE: Absence of Malice (1981); ... And Justice for All (1979); Author! Author! (1982); Bobby Deerfield (1977); Bonfire of the Vanities (1990); Candy (1968); The Champ (1979); Divorce American Style (1967); The Electric Horseman (1979); The Fabulous Baker Boys (1989 – nominated for Academy Award); Falling in Love (1984); Fire Sale (1977); The Firm (1993 – nominated for Academy Award); The Friends of Eddie Coyle (1973); The Front (1976); Fuzz (1972); The Gang Couldn't Shoot Straight (1971); Generation (1969); The Goodbye Girl (1977); The Goonies (1985); The Graduate (1967); The Great Northfield Minnesota Raid (1972); Halls of Anger (1970); Havana (1990); The Heart is a Lonely Hunter (1968); Heaven can Wait (1978); Ishtar (1987); The Little Drummer Girl (1984); Lucas (1986); The Mad Room (1968); A Man called Gannon (1968); The Midnight Man (1974); The Milagro Beanfield War (1988 – Academy Award); Mr Billion (1977); Murder by Death (1976); My Bodyguard (1980); On Golden Pond (1981); The Pope of Greenwich Village (1984); The Pursuit of Happiness (1970); Racing with the Moon (1984); Reds (1981); Scandalous (1983); Shoot Out (1971); Tell them Willie Boy is Here (1969); Tequila Sunrise (1988); Three Days of the Condor (1975); Tootsie (1982); W.W. And the Dixie Dancekings (1975); Waterhole no.3 (1967); Where were you when the lights went out? (1968); Winning (1968); The Yakuza (1974).

RECORDINGS: The Firm. Silva Screen FILMCD152: On Golden Pond. RCA 09026 61326–2.

GUNNING, Christopher (1944–)

British composer

FILMS INCLUDE: *Feature*. Goodbye Gemini (1970); Hands of the Ripper (1971); When the Whales Came (1989). *Documentary*: A New Age for Railways (1979).

RECORDINGS: Hands of the Ripper. Silva Screen FILMCD714; When the Whales Came. Silva Screen FILMCD049.

GURLITT, Manfred (1890–1972)
German composer and conducter who studied composition with Humperdinck. Settled in Japan after World War II and revisited Germany in 1953 to perform some of his works. He composed music to four cultural films for the Terra Society (1936–37).

GUTHRIE, Arlo (1947–)
American ballad singer, son of Woody Guthrie.
FILMS INCLUDE: Alice's Restaurant (1969); Arthur Penn 1922 (1970); Renaldo and Clara (1977); Roadside Prophets (1992); Woodstock (1970).

HADJIDAKIS, Manos (1925–1994)
Greek composer who wrote scores for many Greek and international films. He won an Academy Award for the music and lyrics of the title song for the film *Never on Sunday* (1960).
FILMS INCLUDE: Agioupa (1957); Aliki (1962); America, America (1963); Bed of Grass (1956); Blue (1968); Honeymoon (1979); In the Cool of the Day (1963); The Invincible Six (1968); It Happened in Athens (1961); The Martlet's Tale (1970); Memed My Hawk (1984); Pote Tin Kyriaki (Never on Sunday) (1959); Stella (1956); Susuz Yaz (Dry Summer) (1964); Topkapi (The Light of Day) (1964).
RECORDINGS: America, America. STAN STZ112; Blue. Silva Screen FILMCD176; Never on Sunday. RCA 09026 61326–2; Topkapi. CHESKY CD71.

HAENTZSCHEL, Georg (1907–1992)
German composer who assisted composer Theo Mackeben on the Berlin Radio Hour before moving into film scoring. Also wrote a great deal of light orchestral music for radio orchestras, and during World War II he was the Director of the German Dance and Light Music Orchestra. After the War, he was appointed composer and conductor to the West German Radio in Cologne.
FILMS INCLUDE: Annelia (1941); Emil und die Detektive (1955); Hotel Adlon (1955); Meine Kinder und Ich (1955); Münchhausen (1943); Robinson Soll Nicht Sterben (1957); Via Mala (1944).
RECORDINGS: Annelia. Capriccio 10 400; Münchhausen. Capriccio 10 400; Via Mala. Capriccio 10 400.

HAGEMAN, Richard (1882–1966)
Dutch composer and conductor, resident in America. Travelled to New York in 1906 as an accompanist, and conducted at the Metropolitan Opera, New

York. (1908–22), The Chicago Civic Opera (1922–23) and the Los Angeles Grand Opera (1923). Later worked at Paramount Studios in Hollywood.
FILMS INCLUDE: Fort Apache (1948); The Fugitive (1947); The Great Caruso (1951); Grounds for Marriage (1950); The Howards of Virginia (1940); If I were King (1938 – nominated for Academy Award); The Long Voyage Home (1940); Mourning Becomes Electra (1947); Rhapsody (1953); The Shanghai Gesture (1942); She Wore a Yellow Ribbon (1949); Stagecoach (1939 – part only); This Woman is Mine (1941); The Toast Of New Orleans (1950); Wagon Master (1950).
RECORDINGS: She Wore a Yellow Ribbon. Silva Screen FILM CD176; Stagecoach. Silva Screen FILM CD153.

HAJOS, Karl (1889–1950)
Hungarian composer who lived in America from the 1920s.
FILMS INCLUDE: Appointment with Murder (1948); Dangerous Intruder (1945); Hitler's Hangman (1943); It's a Small World (1950); The Lovable Cheat (1949); Morocco (1930); Stars over Texas (1946); Summer Storm (1944 – nominated for an Academy Award); Werewolf In London (1935); Wild West (1945).

HAMLISCH, Marvin (1945–   )
American composer, arranger and pianist. Wrote his first film score in 1968. Became the first individual ever to win three Oscars in one night at the 1974 Academy Award ceremony – one for the score of *The Sting* and two for *The Way We Were* (one for the score, the other for the title song sung by Barbra Streisand).
FILMS INCLUDE: The April Fools (1969); Bananas (1971); Chapter Two (1979); A Chorus Line (1985); D.A.R.Y.L. (1985); The Experts (1989); Fat City (1970); Flap (1970); Frankie and Johnny (1991); Ice Castles (1978); Irving Berlin's America (1986); The January Man (1988); Kotch (1971); Little Nikita (1988); The Mirror has two Faces (1996); Ordinary People (1980); Pennies from Heaven (1981); The Prisoner of Second Avenue (1975); Romantic Comedy (1983); Same Time, Next Year (1978); Save the Tiger (1972); Seems Like Old Times (1980); Ski Party (1965); Something Big (1971); Sophie's Choice (1982 – nominated for an Academy Award); The Special London Bridge Special (1972); The Spy Who Loved Me (1977); Starting Over (1979); The Sting (1973 – Academy Award); The Swimmer (1968); Take the Money and Run (1969); Three Men and a Baby (1987); The War Between Men and Women (1972); The Way We Were (1973 – two Academy Awards); The World's Greatest Athlete (1973).
RECORDINGS: Ice Castles. Sony SK53380; The Spy Who Loved Me. Silva Screen FILMCD007; The Way We Were. RCA 09026 61326–2.

HANCOCK, Herbie (1940–)

American composer and jazz musician who turned to electronic music in the 1970s, soon after he began to write for films.

FILMS INCLUDE: Action Jackson (1988); Blowup (1966); Colours (1988); Death Wish (1974); Harlem Night (1989); Round Midnight (1986); A Soldier's Story (1984); The Spook Who Sat By The Door (1973).

HARLINE, Leigh (1907–1969)

American composer who joined the Walt Disney studios in 1932 as an arranger and scorer. He won an Academy Award for the song 'When You Wish Upon A Star' from Disney's *Pinocchio*. He left Disney in 1941 and free-lanced for various studios.

FILMS INCLUDE: The Bachelor and the Bobby-Soxer (1947); Behave Yourself (1951); The Big Steal (1949); Black Widow (1954); The Bottom of the Bottle (1955); The Brighton Strangler (1945); Call Me Mister (1951); Crack-up (1946); Down Among The Sheltering Palms (1952); The Enemy Below (1957); The Facts of Life (1960); The Farmer's Daughter (1947); Good Morning, Miss Dove (1955); Guns of Diablo (1964); The Guy Who Came Back (1951); Heavenly Days (1944); His Girl Friday (1940); His Kind of Woman (1951); Holiday for Lovers (1959); The Honeymoon Machine (1961); House of Bamboo (1955); Isle of the Dead (1945); Johnny Angel (1945); Lady Luck (1946); The Last Frontier (1955); The More the Merrier (1943); Mr Blandings Builds His Dream House (1948); My Friend Irma Goes West (1950); No Down Payment (1957); On The Loose (1951); The Pride of the Yankees (1942 – nominated for an Academy Award); The Remarkable Mr Pennypacker (1958); Road to Utopia (1945); The Sky's The Limit (1943); Strange Bedfellows (1964); Susan Slept Here (1954); Teenage Rebel (1956); Ten North Frederick (1958); That's My Bow (1951); These Thousand Hills (1958); They Got Me Covered (1942); The True Story of Jesse James (1957); Visit to a Small Planet (1959); Warlock (1959); The Wayward Bus (1957); The Wonderful World of Brothers Grimm (1962); You Were Never Lovelier (1942 – nominated for an Academy Award).

HARLING, W. Franke (1887–1958)

American composer.

FILMS INCLUDE: Adam had Four Sons (1941); The Bachelor's Daughter (1946); A Bill of Divorcement (1932); The Lady is Willing (1942); One Hour with You (1932); Penny Serenade (1941); The Scarlet Empress (1934); Souls at Sea (1937); Stagecoach (1939 – part only); Three Russian Girls (1944 – nominated for an Academy Award).

HARRIS, Max
Composer who also wrote for television (e.g. *The Spies*).
FILMS INCLUDE: Baby Love (1968); Carry on England (1976); Dreamchild (1985); On the Buses (1971); One of Our Dinosaurs is Missing (1975).

HARRIS, Roy (1898–1979)
American composer and teacher. Wrote fourteen symphonies, one ballet and one film score, for *One-Tenth of a Nation* (1940), which uses chamber music forces.

HARSÁNY, Tibor (1898–1954)
French composer and pianist of Hungarian descent, who received guidance from Bartok but owed his technical training to Kodály. In 1924 he moved to Paris where he helped to found the Société Triton for contemporary chamber music. Wrote one film score in 1933: *La Joie de Vivre*.

HARTLEY, Richard R. (1944–   )
British composer.
FILMS INCLUDE: Aces High (1976); Afraid of the Dark (1991); Bad Timing (1980); Consuming Passions (1988); Dance with a Stranger (1984); Dealers (1989); Galileo (1974); The Good Father (1986); The Lady Vanishes (1979); Parker (1984); Party Party (1983); Princess Caraboo (1994); The Railway Station Man (1992); The Rocky Horror Picture Show (1975); The Romantic Englishwoman (1975); The Secret Rapture (1993); She's Been Away (1989); Sheen (1984); Shock Treatment (1981); Soursweet (1988); The Tree of Hands (1989).

HARUT 'UNYAN, Alexander G. (1920–   )
Armenian composer and pianist who was made a People's Artist of the USSR in 1970. Has written operas, cantatas and other vocal pieces, many based on folksong.

HARVEY, Richard R. (1953–   )
British composer who has also written for television e.g. *Dr Finlay* and *Jake's Progress*.
FILMS INCLUDE: The Assam Garden (1985); Dancing with the Dead (1990); Deadly Advice (1993); Defence of the Realm (1985); The Honorary Consul (1983); House of the Long Shadows (1982); Lady Chatterley's Lover (1981); Ping Pong (1986); Steaming (1984); To the Western World: The Travels of J M Synge and Jack Yeats in Connemara in 1905 (1981); Trucking (1980).
RECORDINGS: The Assam Garden; Dancing with the Dead; Deadly Advice; Defence of the Realm. Silva Screen FILMCD172.

HASKELL, Jimmy
American composer who has written many scores for television films since the 1980s.
FILMS INCLUDE: Animalympics (1979); Apache Uprising (1965); Arizona Bushwhackers (1967); Buckskin (1968); Death Game (1976); Dirty Mary Crazy Larry (1974); Electra Glide in Blue (1973); Fort Utah (1967); The Gun Hawk (1963); Guyana el Crimen del Siglo (1979); The Honkers (1972); Hostile Guns (1967); Johnny Reno (1965); Joyride (1977); King of the Gypsies (1978); Lipstick (1976); Love in a Goldfish Bowl (1961); Night of the Lepus (1972); Red Tomahawk (1966); Rogue's Gallery (1967); She's Back (1989); Surf Party (1963); Town Tamer (1965); Waco (1966); When the North Wind Blows (1974); Zachariah (1970).

HATCH, Tony (1939–   )
British composer (now resident in Australia) of pop songs, mainly for Petula Clark, and music for television including *Crossroads*, *Emmerdale Farm*, *Love Story*, *Man Alive*, *Neighbours* and *Sweeney II*. Married to the singer Jackie Trent.
FILMS INCLUDE: Travels with My Aunt (1972).

HATLEY, Thomas Marvin (1905–1986)
American composer and musical director of the Hal Roach Studio (1930–39) where he scored several Laurel and Hardy films. Left the cinema in the 1940s to concentrate on playing the piano.
FILMS INCLUDE: Blockheads (1938 – nominated for an Academy Award); Broadway Limited (1941); A Chump at Oxford (1939); General Spanky (1936); Merrily We Live (1938); Nobody's Baby (1937); Saps at Sea (1940); Swiss Miss (1938); There goes my Heart (1938 – nominated for an Academy Award); Topper (1937); Topper Takes a Trip (1939); Way out West (1937); Zenobia (1939).

HAWKSHAW, Alan
English composer who has also written for television e.g. *Grange Hill*.
FILMS INCLUDE: The Green Wall (1969); Groupie Girl (1970); The Silent Witness (1978).

HAWKSWORTH, Johnny
British composer and band leader who has also written for television e.g. *Danger U.B.X.*
FILMS INCLUDE: Bang (1967); Goal! World Cup 1966 (1966); The Naked World of Harrison Marks (1965); The Penthouse (1967); Plod (1972); Zeta One (1969).

HAYES, Isaac (1942–)
American composer, singer and actor who played the piano in Memphis clubs and played in several bands including Sir Isaac and the Doo-Dads.
FILMS INCLUDE: Acting on Impulse (1993); Escape from New York (1981); Guilty as Charged (1991); I'm Gonna Git You Sucka (1988); Posse (1993); Prime Target (1991); Robin Hood: Men in Tights (1993); Shaft (1971); Shaft's Big Score! (1972); Three Tough Guys (1974); Truck Turner (1974); Wattstax (1973).
RECORDINGS: Shaft. Telemarc CD80251.

HAYTON, Lenni (1908–1971)
American composer.
FILMS INCLUDE: The Bugle Sounds (1941); Easy to Love (1953); The Harvey Girls (1946); Hello, Dolly! (1969); Meet the People (1943); Salute to the Marines (1943); Singin' in the Rain (1952); Summer Holiday (1946); Star! (1968); Whistling in Dixie (1942); A Yank on the Burma Road (1942); Ziegfeld Follies (1944).

HAZELHURST, Ronnie (1928–)
British composer, band leader and arranger who has written mainly for television including *The Fall and Rise of Reginald Perrin*, *The Last of the Summer Wine* and *The Two Ronnies*.

HEFTI, Neal (1922–)
American composer, band musician and arranger for the bands of Woody Herman, Harry James and Count Basie. Also wrote the theme for the *Batman* TV series.
FILMS INCLUDE: Barefoot in the Park (1967); Boeing Boeing (1965); Duel at Diablo (1965); Harlow (1965); How to Murder Your Wife (1964); Jamboree (1957); Last of the Red Hot Lovers (1972); Lord Love a Duck (1965); The Odd Couple (1967); Oh Dad Poor Dad, Mama's Hung You in the Closet and I'm Feeling so Sad . . . (1966); P.J. (1967); Sex and the Single Girl (1964); Synanon (1965); Won Ton Ton, The Dog Who Saved Hollywood (1975).

HEINDORF, Ray (1908–1980)
American composer, conductor and arranger who was head of Warner Brothers music department where he arranged and conducted musical scores for many films, and occasionally wrote original scores and songs. He won Academy Awards for his orchestrations of *Yankee Doodle Dandy* (1942), *This is the Army* (1943) and *The Music Man* (1962).
FILMS INCLUDE: The Breaking Point (1950); No Time for Sergeants (1957); Stop, You're Killing Me (1952); Up Periscope (1959); The West Point Story (1950); Wonder Man (1945); Young Man with a Horn (1950).

HELY-HUTCHINSON, Victor (1901–1947)
British composer and pianist who became Professor of Music at Birmingham University in 1934 and Director of Music at the BBC in 1944, in succession to Sir Arthur Bliss. Famous for his Carol Symphony.
FILMS INCLUDE: *Documentary*: Battle of Supplies (Strand, 1942); The Call of the Sea, South Africa (CFU, 1944); Camouflage Airview (Verity, 1945); The Gen (RAF Newsreel); New Zealand (CFU, 1945); Teeth of Steel (Technique); When We Build Again (Strand, 1944).

HENZE, Hans Werner (1926–)
German composer who was drafted into the army early in 1944 and seconded to a unit specially formed for the making of propaganda films. After World War II returned to his studies with Fortner and Leibowitz at Darmstadt. Settled in Italy in 1953.
FILMS INCLUDE: L'Amour à Mort (Love unto Death) (1984); Un Amour de Swann (1983); Comrades (1986); Good for Nothing (1978); Der Junge Torless (Young Torless) (1966); Muriel, Ou le Temps d'un Retour (1963); Die Verlorene Ehre der Katharina Blum (1975).

HERRMANN, Bernard (1911–1975)
American composer and conductor who lived in London for several months each year. Associated with the films of Orson Welles and Alfred Hitchcock. Used electric violin and bass in *The Day the Earth Stood Still* – one of the first examples of electronic music in films. He died in his sleep shortly after completing the recording session for his score of *Taxi Driver* (1976); director, Martin Scorsese, dedicated the film to his memory.
FILMS INCLUDE: All that Money can Buy (1941); Anna and the King of Siam (1946); The Battle of Neretra (1970); Beneath the 12 Mile Reef (1963 – used nine harps in the Ocean music sequence); Bezeten – Het Gat in de Muur (Obsessions) (1969); The Birds (1963); Blue Denim (1959); The Bride Wore Black (1968); Cape Fear (1961); Citizen Kane (1941); The Day the Earth Stood Still (1951); The Egyptian (1954); Endless Night (1972); Fahrenheit 451 (1966); Garden of Evil (1954); The Ghost and Mrs Muir (1947); Hangover Square (1945 – Herrmann's *Concerto Macabre* is based on some of the film's music); A Hatful of Rain (1957); It Lives Again (1978); Jane Eyre (1943); Jason and The Argonauts (1963); Journey to the Center of the Earth (1959); Joy in the Morning (1964); The Kentuckian (1955); The Magnificent Ambersons (1942); The Man in the Grey Flannel Suit (1956); The Man Who Knew Too Much (1955); La Mariée était en Noir (1967); Marnie (1964); Mysterious Island (1961); The Naked and The Dead (1958); The Night Digger (1971); North by Northwest (1959); Obsession (1976); On Dangerous Ground (1951); Prince of Players (1954); Psycho (1960); The Seventh Voyage of Sinbad (1958); Sisters (1972); The Snows of Kilamanjaro (1952); Taxi

Driver (1976); Tender is the Night (1961); The Three Worlds of Gulliver (1960); Torn Curtain (1966 – this score was rejected by Hitchcock; Herrmann never recovered from this rejection); The Trouble with Harry (1954); Twisted Nerve (1968); Vertigo (1958); White Witch Doctor (1953); The Wrong Man (1956).
RECORDINGS: Cape Fear. Silva Screen FILMCD162; Citizen Kane. Silva Screen FILMCD180; Jane Eyre. Fox 07822 11 006–2; Jason and the Argonauts. Silva Screen FILMXCD 187; Psycho. Silva Screen FILMCD162.

HESS, Nigel
British composer and nephew of pianist Myra Hess. Has written much for television e.g. *Dangerfield* (1994), *Hetty Wainthrop Investigates* (1995) and *Wycliffe* (1994).

HEYMANN, Werner R. (1896–1961)
German composer, later resident in Hollywood. Worked in Max Reinhardt's theatre and in 1925 became assistant to the musical director of UFA, the German film company. Later became the company's musical director. Went to the USA in 1933, but returned to Germany in the early 1950s.
FILMS INCLUDE: Adorable (1933); Ein Blonder Traum (1932); Bluebeard's Eighth Wife (1935); Le Capitaine Craddock (1931); Le Chemin du Paradis (1930); Die Drei von der Tankstelle (1930); The King and the Chorus Girl (1937); Der Kongress Tanzt (1931); Mademoiselle Fifi (1944); My Life with Caroline (1941); A Night to Remember (1942); Ninotchka (1939); One Million B.C. (1940); Un Rêve Blonde (1932); The Shop Around the Corner (1940); Spione (1928); To Be or Not To Be (1942); Together Again (1944); Topper Returns (1941).

HINDEMITH, Paul (1895–1963)
German composer, viola player and conductor who wrote works in many genres, including operas (e.g. *Mathis der Maler*) and ballets.
FILMS INCLUDE: Clemont de Fouet (1931 – for string trio); Felix der Kator in Zirkus (Opus 44/1, 1926 – for mechanical organ); Vormittagsspuk (1928 – for mechanical piano).

HIRSHFELDER, David
American composer.
FILMS INCLUDE: Shine (1996).

HODDINOTT, Alun (1929–)
Welsh composer who studied with Arthur Benjamin. Has written works in many genres including operas and eight symphonies.
FILMS INCLUDE: *Feature*: The Horsemasters (1961); Sword of Sherwood Forest

(1960). *Documentary*: Pembrokeshire, My Country (1960); The Secret World of Odilon Redilon (1973 – uses excerpts from Hoddinott's concert works); Steel be my Sister (1975).

HODGE, Jonathan
FILMS INCLUDE: Embassy (1972); Great (1975); Villain (1971); Z.P.G. (1971).

HOFFERT, Paul (1943–)
Canadian composer.
FILMS INCLUDE: Circle of Two (1980); Fanny Hill (1983); Flick (1969); The Groundstar Conspiracy (1972); H G Wells' The Shape of Things to Come (1979); High-Ballin' (1979); Outrageous (1977); Sunday in the Country (1974).

HOLDRIDGE, Lee (1944–)
American composer who has also written for television. Born in Port-au-Prince, Haiti.
FILMS INCLUDE: The Beastmaster (1982); Big Business (1988); Cyborg Agent (1992); Dead Men Don't Wear Plaid (1981); E'Lollipop (1975); The Greatest (1977); Jeremy (1973); Jonathan Livingston Seagull (1973); Mahogany (1975); Micki and Maude (1984); Moment by Moment (1978); Mr Mom (1983); My Sweet Lady (Sunshine Part II) (1975); Old Gringo (1989); Oliver's Story (Love Story) (1978); The Pack (1977); Pastime (1991); The Sidelong Glances of a Pigeon Kicker (1970); Splash (1984); Sylvester (1985); Tilt (1978); Transylvania 6-5000 (1985); Walk Like a Man (1987); Winterhawk (1975).
RECORDINGS: Old Gringo. GNP GNPD8017; Transylvania 6-5000. Silva Screen FILMCD127.

HOLLANDER, Frederick (1896–1976)
German composer who composed for Max Reinhardt and for his own theatre in Berlin. Wrote scores and many songs for German and Hollywood films including 'Falling in Love Again' (*The Blue Angel*, 1930).
FILMS INCLUDE: The Blue Angel (1930); Bluebeard's Eighth Wife (1938); Destry Rides Again (1939); Die Grosse Sehnsucht (1930); Ian Suzanne (1934); Ich und die Kaiserin (1933 – which he also directed); The Man Who Came to Dinner (1942); Der Mann, Der Seinen Muder Sucht (1931); Million Dollar Baby (1941); The Only Girl (1933); The Red Stallion (1946); Das Strumpfband der Kaiserin (1932).
RECORDINGS: The Blue Angel. RCA 7421–38656–2.

HOLLINGSWORTH, John (1916–1963)
British music director. Associate conductor of the Royal Air Force Symphony Orchestra during World War II. His first work for films was in 1942 when he conducted the orchestra in the recording of Leighton Lucas's score for *Target for Tonight*. His introduction to feature films came in 1945 when he became assistant music director to Muir Mathieson with whom he collaborated on the music for *Brief Encounter*.

HOLST, Gustav (1874–1934)
British composer who wrote 'The Planets' and 'St Paul's Suite'. Composed music for one film *The Bells* which was produced at Wembley by Associated Sound Film Industries in about 1931.

HONEGGER, Arthur (1892–1955)
French composer who was a member of 'Les Six'. Remembered for his unusual works including the poems 'Rugby' and 'Pacific 231'. Worked extensively for the French cinema, and wrote the score for the British film *Pygmalion* in 1938, a commission which was originally offered to Walton.
FILMS INCLUDE: Antoine Bourdelle (1950); Crime et Châtiment (1934); L'Idée (1934); Mayerling (1936); Les Misérables (1934); Napoléon (1927); Pygmalion (1938); Le Roi de Camargue (1934); La Rouse (1923); Le Village Perdu (1947); Le Visage de la France (1937).
RECORDINGS: L'Idée. Marco Polo 8 223460; Mayerling. Marco Polo 8 223467; Les Misérables. Marco Polo 8 223134; Napoléon. Marco Polo 8 223134.

HOPKINS, Anthony (1921–   )
British composer, pianist and broadcaster who has written several chamber operas.
FILMS INCLUDE: The Angel Who Pawned Her Harp (1953); Billy Budd (1962); The Blue Peter (1954); Cast a Dark Shadow (1955); Child's Play (1954); Decameron Nights (1953); The Pickwick Papers (1952); Seven Thunders (1957); Vice Versa (1947).

HOPKINS, Kenyon (1932–   )
American composer.
FILMS INCLUDE: Baby Doll (1956); Doctor, You've got to be Kidding! (1966); Downhill Racer (1969); The First Time (1968); The Fugitive Kind (1959); The Hustler (1961); Lilith (1964); A Lovely Way to Die (1968); Mister Buddwing (1965); The Strange One (1957); This Property is Condemned (1966); Twelve Angry Men (1956); Wild in the Country (1961); Wild River (1960); The Yellow Canary (1963).

HORNER, James (1953–)

American composer who spent his early years in England. His score for *Star Trek II* launched his film music career in 1982.

FILMS INCLUDE: Aliens (1986 – nominated for an Academy Award); An American Tail (1986); Apollo 13 (1995); Battle Beyond the Stars (1980); Bopha! (1993); Brainstorm (1983); Braveheart (1995); Casper (1995); Clear and Present Danger (1994); Cocoon (1985); Commando (1985); Deadly Blessing (1981); The Dresser (1983); A Far Off Place (1993); Field of Dreams (1989); Glory (1989); Gorky Park (1983); Heaven Help Us (1984); Humanoids from the Deep (1980); Jack the Bear (1993); The Journey of Natty Gann (1985); Jumanji (1995); Krull (1983); The Lady in Red (1979); The Man Without a Face (1993); My Heroes have always been Cowboys (1991); Once upon a Forest (1993); The Pagemaster (1994); Pelican Brief (1993); The Pursuit of D.B. Cooper (1981); The Rocketeer (1991); Something Wicked This Way Comes (1982); Star Trek III – The Search for Spock (1984); Star Trek – The Wrath of Khan (1982); Swing Kids (1993); Testament (1983); Uncommon Valour (1983); Volunteers (1985); We're Back! A Dinosaur's Story (1993); Willow (1988); Wolfen (1981).

RECORDINGS: Aliens. Varèse Sarabande VSD47263; Apollo 13. Varèse Sarabande VSD5671; Braveheart. Silva Screen FILMXCD 187; Casper. MCA MCD1 1240; Gorky Park. Varèse Sarabande VSD47260; Jumanji. Epic 481561–2; Star Trek III. GNP GNPD8022.

HORWOOD, Bo

American composer.

FILMS INCLUDE: Happy Birthday to Me (1980); The Killing of a Chinese Bookie (1976); Love Streams (1984); Minnie and Moskowitz (1971); My Bloody Valentine (1981); Opening Night (1977); Terror Train (1979); A Woman Under the Influence (1974).

HOWARD, James Newton (1951–)

American composer who played with the band Mama Lion in the 1970s. Also worked as a session pianist and arranger for Elton John's band.

FILMS INCLUDE: Alive (1993); American Heart (1992); Dave (1993); Diggstown (1992); Falling Down (1993); The Fugitive (1993 – nominated for an Academy Award); Glengarry Glen Ross (1992); Grand Canyon (1991); Hear Office (1986); Just Cause (1995); The Man in the Moon (1991); Outbreak (1995); The Saint of Fort Washington (1993); Waterworld (1995); Wyatt Earp (1994).

RECORDINGS: Dave. GIAN 74321 15292–2; Outbreak. Varèse Sarabande VSD5599; Waterworld. MCA MCD 11282.

HUGHES, Spike (1908–1987)
British composer, critic and conductor who studied with Egon Wellesz in Vienna.
FILMS INCLUDE: *Feature*: Fiddlers Three (1944). *Documentary*: Capital Visit (1955); Lancashire Coast (1957).

HUPPERTZ, Gottfried
German composer who wrote scores for early films.
FILMS INCLUDE: Kriemhild's Revenge (1923); Metropolis (1926); Siegfried (1923).

HURD, Michael (1928–   )
British composer, author and conductor. Has written music in many genres.
FILMS INCLUDE: Amy! (1980); Flickorna (1968); Scrubbers (1982); Sunday Pursuit (1990).

HYDEN, Walford (1892–   )
British composer and authority on Spanish music.
FILMS INCLUDE: Caravan (1946).

HYMAN, Richard (1927–   )
American composer and jazz pianist who has scored some of Woody Allen's films.
FILMS INCLUDE: Alan and Naomi (1992); Broadway Danny Rose (1984); The Great Rocky Mountain Jazz Party (1979); Leader of the Band (1987); The Purple Rose of Cairo (1985); Radio Days (1987); Scott Joplin (1977); Stardust Memories (1980); Zelig (1983).

IBERT, Jacques (1890–1962)
French composer who studied composition with Paul Vidal. Two of his seven operas were written in collaboration with Arthur Honegger.
FILMS INCLUDE: La Charrette Fantôme (1938); Don Quichotte (1933); Golgotha (1935); Invitation to the Dance: Circus (1956); The Italian Straw Hat (1928); Macbeth (1948); Panique (1947).
RECORDINGS: Don Quichotte. Marco Polo 8 223287; Golgotha. Marco Polo 8 223287; Macbeth. Marco Polo 8 223287.

IFUKUBE, Akira (1914–   )
Japanese composer who studied forestry before turning to music. Besides composing he has written and published a treatise on orchestration.
FILMS INCLUDE: Biruma Npo Tategoto (The Burmese Harp) (1956); Chikyu Boeigun (1957); Daikaiju Barn (1958); Gojira (Godzilla) (1954); Gojira Tai

Gaigan (1972); Gojira Tai Mosura (1964); Ido Zero Daisakusen (1969); Kaiju Soshingeki (Destroy all Monsters) (1968); Kessen Nankai No Daikaiju (1970); Kingkongkongu no Gyakushu (1967); Rodan (1956); The Saga of Anatahan (1953); Shin no Shikotei (1962); Uchu Dai Senso (1959).

IKEBE, Shin-Ichiro (1943–)
Japanese composer.
FILMS INCLUDE: Akira Kurosawa's Dreams (1990); The Ballad of Narayama (1983); Kagemusha (1980); Zeger (1987).

IRELAND, John (1879–1962)
British composer who wrote orchestral music and many songs, together with chamber music and a piano concerto. Wrote one film score, *The Overlanders*, made in Australia (1946). Ireland was later approached for another film score, Cavalcanti's *Toilers of the Sea*. However, this came to nothing when Cavalcanti left Ealing Studios.
RECORDINGS: The Overlanders. Chandos CHAN8994; Silva Screen FILMCD 177.

IRVING, Ernest (1878–1953)
British composer and music director who worked in London between 1900–40, and Ealing film studios 1935–53, engaging several leading British composers to write film music.
FILMS INCLUDE: I Believe in You (1952); The Proud Valley (1939); Whisky Galore (1948).
RECORDINGS: Whisky Galore. Silva Screen FILMCD 177.

ISAACS, Leonard
British composer who wrote music for short films including *The Gen* (the RAF newsreel series) and *Cornish Valley* (Greenpark, 1944).

ISHAM, Mark (1951–)
American composer and renowned jazz trumpeter. Experimented with electronic instruments.
FILMS INCLUDE: The Browning Version (1994); Cool World (1993); Fire in the Sky (1993); The Hitcher (1986); Mrs Soffel (1984); The Net (1995); Never Cry Wolf (1983); Of Mice and Men (1992); The Public Eye (1992); A River Runs Through It (1992); Romeo is Bleeding (1993); The Secret Policeman's Other Ball (1982); Short Cuts (1993); Time Cop (1994); The Times of Harvey Milk (1984); Trouble in Mind (1985); An Unsuitable Job for a Woman (1981).
RECORDINGS: The Browning Version. Milan 74321 21301–2; Fire in the Sky. Varèse Sarabande VSD5417; A River Runs Through it. Milan 74321 12409–2.

JACKSON, Howard (1900–)
American composer and arranger.
FILMS INCLUDE: Black Gold (1963); The Body Disappears (1941); Broadway (1929); Claudelle Inglish (1961); Code of Silence (1985); Count of Hours (1953); Cry Terror! (1957); The Delta Force (1986); Gold of Seven Saints (1961); The Great Garbo (1929); House of Women (1961); Invasion U.S.A. (1985); The King Steps Out (1936); Merrill's Marauders (1961); Philbert (1963); Run for Cover (1954); Sergeant Rutledge (1960); Thar She Blows! (1953); Wakamba (1955); Yellowstone Kelly (1959).

JACOB, Gordon (1895–1984)
British composer, teacher and conductor. Taught many famous pupils at the Royal College of Music including Malcolm Arnold, Imogen Holst and Elizabeth Maconchy. Wrote music in many genres including two symphonies and two viola concertas. Entered films in 1943.
FILMS INCLUDE: *Feature*: Esther Waters (1948); For Those in Peril (1944); The Way We Live (1946). *Documentary*: Before the Raid (CFU, 1943); The Big Pack (RAF Film Unit, 1944); Close Quarters (CFU, 1943); Journey Together (RAF Film Unit, 1945); Maintenance Command (RAF Film Unit, 1944); On the Face of It (Verity, 1944).

JANSEN, Pierrie (1930–)
French composer who is associated with many of the films of Claude Chabrol.
FILMS INCLUDE: Les Biches (1968); Blood Relatives (1977); Les Bonnes Femmes (1960); Le Boucher (1970); Boulevard des Hirondelles (1993); Le Cheval d'Orgueil (1980); La Decade Prodigieuse (1971); La Dentellière (1977); Docteur Popaul (1972); La Femme Infidèle (1968); Flammes sur L'Adriatique (1968); Les Innocents aux Mains Sales (1975); Juste Avant la Nuit (1971); Landru (1962); Les Noces Rouges (1973); Phlia (1962); Killer! (1969); La Route de Corinthe (1967); La Rupture (1970); Le Sauveur (1971); Le Scandale (1967); Le Tigre aime la Chair Fraîche (1964); Violette Nozière (1977).

JANSSEN, Werner (1899–1990)
American composer.
FILMS INCLUDE: Blockade (1938); Eternally Yours (1939 – nominated for an Academy Award); The General Died at Dawn (1936); Guest in the House (1944); A Night in Casablanca (1946); Ruthless (1948); Slightly Honourable (1940); The Southerner (1945 – nominated for an Academy Award).

JARRE, Maurice (1924–)
French composer who began his association with the cinema by scoring the short films of Resnais, Franju and others. Won Academy Awards for the scores of *Lawrence of Arabia* (1962 – a commission originally offered to Malcolm

Arnold, William Walton, Benjamin Britten and Aram Khachaturian), *Doctor Zhivago* (1965) and *A Passage to India* (1984), all composed for director David Lean.

FILMS INCLUDE: Ash Wednesday (1973); Barbarella (1967); Behold a Pale Horse (1964); The Big Gamble (1961); Die Blechtrommel (1979); The Bride (1985); La Caduta Degli Dei (The Damned) (1969); The Collector (1965); Crack in the Mirror (1960); Le Dernier Matin d'Albert Camus (1964); Les Dimanches de Ville d'Avray (1962); Doctor Zhivago (1965); Les Drageurs (1959); Dreamscape (1983); The Effect of Gamma Rays on Man-in-the-Moon Marigolds (1972); El Condor (1970); Enemy Mine (1985); The Extraordinary Seaman (1968); Die Fleschung (Circle of Deceit) (1981); Fatal Attraction (1987); Fearless (1993); Firefox (1982); The Fixer (1968); Gambit (1966); Grand Prix (1966); Grandeur Nature (1973); Great Expectations (1975); Hôtel des Invalides (1952); Isadora (1968); The Island at the Top of the World (1973); Jesus of Nazareth (The Life of Jesus) (1977); Judex (1963); The Last Flight of Noah's Ark (1980); The Last Tycoon (1976); Lawrence of Arabia (1962); The Life and Times of Judge Roy Bean (1972); Lion of The Desert (1980); The Longest Day (1962); The Mackintosh Man (1973); Mad Max – Beyond Thunderdome (1985); The Magician of Lublin (1978); La Main Chaude (1960); The Man Who Would Be King (1975); Mandingo (1975); March or Die (1977); Mr Jones (1993); The Night of the Generals (1966); The Only Game in Town (1969); A Passage to India (1984); Plaza Suite (1970); Pope Joan (1972); Posse (1975); Le Président (1961); The Prince and The Pauper (1977); The Professionals (1966); Le Puits aux Trois Verités (1961); Resurrection (1980); Al Risalah (The Message) (1976); Ryan's Daughter (1970); Shogun (1980); Shout at the Devil (1976); Soleil Rouge (1971); Success (1979); Taps (1981); La Tête Contre Les Murs (1959); Thérèse Dequeyroux (1962); Top Secret (1984); Topaz (1969); The Train (1964); Vel d'Hiv (1959); Villa Rides (1968); A Walk in the Clouds (1995); Weekend at Dunkirk (1964); Winter Kills (1979); Witness (1985); The Year of Living Dangerously (1982); Les Yeux sans Visage (1960); Young Doctors in Love (1982).

RECORDINGS: Behold a Pale Horse. Milan 262 321; Dr Zhivago. Milan 74321 10131–2; Fatal Attraction. GNP GNPD8011; Lawrence of Arabia. Milan 74321 10131–2; Ryan's Daughter. Milan 74321 10131–4.

JAUBERT, Maurice (1900–1940)

French composer who worked with famous directors including René Clair and who scored some of France's most famous films. A former lawyer, he was killed in action in World War II.

FILMS INCLUDE: *Feature*: Bizarre Bizarre (1939); Le Dernier Milliadaire (1934); Le Fin du Jour (1939); Le Jour se Lève (1939); Pays du Scalp (1929); Quai des Brumes (1938); Quatorze Juillet (1932); Tarakanova (1938); We Live in Two Worlds (1937 – directed by Cavalcanti); Zero de Conduite (1933).

Documentary: Easter Island (1934); La Vie D'un Fleuve; We Live in Two Worlds (GPO Film Unit, 1937).

JERSILD, Jorgen (1913–)
Danish composer.
FILMS INCLUDE: Gertrud (1964).

JOHNSON, Jay Jay (1924–)
American jazz trombone player and composer who played with the Count Basie Orchestra. Has written scores for films and television since 1970.

JOHNSON, Laurie (1927–)
British composer, well-known for the themes of the television series *The Avengers* and *The Professionals*. Also arranged music for band leaders including Ambrose, Ted Heath and Geraldo.
FILMS INCLUDE: And Soon the Darkness (1970); The Beauty Jungle (1964); The Belstone Fox (1973); Bitter Harvest (1963); Captain Kronos, Vampire Hunter (1972); Diagnosis: Murder (1974); Dr Strangelove; or, How I Learned to stop Worrying and Love The Bomb (1963); East of Sudan (1964); The Firechasers (1970); First Men in the Moon (1964); Girls at Sea (1958); The Good Companions (1956); Hedda (1975); Hot Millions (1968); I Aim at the Stars (1960); It Lives Again (1978); It Shouldn't Happen to a Vet (1976); Lock Up Your Daughters! (1969); The Maids (1974); Mister Jerico (1969); The Moonraker (1957); No Trees in the Street (1958); Operation Bullshine (1959); Spare the Rod (1961); Tiger Bay (1959); What a Whopper! (1961); You Must be Joking (1965).
RECORDINGS: The First Men in the Moon. Cloud Nine ACN 7015.

JOHNSTON, Arthur J. (1898–1954)
American composer who worked for Irving Berlin as an orchestrator and who went with him to Hollywood in 1929. Wrote many songs for Bing Crosby.
FILMS INCLUDE: Belle of the Nineties (1934); College Coach (1932); College Human (1933); The Girlfriend (1935); Hello Everybody (1933); Murder of the Vanities (1934); Pennies from Heaven (1936); Sailing Along (1938); Song of the South (1947); Theresa Million (1935); Too Much Harmony (1933).

JOHNSTON, Benjamin B (1926–)
American composer who worked as a dance band pianist before studying composition.
FILMS INCLUDE: Museum Piece (1968–69).

JONES, Kenneth V (1924–)
British composer who has worked in the USA.
FILMS INCLUDE: *Feature*: The Bandit of Zhobe (1959); Blind Man's Bluff (1977); The Brute (1976); Cairo (1963); The Carringford School Mystery (1958); The Girl on the Boat (1962); The Horse's Mouth (1958); Intent to Kill (1958); Jazzboat (1959); Leopard in the Snow (1977); Maroc 7 (1966); Paganini Strikes Again (1973); Professor Popper's Problems (1974); The Projected Man (1966); Psyche 59 (1963); Sea Wife (1956); The Siege of Pinchgut (1959); A Story of David (1960); Ten Seconds to Hell (1958); The Tomb of Ligeia (1964); Tower of Evil (1972); The Trials of Oscar Wilde (1960); What changed Charlie Farthing (1974); Whoever Slew Auntie Roo? (1971); Yorkshire Imperial on Thames (1957). *Documentary*: The Age of Invention (1975); A Day of One's Own (1955); Down to Sussex (1965); Fourth Report on Modernisation (1963); A Hundred Years Undergrowth (1964); Midland Country (1974); Omnibus for All (1963); On Track for the Eighties – Rail Report 13 (1980); Overhaul (1957); Sea Road to Britain (1974); The Stage is Yours (1979); They Take the High Road (1960); Third Report on Modernisation (1961); Undergrowth Centenary (1964).

JONES, Quincy (1933–)
American composer who started his professional career at 17 as a trumpeter and arranger for Lionel Hampton. He later played and arranged for Dizzy Gillespie, Count Basie and others. Won an Emmy award for his score to the TV series *Roots* (1977). Has continued as an arranger producing much of Michael Jackson's material in the 1980s.
FILMS INCLUDE: The Anderson Tapes (1971); Banning (1967); Bob & Carol & Ted & Alice (1969); Brother John (1970); Cactus Flower (1969); The Color Purple (1985); Come Back Charleston Blue (1972); The Counterfeit Killer (1968); A Dandy in Aspic (1968); The Deadly Affair (1966); Enter Laughing (1966); For Love of Ivy (1968); The Getaway (1972); The Heist (1971); The Hell with Heroes (1968); The Hot Rock (1972); In Cold Blood (1967 – nominated for an Academy Award); In the Heat of the Night (1967); The Italian Job (1969); John and Mary (1969); Listen up: The Lives of Quincy Jones (1990); The Lost Man (1969); McKenna's Gold (1968); Made in Paris (1965); Mirage (1965); The New Centurions (1972); The Out of Towners (1969); The Pawnbrokers (1964); The Return of Ironside (1993); The Slender Thread (1965); The Split (1968); Walk, Don't Run (1978); The Wiz (1978).

JONES, Ron
American composer who has written music for the Hanna-Barbera cartoons *Scooby Doo* and *The Flintstones*, and series such as *The A-Team*. He has also scored several episodes of *Star Trek: The Next Generation*.

JONES, Trevor (1949–   )
South African born composer who has written scores for British and American films and television series.
FILMS INCLUDE: Angel Heart (1987); Black Angel (1980); Bovver Boots (1977); Brothers and Sisters (1980); Cliffhanger (1993); The Dark Crystal (1982); The Dollar Bottom (1981); Excalibur (1981); In the Name of the Father (1993); Labyrinth (1986); The Last of the Mohicans (1992); Runaway Train (1985); Savage Island (1983); Sea of Love (1989); Smile Until I Tell You to Stop (1979); A Stolen Portrait (1980); Those Glory Glory Days (1983); Time Bandits (1981).
RECORDINGS: Cliffhanger. Silva Screen FILMCD139; Excalibur. Silva Screen FILMCD156.

JOSEPHS, Wilfred (1927–   )
British composer who studied with Arthur Milner. Abandoned dentistry for music in 1963. He composed much film and television music.
FILMS INCLUDE: *Feature*: All Creatures Great and Small (1974); Callan (1974); Cash on Demand (1961); Dark Places (1973); The Deadly Bees (1966); Doomsday at Eleven (1962); Fanatic (1965); Mata Hari (1984); My Side of the Mountain (1968); Night without Pity (1962); Swallows and Amazons (1974); Two-Letter Alibi (1961); The Uncanny (1977); The Webster Boy (1962). *Documentary*: Rail (1967).

JUROVSKÝ, Šimon (1912–1963)
Slovak composer and administrator. Music producer and head of music broadcasting for Bratislava Radio (1941–50).

KABALEVSKY, Dmitry B. (1904–1987)
Russian composer and pianist who worked in the silent cinema (1922–25). His Piano Concerto (1929) won him fame in Russia. Also wrote four symphonies, the third of which was a requiem for Lenin.
FILMS INCLUDE: Academician Ivan Pavlov (1949); Aerograd (Frontier) (1936); Bleak Morning (1959); Flames on the Volga (1955); The Godfly (1955); 1918 (1958); The Sisters (1957).

KAEMPFERT, Burt (1923–1980)
German composer and bandleader.
FILMS INCLUDE: A Man Could get Killed (1966); You Can't Win 'em All (1970).

KALNIŅŠ Imants (1941–   )
Latvian composer who has written four symphonies and incidental music.

KAMEN, Michael (1948–   )
American composer now living in London, who has written for the cinema and television. Has worked with major names in the pop world including Bob Dylan, Eric Clapton and Kate Bush. Bryan Adams also features in several Kamen film scores.
FILMS INCLUDE: Adventures of Baron Munchausen (1989); Angelo my Love (1982); Between the Lines (1977); Boardwalk (1979); Brazil (1985); The Dead Zone (1983); Die Hard (1988); Die Hard 2 (1990); Last Action Hero (1993); 'Let him have It' (1991); Lethal Weapon (1987); Lethal Weapon 2 (1989); Lethal Weapon 3 (1987); Licensed to Kill (1989); Life Force (1985); Mona Lisa (1986); The Next Man (1976); One Hundred and One Dalmatians (1996); Pink Floyd The Wall (1982); Polyester (1981); Robin Hood: Prince of Thieves (1991); Shanghai Surprise (1986); Stunts (1977); The Three Musketeers (1993); Venom (1981); Wilder Napalm (1993).
RECORDINGS: Brazil. Milan 74321 11124–2; The Dead Zone. Milan 74321 23976–2; Die Hard. Varèse Sarabande VSD2508; Lethal Weapon. Telarc CD80251; Robin Hood: Prince of Thieves. Telarc CD80342.

KANDER, John (1927–   )
American composer who, with Fred Ebb, wrote *Cabaret*.
FILMS INCLUDE: Cabaret (1972); Places in the Heart (1984); Something for Everyone (1970); Still of the Night (1982).

KAPER, Bronislau (1902–1983)
Polish composer who lived in the USA from the 1930s. Scored early German sound films, usually in collaboration with Austrian composer Walter Jurman. Contributed songs for Hollywood films, often in collaboration with lyricist Gus Kahn.
FILMS INCLUDE; Ada (1961); The Adventures of Quentin Durward (1955); The Angel wore Red (1960); Auntie Mame (1958); The Barretts of Wimpole Street (1956); The Brothers Karamazov (1958); Butterfield 8 (1960); Comrade X (1940); Cosa Nostra an arch enemy of the FBI (1967); Counterpoint (1967); Don't go near the Water (1957); A Flea in her Ear (1968); Forever, Darling (1955); The Glass Slipper (1954); The Great Sinner (1949); Green Mansions (1958); Grounds for Marriage (1950); Home from the Hill (1960); It's a Big Country (1950); Jet Pilot (1957); Kisses for my President (1964); A Life of her Own (1950); Lili (1952 – Academy Award); Lord Jim (1964); Melodie der liebe (Right to Happiness) (1932); Mutiny on the Bounty (1962); The Power and the Prize (1956); The Prodigal (1955); Rage in Heaven (1941); The Red Badge of Courage (1951 – Academy Award); Rhapsody (1953); The

Scapegoat (1958); Somebody up there likes me (1956); The Stranger (1946); The Swan (1956); Them (1954); Tobruk (1966); Two-Faced Woman (1941); Two Loves (1961); The Way West (1967); White Cargo (1942); A Woman's Face (1941).
RECORDINGS: The Brothers Karamazov. Facet FE101; Butterfield 8. Facet FE101; Mutiny on the Bounty. Facet FE101.

KAPLAN, Sol (1913–1990)
American composer and pianist who also wrote for television.
FILMS INCLUDE: Alice in Wonderland (1949); The Burglar (1957); Diplomatic Courier (1952); Explosion (1969); Girl of the Night (1960); Happy Anniversary (1959); The House on Telegraph Hill (1951); I'd Climb the Highest Mountain (1951); Judith (1965); Kangaroo (1951); Lies My Father Told me (1975); Living Free (1972); Over the Edge (1979); Port of New York (1949); Rawhide (1951); Red Skies of Montana (1952); The Spy Who Came in from the Cold (1965); Tell-Tale Heart (1941); The Victors (1963).

KARAINDROU, Eleni
Greek composer who developed an interest in films after her family moved to live next door to an open air cinema in Athens. Between 1953–67 she studied piano and theory, but was then forced to leave the country by the military junta and settled in Paris. She returned to Athens in 1974 where she has worked with director Christoforo Christofis, Leftens Xanthopoulos and Theo Angelopoulos.
FILMS INCLUDE: The Beekeeper (1986); Happy Homecoming Comrade (1986); Landscape in the Mist (1990); Rosa (1982); The Suspended Step of the Stork (1991); Ulysses' Gaze (1995); Wandering (1982).
RECORDINGS: The Beekeeper. ECM 847069–2; Landscape in the Mist. ECM 847069–2; Ulysses' Gaze. ECM449 153–2.

KARAS, Anton (1906–1985)
Viennese composer whose zither music featured in The Third Man (1949).

KARETNIKOV, Nikolay (1930–1994)
Soviet composer and pianist. From 1958 he composed many scores for the theatre, cinema and television, and has appeared as a pianist and conductor of his own work, in both concert hall and film studio. Has also worked in the electronic studio.
FILMS INCLUDE: The Flight (1971).

KARLIN, Fred (1936–)
American composer for the cinema and television.
FILMS INCLUDE: Baby Blue Marine (1976); The Baby Maker (1970); Believe in Me (1971); California Dreaming (1979); Chosen Survivors (1974); Cloud Dancer (1979); Cover Me Babe (1969); Every Little Crook and Nanny (1972); Futureworld (1976); The Gravy Train (1974); Greased Lightning (1977); Leadbelly (1976); The Little Ark (1971); Lovers and Other Strangers (1970); Loving Couples (1980); The Marriage of a Young Stockbroker (1971); Mean Dog Blues (1978); Mixed Company (1974); The Spike Gang (1974); The Stalking Moon (1968); The Sterile Cuckoo (1969); Up the Down Staircase (1967); Westworld (1973); Yours, Mine and Ours (1968).

KAY, Edward (1898–1973)
American composer who has written many scores for the cinema.
FILMS INCLUDE: The Admiral was a Lady (1950); The Big Tip Off (1955); Block Busters (1944); Dark Alibi (1946); Drums of the Desert (1940); Fear (1946); Gentleman Joe Palooka (1946); Joe Palooka in the Big Fight (1949); Johnny Rocco (1958); King of the Zombies (1941); Las Vegas Shakedown (1955); Law of the Jungle (1942); Night Freight (1955); Northern Patrol (1953); Port of Hell (1954); The Red Dragon (1945); Roar of the Press (1941); Security Risk (1954); Tangier Incident (1953); Thunder Pass (1954); The Toughest Man Alive (1955); The Trap (1946); Yaqui Drums (1956); Yukon Vengeance (1954).

KAYLIN, Samuel (1892–)
American composer who was born in Russia and who studied with Schoenberg. Was composer and musical director for Twentieth Century Fox studios between 1929 and 1941.
FILMS INCLUDE: Arizona Wildcat (1938); Charlie Chan at Monte Carlo (1938); Charlie Chan at the Circus (1936); Charlie Chan at the Olympics (1937); Charlie Chan at the Opera (1936); Charlie Chan at the Race Track (1936); Charlie Chan at Treasure Island (1939); Charlie Chan in City of Darkness (1939); Charlie Chan in Egypt (1935); Charlie Chan in Honolulu (1939); Charlie Chan in London (1934); Charlie Chan in Panama (1940); Charlie Chan in Paris (1935); Charlie Chan in Reno (1939); Charlie Chan in Shanghai (1935); Charlie Chan on Broadway (1937); Charlie Chan's Murder Cruise (1940); Charlie Chan's Secret (1936); Dante's Inferno (1935); Mr Moto in Danger Island (1939); Mr Moto Takes a Chance (1938); Mr Moto Takes a Vacation (1939); Mr Moto's Gamble (1938); Mr Moto's Last Warning (1939); Mysterious Mr Moto (1938); Thank You, Mr Moto (1938); Think Fast, Mr Moto (1937).

KAUN, Bernhard (1899–1980)
German-born composer in Hollywood where he specialised in music for early horror films.
FILMS INCLUDE: Dr X (1932); Frankenstein (1931); The Mystery of the Wax Museum (1933); The Return of Dr X (1939); Return of the Terror (1934); The Smiling Ghost (1941); Special Delivery (1955); The Walking Dead (1936).

KERN, Jerome (1885–1945)
American composer and songwriter who also created stage musicals. Settled in Hollywood in 1930 where he began to write original songs and scores for many films. His first film score was an accompaniment to the silent serial *Gloria's Romance* (1916).
FILMS INCLUDE: Can't Help Singing (1944); Centennial Summer (1946); Cover Girl (1944); Roberta (1935); Showboat (1935 and 1951); Swing Time (1936); Till the Clouds Roll (1946).
RECORDINGS: Can't Help Singing. Philips 442 129–2PH; Centennial Summer. Philips 442 129–2PH; Show Boat. EMI CDODOEN21.

KHACHATURIAN, Aram (1903–1978)
Russian composer who studied composition with Myaskovsky at the Moscow Conservatory. Wrote the ballets *Gayaneh* (1942) and *Spartacus* (1954), together with some twenty-five scores for Soviet films, beginning with *Pepo* in 1934 and ending with *Men and Animals* in 1960.
FILMS INCLUDE: Admiral Ushakov (1953); Attack from the Sea (1953); The Battle of Stalingrad (1949); Girl No 217 (1944); Men and Animals (1960); Othello (1955); Pepo (1934); The Russian Question (1948); Salavat Yulayev (1941); Saltanat (1955); 2001: A Space Odyssey (1968 – contribution).
RECORDINGS: The Battle of Stalingrad. ASV CDDCA859; Othello. Marco Polo 8 223314.

KHACHATURIAN, Karen (1920–)
Russian composer, nephew of Aram Khachaturian, who studied partly with Shostakovich at the Moscow Conservatory. Wrote an oratario dedicated to Lenin's memory.

KHAN, Alik Akbar (1922–)
Indian/American composer.
FILMS INCLUDE: Cruel Wind (1952); Devi – The Goddess (1960); The Sword and The Flute (1959).

KHOLMINOV, Alexander N. (1925–)
Russian composer who has written operas, cantatas and songs, many of them dealing with contemporary themes.

KHRENNIKOV, Tikhon (1913–)
Russian composer who made his debut as a composer-pianist with his Piano
Concerto (Op.1) in 1933. Also associated with the Vakhtangov Theatre for
which he wrote many incidental scores. Wrote music for twelve films.
FILMS INCLUDE: Vernye Druzya (1954).

KILAR, Wojcieck (1932–)
Polish composer who studied partly with Nadia Boulanger in Paris. Has
written extensively for the Polish cinema, working with such directors as
Andrzej Wajda and Krzystof Zanussi. Came to prominence in 1992 with his
score for Coppola's *Dracula*.
FILMS INCLUDE: Barwy Ochronne (Camouflage) (1977); Bram Stoker's
Dracula (1992); Constans (1980); Iluminacja (1972); Kontrakt (1980);
Korczak (1990); Lalka (The Doll) (1968); Orawa; Paciorki Jejdnego Rozanca
(The Beads of One Rosary) (1979); Le Roi et L'Oiseau (1980); Rok Spo-
kojnego Slonca (The Year of the Quiet Sun) (1984); Zycie Rodzinne (Family
Life).
RECORDINGS: Bram Stoker's Dracula. Epic 472746–2.

KING, Denis (1939–)
British composer.
FILMS INCLUDE: Privates on Parade (1982); Sista Dansen (1993); Stainless Steel
and Star Spies (1980); Strictly Private (1982).

KINSEY, Tony
British composer.
FILMS INCLUDE: On the Bridge (1980).

KIRCHEN, Basil
British composer.
FILMS INCLUDE: The Abominable Dr Phibes (1971); Assignment (1967); I Start
Counting (1969); The Mutations (1973); Negatives (1968); The Shuttered
Room (1966); The Strange Affair (1968).

KISIELEWSKI, Stefan (1911–)
Polish composer and writer who studied Polish literature and philosophy
besides music. Has shown a preference of writing music for the chamber
orchestra.

KITARO (1953–)
Japanese composer and recording artist.
FILMS INCLUDE: Catch Your Dreams (1983); Heaven and Earth (1993); Samuel
Lount (1985).

KLEGA, Miroslav (1926–)
Czech composer who has written music for the theatre, cinema, radio and television.

KLUSAK, Jan (1934–)
Czech composer.
FILMS INCLUDE: Martyrs of Love (1966); Pearls of the Deep (1965); A Report on the Party and the Guests (1966); Valerie and Her Week of Wonders (1970).

KNIEPER, Jurgen (1941–)
German composer.
FILMS INCLUDE: Der Amerikanische Freund (The American Friend) (1977); Die Angst Des Tormanns Beim Elfmeter (The Goalkeeper's Fear of the Penalty) (1971); L'Avenir D'Emilie (1984); The Blond (1994); Christiane F. wir Kinder Vom Bahnhof Zoo (1981); Deutschland Bleiche Mutter (Germany, Pale Mother) (1980); Deutschlandgeshichten – . . . Können Mir Doch Arbeit Geben, Die Philiste . . . (1979); Einmal Ku'Damm und Zurück (A Berlin Love Story) (1983); End of the Night (1990); Falsche Bewegung (Wrong Movement) (1975); Gudrun (1992); Madregilda (1993); Der Scharlachrote Buchstabe (The Scarlet Letter) (1972); The State of Things (Der Stand Der Dinge) (1982).

KNIPPER, Lar K. (1898–1974)
Russian composer who partly studied music in Germany. Also held occasional posts in the music section of the Red Army. Wrote incidental music, many songs and choruses.

KNOPFLER, Mark (1949–)
British composer, guitarist and singer. A founder member of the rock band Dire Straits.
FILMS INCLUDE: Cal (1984); Comfort and Joy (1984); Last Exit to Brooklyn (1989); Local Hero (1983); The Princess Bride (1987).
RECORDINGS: The Princess Bride. Telarc CD86342.

KOECHLIN, Charles (1867–1950)
French composer, teacher and musicologist who studied with Massenet and Fauré. Wrote a great deal of music, much of which is still rarely heard. Some was written for, or suggested by, films, e.g. Op.132 (1933) is the 'Seven Stars' Symphony', comprising seven movements each devoted to a film star: Douglas Fairbanks, Lilian Harvey, Greta Garbo, Clara Bow, Marlene Dietrich, Emil Jennings, Charlie Chaplin.
FILMS INCLUDE: Les Confidences d'un Joveur de Clarinette (1934); Croisières avec L'Escadre (1933 – unused); Victoire de la Vie (1938).

KOMEDA, Krzyszlof (1931–1969)
Polish composer.
FILMS INCLUDE: Bariera (1966); Cul-de-Sac (1966); Dance of the Vampires (1967); Dwaj Ludzie Z Szafa (Two Men and a Wardrobe) (1957); Mennesker Modes Og Sod Musik Opstr I Hjertet (People Meet) (1967); Niewinni Czardzieje (Innocent Sorcerers) (1960); Noz W Wodzie (Knife in the Water) (1962); Riot (1968); Rosemary's Baby (1968); Ssaki (Mammals) (1962); Sult – Dk No Se (Hunger) (1966).

KONT, Paul (1920–)
Austrian composer and conductor who partly studied with Milhaud, Honegger and Messiaen in Paris.

KOPP, Rudolph (1887–1971)
Composer who wrote for films between 1933–1953 at Paramount Pictures. Was born in Austria and went to the USA.
FILMS INCLUDE: Ambush (1948); Arena (1952); Bannerline (1951); Calling Bulldog Drummond (1951); Cleopatra (1934 – directed by Cecil B. de Mille); The Crusades (1935); Desperate Search (1952); The Doctor and the Girl (1949); The Great Diamond Robbery (1953); Gypsy Colt (1953); The Hoaxters (1952); Mystery Street (1949); Sign of the Cross (1932); Tenth Avenue Angel (1948); Vengeance Valley (1951); The Voice of Bugle Ann (1936).

KOPPELL, Herman (1908–)
Danish composer and pianist of Polish parentage. Took refuge in Sweden during World War II – this made a deep impression on his work which is evident in the score he provided for a 1944 documentary film dealing with the plight of the Danish Jews who had escaped to Sweden. The Koppels are among the foremost musical families of Denmark; Herman's son, Thomas, is a pianist and composer as well as the leader of the highly successful Danish rock group Savage Rose.

KORNGOLD, Erich W. (1897–1957)
Austro-Hungarian composer and conductor who went to the USA in the 1930s. A child prodigy, he played his cantata 'Gold' to Mahler at the age of ten and the following year he composed the pantomime 'Der Schneemann' which caused a sensation when it was first performed in 1910. He wrote scores for Warner Brothers and won Academy Awards for *Anthony Adverse* (1936) and *The Adventures of Robin Hood* (1938). He regarded his film scores as operas without singing. His score for *Deception* (1946) contained a one-movement cello concerto, especially written for the film. This later became Korngold's Cello Concerto in C (Op. 37).
FILMS INCLUDE: The Adventures of Robin Hood (1938); Another Dawn (1937);

Anthony Adverse (1936); Between Two Worlds (1944); Captain Blood (1935); The Constant Nymph (1943); Deception (1946); King's Row (1941); A Midsummer Night's Dream (1935 – arrangements of music by Mendelssohn); The Private Lives of Elizabeth and Essex (1939); The Sea Hawk (1940); The Sea Wolf (1941); The Story of Louis Pasteur (1936).

RECORDINGS: The Adventures of Robin Hood. Varèse Sarabande VSD47202; Another Dawn. Marco Polo 8 223871; Anthony Adverse. Varèse Sarabande VSD5285; Captain Blood. Marco Polo 8 223607; King's Row. Varèse Sarabande VSD47203; The Private Lives of Elizabeth and Essex. Milan 873 122; The Sea Hawk. Varèse Sarabande VSD47304; The Sea Wolf. EMI CD ODEON13.

KOSMA, Joseph (1905–1969)

Hungarian composer, resident in France from 1933. Wrote many scores, especially for the films of Renoir and Carné, and numerous popular songs including 'Autumn Leaves'.

FILMS INCLUDE: L'Amant de Lady Chatterley (1955); Les Amants de Verone (1949); Au Grand Balcon (1949); Aubervilliers (1947); La Belle Que Voilà (1950); Black Jack (1950); Calle Mayor (1956); Le Caporal Epingle (1962); Le Cas Du Docteur Laurent (1957); La Chatte (1958); La Chatte Sort Ses Griffes (1960); Le Déjeuner sur L'Herbe (1959); Des Maisons et des Hommes (1953); The Doctor's Dilemma (1958); Un Drôle de Paroissien (1963); Dupont Barbes (1952); L'Ecole Buissonnière (1948); En Passant par La Lorraine (1951); Les Enfants de L'Amour (1953); La Française et L'Amour (1960); Les Fruits Amers (1967); Les Fruits Sauvages (1954); Goubbiah, Mon Amour (1956); Un Grand Patron (1951); Le Grand Rendez-Vous (1950); The Green Glove (1951); Hans le Marin (1949); Huis-Clos (1954); In The French Style (1963); L'Inconnue de Montral (1951); Innocents in Paris (1953); Le Long des Trottoirs (1956); Les Louves (1957); La Marie du Port (1949); La Marseillaise (1937); Mon Ami Pierre (1951); M'Sieur la Caille (1955); The Pavements of Paris (1961); Le Petit Théâtre de Jean Renoir (1969); Harbour of Desire (1955); La Poupe (1962); La Règle du Jeu (1939); Le Roi et L'Oiseau (1980); Le Sang des Bêtes (1948); Snobs (1961); La Pavane des Poisons (1956); Souvenirs Perdus (1950); Tamango (1958); Le Testament du Docteur Cordelier (1961); Trois Telegrammes (1950).

KOVAL, Marian V. (1907–1971)

Russian composer whose style has its roots in Russian folk music.

KOZLOVSKY, Alexey (1905–1977)

Russian composer and conductor.

KRAUSHAAR, Raoul (1908–)
French American composer, conductor and writer, who wrote for various performers including Gene Autry and Roy Rogers.
FILMS INCLUDE: Abbott and Costello (1952); Back from the Dead (1957); Billy the Kid vs. Dracula (1965); Bitter Creek (1954); The Black Whip (1956); Blood Arrow (1957); Copper Sky (1957); Curucu, Beast of the Amazon (1956); Desert Hell (1958); An Eye for an Eye (1966); Invaders from Mars (1953); Jack and the Beanstalk (1951); Jesse James Meets Frankenstein's Daughter (1965); New Faces (1953); The Outlaw's Daughter (1954); The Restless Breed (1957); Rose of Cimarron (1947); Stork Bites Man (1947); Texas Bad Man (1953); Texas City (1952); Thriller – En Grym Film (1974); Two Guns and a Badge (1954); The Unknown Terror (1957); Vigilante Terror (1953); Whistling Hills (1951).

KŘIVINKA, Gustav (1928–)
Czech composer who was interested in Moravian folk music.

KRYUKOV, Vladimir N. (1902–1960)
Russian composer and teacher.
FILMS INCLUDE: The Forty-First (1956); The Grasshopper (1955); Heroes of Shipka (1955); The Idiot (1958); The Letter that was Never Sent (1959); Revolutionists (1936); Symphony of Life (1949); We are from Kronstadt (1936); Without Prejudice (1949).

KUBIK, Gail (1914–1984)
American composer who partly studied composition with Walter Piston at Harvard University. Director of music for the film bureau at the Office of War Information (1942–3) and a composer-conductor for the US Air Force Motion Picture Unit (1943–6).
FILMS INCLUDE: *Feature*: C-Man (1945); The Desperate Hours (1955); Gerald McBoing Boing (1950); I Thank a Fool (1962); The Miner's Daughter (1950); Two Goals and a Guy (1951). *Documentary*: Air Pattern Pacific (1944); Memphis Belle (1943); Men and Ships (US Maritime Commission, 1940); Paratroops (1942); Thunderbolt (1945); The World at War (1942).

KÜNNEKE, Eduard (1885–1953)
German composer who was a composition pupil of Max Bruch. Later used jazz in some of his compositions. Wrote over thirty comic operas and operattas.

KVERNADZE, Bidzina (1928–)
Georgian composer and teacher who has written ballets and two piano concertos.
FILMS INCLUDE: Natvris Khe (1976).

LABROCA, Mavis (1896–1973)
Italian composer and critic who studied with Respighi and Malipiero.

LAGIDZE, Revas L. (1921–   )
Georgian composer and violinist who has written musical comedies and operas.

LAI, Francis (1932–   )
French composer.
FILMS INCLUDE: Un Autre Homme Une Autre Chance (1977); Baby Sitter (Un Maleddetto Pasticcio) (1975); The Beautiful Story (1991); Bilitis (1976); The Bobo (1967); La Bonne Année (1973); Child Under a Leaf (1974); Le Corps de Mon Ennemi (1976); La Course du Lièvre à Travers les Champs (1972); Dans la Poussière du Soleil (1971); Du Soleil Plein les Yeux (1969); Edith et Marcel (1983); Emmanuelle II, L'Anti-vierge (1975); The Games (1969); Hannibal Brooks (1968); Hello-Goodbye (1970); Un Homme et Une Femme (A Man and A Woman) (1966 – Academy Award); House of Cards (1968); Il y a des Jours . . . et des Lunes (1990); I'll Never Forget What's 'is Name (1967); International Velvet (1978); Keys to Freedom (1989); La Leçon Particulière (1968); La Louve Solitaire (1967); Love Story (1970); Madame Claude 2 (1981); Marie (1985); Masculin Féminin 15 Faits Précis (1966); Mayerling (1968); Mon Amour Mon Amour (1967); My New Partner 2 (1990); Le Passager de la Pluie (1969); Le Petit Matin (1970); Les Pétroleuses (1971); Provincial (1990); Reigen (Dance of Love) (1973); Les Ripoux (1984); Si c'etait à Refaire (1976); Stranger in the House (1992); Three into Two won't go (1968); Too Beautiful for You (1989); Tout Ça . . . Pour Ça . . . !!! (1993); Toute une Vie (1974); La Vie, L'Amour, La Mort (1968); Visit to a Chief's Son (1974); Vivre Pour Vivre (1967); Le Voyou (1970).
RECORDINGS: Love Story. Telerc CD80168.

LAJTHA, László (1892–1963)
Hungarian composer, conductor and writer who was associated with Bartók's and Kodály's folk music movement.
FILMS INCLUDE: *Feature*: Hortobágy (Murder in the Cathedral – after Eliot). *Documentary*: Shapes and Sounds.

LAMBERT, Constant (1905–1951)
British composer, conductor, critic and writer. Wrote ballets and was musical director for the Sadler's Wells Ballet Company.
FILMS INCLUDE: *Feature*: Anna Karenina (1947). *Documentary*: Merchant Seamen (CFU, 1941).
RECORDINGS: Anna Karenina. London 448 954–2LPF.

LAMBRO, Phillip (1935–)
American composer.
FILMS INCLUDE: And now Miguel (1965); Blood Voyage (1976); Chinatown (1974 – but not used); Crypt of the Living Dead (1972); Murph the Surf (1974).

LANCHBERRY, John (1923–)
English composer and conductor, principally of the Royal Ballet for whom he did much arranging including *The Tales of Beatrix Potter*.
FILMS INCLUDE: Black Orchid (1952); Blackout (1950); Colonel March Investigates (1953); Deadly Nightshade (1953); Double Exposure (1954); No Trace (1950).

LANE, Burton (1912–1997)
American composer of songs, best known for *Finian's Rainbow* and *On a Clear Day You Can See Forever*.
FILMS INCLUDE: The Adventures of Huckleberry Finn (1960); Affair in Havana (1957); Finian's Rainbow (1968); Give a Girl a Break (1953); Heidi's Song (1982); Jupiter's Darling (1954); On a Clear Day You Can See Forever (1970); Royal Wedding (1950).

LANGE, Arthur (1889–1956)
American composer and musical director.
FILMS INCLUDE: Along Came Jones (1945); Bad Company (1931); The Big Gamble (1931); Chasing Rainbows (1930); The Common Law (1931); Free and Easy (1930); The Great Ziegfeld (1936); Lady of Burlesque (1943); The Mad Magician (1954); On the Avenue (1937); Prestige (1932); The Pride of St Louis (1952); Ring of Fear (1954); The Steel Lady (1953); Under Your Spell (1936); Woman on the Run (1950).

LARSSON, Lars-Erik (1908–1987)
Swedish composer and conductor. Wrote much music for broadcasting, the theatre and films, together with three symphonies.
FILMS INCLUDE: The Great Adventure (1953); Make Way for Lila (1961).

LA SALLE, Richard
American composer.
FILMS INCLUDE: Ambush Bay (1966); Apache Rifles (1964); Arizona Raiders (1965); The Big Night (1960); The Boy who Caught a Crook (1961); The Day Mars Invaded Earth (1963); Deadly Duo (1962); Diary of a Madman (1963); The Flight that Disappeared (1961); The Firebrand (1962); Fort Courageous (1965); Gun Street (1962); Hands of a Stranger (1962); Incident in an Alley (1962); Secret of a Deep Harbour (1961); Speed Crazy (1959); Super-

beast (1972); The Time Travellers (1964); Twice Told Tales (1963); War Party (1965); A Yank in Vietnam (1964).

LASZLO, Alexander (1895–1970)
Hungarian/American composer.
FILMS INCLUDE: Alimony (1948); Amazon Quest (1949); The Atomic Submarine (1959); Black Magic (1944); Dangerous Passage (1944); Double Exposure (1944); The Great Flamarion (1945); High Powered (1945); Joe Palooka, Champ (1946); One Exciting Night (1945); People are Funny (1946); Song of India (1949); Stranger Impersonation (1946); Tarzan's Magic Fountain (1949); They made me a Killer (1946).

LAVA, William (1911–1971)
American composer who worked with Steiner, Waxman and Mancini.
FILMS INCLUDE: Assignment to Kill (1967); Chamber of Horrors (1966); Chubasco (1968); Dracula vs. Frankenstein (1970); The Good Guys and the Bad Guys (1969); Greta, the Misfit Greyhound (1963); Hell Bent for Leather (1959); The Horse with the Flying Tail (1960); The Hound that thought he was a Raccoon (1960); In Enemy Country (1967); The Littlest Outlaw (1954); PT 109 (1962); Retreat, Hell! (1952); Seven Ways from Sundown (1960); Stormy, The Thoroughbred with an Inferiority Complex (1953); The Tattooed Police Horse (1964); Wall of Noise (1963); Zorro the Avenger (1958).

LAVAGNINO, Angelo Francesco (1909–1987)
Italian composer who studied composition with Rossi in Milan.
FILMS INCLUDE: America Paese di Dio (So This is God's Country?) (1966); Le Avventure di Giacomo Casanova (1954); Beatrice Cenci (1969); La Bella Mugnaia (The Miller's Wife) (1955); I Briganti Italiani (1961); Campanadas a Medianoche (Chimes at Midnight) (1966); Il Castello dei Morti Vivi (1964); Il Colosso di Rodi (1961); Conspiracy of Hearts (1960); Continente Perduto (1954); I Criminali Della Galassia (Wild, Wild Planet) (1965); Daisy Miller (1974); I Dieci Gladiatori (1963); La Donna Del Fiume (1954); Ercole Sfida Sansone (1964); Il Figlio del Capitano Blood (1962); Golia e Il Cavaliere Mascherato (1963); Gorgo (1960); The High Bright Sun (1965); Hot Enough for June (1964); L'Impero del Sole (1956); L'Incano Della Foresta (1958); L'Invincibile Cavaliere Mascherato (1963); Jennie Lees Ha Una Nuova Pistola (1965); Jovanka e le Altre (Five Branded Women) (1960); Kali-Yug la Dea Della Vendetta (1963); Legend of the Lost (1957); Maciste Contro il Vampiro (1961); Madame Sans-Gêne (1961); Mamo (1954); Marcoa o Crepa (1962); Il Mistero del Tempio Indiano (1963); La Muraglia Cinese (Behind the Great Wall) (1958); The Naked Maja (1958); Nel Segno di Roma (1958); Odissea Nuda (1961); Oggi a me ... Domani a te! (1968); Ombre Biachi (1959); Orazi e Curiazi (1961); Othello (1952); Passionate Summer (1958); Qualcosa

Striscia Nel Buio (1970); Il Relitto (The Wastrel) (1960); La Risaia (Rice Girls) (1955); La Rivolta Degli Schiavi (The Revolt of the Slaves) (1961); Saffo, Venere di Lesbo (1960); I Tabu (1963); Ulisse Contro Ercole (1961); Gli Ultimi Giorni di Pompei (1959); Gli Uomini dal Passo pesante (1966); L'Uomo di Toledo (1966); Ursus e la Ragazza Tartara (1961); The Wind Cannot Read (1958); Zorro Contro Maciste (1963).
RECORDINGS: Othello. Varèse Sarabande CSD5420.

LAVIN, Carlos (1883–1962)
Chilean composer and ethnomusicologist. Studied music in Paris and Berlin.

LAVISTA, Raul
Mexican composer.
FILMS INCLUDE: El Angel Exterminador (1962); The Beast of Hollow Mountain (1956); The Big Boodle (1956); La Cucaracha (1958); Daniel Boone, Trail Blazer (1957); Enchanted Island (1958); For the Love of Mike (1960); A Life in the Balance (1954); The Little Savage (1959); Los Marcados (1971); Simon del Desierto (1965); Sofia (1948); El Zarco (1959).

LEE, Lester (1905–1956)
American composer.
FILMS INCLUDE: Abbot and Costello meet Captain Kidd (1952); Double Cross-bones (1950); Jack and the Beanstalk (1951); Let's do it Again (1953); Miss Sadie Thompson (1953); Slightly French (1948); Symphony of Six Million (1932); Travelling Saleswoman (1948).

LE FEVRE, Raymond (1907–   )
French composer.
FILMS INCLUDE: L'Affaire d'une Nuit (1960); L'Affaire Maurizius (1954); Ali Baba et les Quarante Voleurs (1954); Avec Quoi Soulèves-tu L'Edredon? (1974); Les Bons Vivants (1966); Candide ou L'Optimisme au XXè Siècle (1960); Casque D'Or (1952); Club Priv Pour Couples Avertis (1974); Colonel Chabert (1942); Destines (1953); Le Dortoir des Grandes (1953); Le Dos Au Mur (1958); Edouard et Caroline (1951); Espions à L'Affut (1965); Faibles Femmes (1959); La Française et L'Amour (1960); Les Fruits de L'T (1955); Le Garçon Sauvage (1951); Le Gorille a Mordu L'Archevêque (1962); Les Grandes Manoeuvres (1955); Je Suis Frigide... Pourquoi? (1972); Lady Paname (1950); Les Liaisons Particulières (1969); Les Lionceaux (1960); Marie-Octobre (1959); Michel Strogoff (1956); La Minute de Vrit (1952); Nathalie (1957); La Nuit la Plus Chaude (1968); Les Petits matins (1962); Porte des Lilas (1957); Le Roi (1949); Le Secret de Mayerling (1949); Sexuelle-ment Votre (1975); Tartarin de Tarascon (1934); La Vie à Deux (1958); Voulez-Vous Danser Avec Moi? (1959).

LE GALLIENNE, Dorian (1915–1963)
Australian composer and critic who came to England to study with Gordon Jacob. Wrote ballets and incidental music.

LEGRAND, Michel (1931–   )
French composer who gained international recognition with his score for *Les Parapluies de Cherbourg* (1964). Won an Oscar for the song 'The Windmills of Your Mind' (in the 1968 film *The Thomas Crown Affair*) and another for some of *The Summer of '42* (1971).
FILMS INCLUDE: L'Amérique Insolite (1960); Appelez-Moi Mathilde (1969); As Summer Dies (1985); Atlantic City, U.S.A. (1980); La Baie Des Anges (Bay of the Angels) (1962); Bequest to the Nation (1973); Best Friends (1982); Blind Love (1977); Breezy (1973); Castle Keep (1969); Le Cave se Rebiffe (The Counterfeiters of Paris) (1961); Charmants Garçons (1957); Cinq Jours en juin (Five Days in June) (1989); Cléo de 5 a 7 (1962); Cops and Robbers (1973); Corrida pour un Espion (The Spy who went into Hell) (1965); La Dame dans L'Auto avec des Lunettes et un Fusil (The Lady in the Car) (1970); Darling Lili (1969); Les Demoiselles ont eu 25 ans (1993); A Doll's House (1973); Eternity (1990); Eva (1962); L'Evenment le Plus Important Depuis que L'Homme a Marché sur la Lune (1973); Une Femme est Une Femme (A Woman is a Woman) (1961); La Flute a Six Schtroumpfs (1975); Gable and Lombard (1976); The Go-Between (1971); Gulliver's Travels (1976); The Happy Ending (1969); Un Homme est Mort (1972); How to save a Marriage and Ruin Your Life (1967); The Hunter (1980); Ice Station Zebra (1968); Le Joli Mai (1962); Lady Oscar (1978); Lady Sings the Blues (1972); Le Mans (1971); Eine Liebe in Deutschland (A German Love Story) (1963); Les Mariés de L'An II (1970); Michel's Mixed Up Bird (1978); Monnaie de Singe (1965); The Mountain Men (1979); Never Say Never Again (1983); Ode to Billy Joe (1976); One is a Lonely Number (1972); L'Or et le Plomb (1964); The Other Side of Midnight (1977); Peau d'Ane (1970); The Pickle (1993); Pieces of Dreams (1970); La Piscine (The Swimming Pool) (1968); Play Dirty (1968); Portnoy's Complaint (1972); Pretty Polly (1967); Qu'est-ce Que Fait Courir David? (What Makes David Run?) (1982); Rafles sur la Ville (1958); Une Ravissante Idiote (1964); Le Sauvage (Lovers Like Us) (1975); Secret Places (1984); Slapstick of Another Kind (1982); The Summer of '42 (1971); Sweet November (1968); Switching Channels (1988); The Thomas Crown Affair (1968); The Three Musketeers (1973); Time for Loving (1971); Le Triporteur (1957); Vérités et Mensonges (1973); La Vie de Château (1965); Vivre sa Vie (1962); Wuthering Heights (1970); Yentl (1983).
RECORDINGS: Never Say Never Again. Silva Screen FILMCD145; Les Parapluies de Cherbourg. RCA 0 9026 61326–2; Summer of '42. Telearc CD80168; Yentl. Philips 422 401–2PH.

LEIGH, Walter (1905–1942)
British composer; was killed in World War II with the Tank Corps at Tobruk. Studied partly with Hindemith in Berlin. Composed scores for mainly documentary films, many of them now classics. His son, Julian, has also written documentary film music e.g. *Four Back Rooms* (1957).
FILMS INCLUDE: *Documentary*: Dawn of Iran (1937); The Face of Scotland (1938); The Fairy of the Phone (1936); The Fourth Estate (1940); Pett and Pott (1934); 6.30 Collection (1934); Song of Ceylon (1934); Squadron 992 (1940); Work-a-Day (Advertising film).

LEIPOLD, John
American composer who worked for Columbia, Paramount and RKO.
FILMS INCLUDE: Border Vigilantes (1941); Desperadoes (1943); Geronimo (1940 – with Carbonara); Good Luck, Mr Yates (1943); The Heat's On (1943); In Old Colorado (1941); Knights of the Range (1940 – with Young); Pirates on Horseback (1941); The Scarlet Express (1934 – with Harline); The Showdown (1940); Wide Open Town (1941).

LENOIR, Jean (died 1976)
French composer.
FILMS INCLUDE: Deuxième Bureau (1935).

LEOZ, Jesús G. (1904–1953)
Spanish composer who wrote for the cinema.

LEPPARD, Raymond (1927–)
British composer and conductor, specialising in 17th and 18th century music. Settled in the USA in 1976.
FILMS INCLUDE: Alfred the Great (1969); The Hotel New Hampshire (1984); Laughter in the Dark (1969); Lord of the Flies (1963).

LE ROUX, Maurice (1923–)
French composer.
FILMS INCLUDE: Amère Victoire (Bitter Victory) (1957); Le Ballon Rouge (1956); Broadway by Night (1957); La Chamade (1968); Contes Immoraux (1974); Martin Soldat (1966); Le Piège (1958); Les Possédées (1956); Vu du Pont (A View from the Bridge) (1961).

LEVY, Louis (1893–1957)
British composer and musical director. A pioneer of the early silent film days, he started his career in 1910, and in 1916 became musical director at the New Gallery Cinema in London. Worked with Gaumont and Gainsborough

for 1928–47, supervising all musical productions. Scored *Nanook of the North* (1920).

FILMS INCLUDE: Alias Bulldog Drummond (1935); The Citadel (1938); East Meets West (1936); First a Girl (1936); Haunted Honeymoon (1941); Head over Heels in Love (1937); It's Love Again (1936); Man of Affairs (1937); Night Trail (1941); Passing of the Third Floor Back (1936); Secret Agent (1936); Seven Sinners (1936); Transatlantic Tunnel (1935); The Woman Alone (1937); Woman in a Dressing Gown (1957).

LEWIS, John (1920–)
American jazz pianist and composer.
FILMS INCLUDE: Jivin in Be-Bof (1947); The Lamp in Assassin Mews (1962); A Milanese Story (1962); No Blade of Grass (1970); No Sun in Venice (1958); Odds Against Tomorrow (1959); Sait-on Jamais? (1957); Song of the Spirit (1988); This Game of Golf (1974).

LEWIS, Michael J. (1939–)
British composer who has also composed for television.
FILMS INCLUDE: Baxter! (1972); Blood Beach (1980); The Hound of the Basker-villes (1983); The Island of Adventure (1982); Julius Caesar (1970); The Legacy (1978); The Madwoman of Chaillot (1969); The Medusa Touch (1978); The Naked Face (1984); North Sea Hijack (1979); The Passage (1978); Running Scared (1972); Russian Roulette (1975); Sphinx (1980); The Stick Up (1977); Theatre of Blood (1973); Unman, Wittering and Zigo (1971); Yes. Giorgio (1982).
RECORDINGS: The Madwoman of Chaillot. Varèse Sarabande VSD5207.

LIGETI, György (1923–)
Austrian composer of Hungarian birth. Written much electronic music. Composed a section of the score for the film *2001: A Space Odyssey*.

LILLEY, Joseph J. (1914–)
American composer and musical director.
FILMS INCLUDE: At War with the Army (1950); Blue Hawaii (1961); Dear Wife (1949); The Disorderly Orderly (1964); Duffy's Tavern (1945); Easy Come, Easy Go (1966); Fun in Acapulco (1963); G.I. Blues (1960); Girls! Girls! Girls! (1962); The Great Lover (1949); Here Come the Waves (1944); Holiday Inn (1942); Li'l Abner (1959); Mr Music (1950); Paint Your Wagon (1969); Papa's Delicate Condition (1963); Paradise, Hawaiian Style (1965); Paris Holiday (1958); Red Garters (1954); Red, Hot and Blue (1949); Road to Bali (1952); Road to Rio (1947); Road to Utopia (1945); Roustabout (1964); The Seven Little Foys (1954); That Certain Feeling (1956); Welcome Stranger (1946); White Christmas (1954); Who's Minding the Store? (1963).

LINN, Michael (died 1995)
American composer.
FILMS INCLUDE: Agatha Christie's Ordeal by Innocence (1984); The Ambassador (1984); American Ninja (1985); Breakin' (1984); Eating Raoul (1982); Making the Grade (1984); Maria's Lovers (1984); Missing in Action 2 – The Beginning (1984); Over the Brooklyn Bridge (1983); Rappin' (1985); Superstition (1982).

LISKA, Zdenek (1922–1983)
Czech composer.
FILMS INCLUDE: The Angel Levine (1970); Baron Munchausen (1961); Bozska Ema (1979); Hrst Plna Vody (1969); Spalovac Mrtvol (1968); Udoli Vcel (1968); Vrazda po Cesky (1966).

LLOYD WEBBER, Andrew (1948–)
British composer of highly successful musicals.
FILMS INCLUDE: Gumshoe (1971); The Odessa File (1974).

LLOYD, Jonathan (1948–)
British composer who lived in Paris (1964–70) and attended Ligeti's classes at Tanglewood (1973). A busker and street musician (1974–6). Has written music to *Blackmail* – Hitchcock's silent thriller (1992–3).

LoDUCA, Joseph
American composer and guitarist who has won eight Emmy Awards for his television work.
FILMS INCLUDE: Army of Darkness: Evil Dead III (1992); Crimewave (1985); The Evil Dead (1982); Evil Dead II (1987); Moontrap (1989); Necronomicon (1993).
RECORDINGS: Army of Darkness: Evil Dead III. Varèse Sarabande VSD5411; The Evil Dead. Varèse Sarabande VSD5362; Evil Dead II. TER CDTER1142.

LOESSER, Frank (1910–1969)
American songwriter. Associated with films for 1930, he began as a lyricist and, from 1947, he wrote both words and music.
FILMS INCLUDE: College Swing (1938); Destry Rides Again (1939); Guys and Dolls (1955); Hans Christian Andersen (1952); How to Succeed in Business Without Really Trying (1966); Let's Dance (1950); Man About Town (1939); The Perils of Pauline (1947); Where's Charley? (1952).
RECORDINGS: Hans Christian Andersen. RCA 09026 68131–2.

LOEWE, Frederick (1901–1985)
Austrian composer, resident in America. Usually associated with Alan Jay Lerner.
FILMS INCLUDE: Brigadoon (1954); Camelot (1967); Gigi (1957); The Little Prince (1974); My Fair Lady (1964); Paint Your Wagon (1969).
RECORDINGS: Brigadoon. EMI CDODEON16; Gigi. First Night Records OCRCD07; My Fair Lady. Ter Classics CDTER21211.

LONDON, Kurt (1899–   )
German musician, technician and writer who studied philosophy, music and literature in Berlin, Heidelberg, Wurzburg and Freiburg. Became associated with film music in 1929 when he was appointed chief editor of *Der Film*. Also composed for German films. Came to London in 1935 where his book *Film Music* was published in 1936. This became the standard textbook on the subject for many years.

LOS RIOS, Waldo de
Composer.
FILMS INCLUDE: La Corrupcion de Chris Miller (1972); Murders in the Rue Morgue (1971); Pampa Salvaje (1966); Quien Puede matar a un Nino? (1975); La Residencia (1969); A Town Called Bastard (1971).

LUCAS, Leighton (1903–1982)
British composer and conductor who began his career as a dancer.
FILMS INCLUDE: *Feature*: The Dam Busters (1954 – part); Hyde Park Corner (1935); Ice Cold in Alex (1958); Portrait of Clare (1950); Serious Charge (1959); Son of Robin Hood (1958); Stage Fright (1949); Yangtse Incident (1956 – part). *Documentary*: A Date with a Tank (AFU, 1945); The Key to Scotland (Strand, 1935); Pacific Thrust (Greenpark, 1944); Ship Busters (RAF Film Unit, 1945); Target for Today (CFU, 1941); This is York (1953); We of the West Riding (Greenpark, 1946).
RECORDINGS: Stage Fright. Silva Screen FILMCD159.

LUTOSLAWSKI, Witold (1913–1994)
Polish composer, pianist and conductor who also studied in mathematics at Warsaw University. Prisoner-of-war of the Germans in 1939 but escaped and worked as a pianist in Warsaw cafes (1940–45). Later travelled to the USA and Britain to teach and give seminars.
FILMS INCLUDE: Odra do Baltyku (1945); Suita Warszawska (1946).

LUTYENS, Elisabeth (1906–1983)
British composer who partly studied in Paris. One of the first English composers to use the 12-note system of composition. Composed nearly two hundred scores for films, radio and incidental music for plays.

FILMS INCLUDE: *Feature*: Bermuda Affair (1956); Don't Bother to Knock (1961); Dr Terror's House of Horrors (1964); The Earth Dies Screaming (1964); The Malpas Mystery (1960); Mijn Nachten Met Susan, Olga, Albert, Julie, Piet and Sandra (1975); Never Take Sweets from a Stranger (1960); Out of True (1951); Paranoiac (1962); The Psychopath (1966); The Skull (1965); Spaceflight IC-1 (1965); The Terrornauts (1967); Theatre of Death (1966); To be a Woman (1951); The Travel Game (1958); The Twilight Forest (1957); The Way to Wimbledon (1952); World Without End (1953). *Documentary*: Any Man's Kingdom (1956); Europe by Train (1965); Heart of England (1954); Jungle Mariner (1944); Off the Beaten Track (1968); Three is Company (1959); The Travel Game (1958); The Way from Germany (1946).

MAAS, Dick (1931–)

Dutch composer, director, screenwriter and producer. Also a former cartoonist. FILMS INCLUDE: Abel (1985); Amsterdamned (1988); Flodder (1986); Flodder does Manhattan (1992); De Lift (1983); De Noorderlingen (The Northerners) (1993); Oh Boy! (1993); Wings of Fame (1990).

McCABE, John (1939–)

British composer and pianist who has also written music for television productions (e.g. *All for Love* and the *Hammer House of Mystery and Suspense*). FILMS INCLUDE: Fear in the Night (1972).

McCARTHY, Dennis

American composer and conductor. Also an arranger for Glen Campbell and an orchestrator for Alex North. Has composed much for television including *Star Trek: The Next Generation* (1987), *Star Trek: Generations* (1994) and *Star Trek: Deep Space Nine* (1993). RECORDINGS: Star Trek: Generations. GNP GNPD8040.

McCARTNEY, Paul (1942–)

British composer and songwriter. A member of The Beatles, he wrote many of the group's songs in collaboration with John Lennon. Later formed the band Wings. FILMS INCLUDE: The Family Way (1966); Give My Regards to Broad Street (1984); A Hard Day's Night (1964); Help! (1965); The Honorary Consul (1983); Let it Be (1970); Live and Let Die (1973); Magical Mystery Tour (1967); Twice in a Lifetime (1985); Yellow Submarine (1968). RECORDINGS: The Family Way. Carlton Classics MCD97.

MACERO, Teo (1925–   )
American composer.
FILMS INCLUDE: AKA Cassius Clay (1970); Bridges-go-Round (1958); End of the Road (1969).

McGUFFIE, Bill (died 1987)
Scottish composer.
FILMS INCLUDE: The Asphyx (1972); The Boys (1962); The Challenge (1959); The Cherry Picker (1972); The Comedy Man (1963); Corruption (1967); Cup Fever (1965); Daleks – Invasion Earth 2150 A.D. (1966); During One Night (1961); The Golden Rabbit (1962); The Leather Boys (1963); The Long Shadow (1961); The Unstoppable Man (1960).

McHUGH, James (1894–1969)
American composer and songwriter e.g. On the Sunny Side of the Street.
FILMS INCLUDE: Ask any Girl (1959); Buck Benny Rides Again (1940); The Cock-Eyed World (1929); Do You Love Me? (1946); Happy Go Lucky (1942); Mad about Music (1938); A Private's Affair (1959); Something for the Boys (1944); Sunny Side of the Street (1951); You'll Find Out (1940).
RECORDINGS: Happy Go Lucky. Koch International 37241–2.

McKENZIE, Mark
American composer and orchestrator of film scores by other composers e.g. Bruce Broughton, John Barry, Danny Elfman and Dennis McCarthy.
FILMS INCLUDE: Dr Jekyll and Ms Hyde (1995); Frank and Jesse (1994); Son of Darkness: To Die For 2 (1991); Warlock: The Armageddon (1993).
RECORDINGS: Dr Jekyll and Ms Hyde. Intrada MAF7063D; Frank and Jesse. Intrada 7059D; Warlock: The Armageddon. Intrada MAF7049D.

MACKEY, Percival (1894–   )
British composer and music director. At the age of 18 he went to Ireland, where he toured with the Royal Irish Animated Picture Company with a three-piece band, accompanying a touring film show. Wounded in France during World War I. Worked in many cinema orchestras, eventually forming his own dance band and making a large number of gramophone records. For a time he was an orchestrator with Jack Hylton's band. His first score for a sound film was *This Week of Grace* (1933 – starring Gracie Fields) which was followed by music for the first film made by Alexander Korda in Britain, *Service for Ladies*, starring Leslie Howard.
FILMS INCLUDE: Accused (1936); Almost a Gentleman (1938); Bob's Your Uncle (1941); Charing Cross Road (1935); Cheer Up (1935); Danny Boy (1941); Death at Broadcasting House (1934); The Echo Murders (1945); Facing the Music (1941); Girls Please (1931); Headlines (1943); Jailbirds (1940); Jump

For Glory (1937); Lilly of Laguna (1937); Old Mother Riley in Paris (1938); SOS (1935); These Charmed People (1931); Up with the Lark (1943); What do we do now? (1946).

McKUEN, Rod (1933–)
American composer.
FILMS INCLUDE: Emily (1976); Joanna (1968); The Prime of Miss Jean Brodie (1968); Rock, Pretty Baby (1957); Scandalous John (1971); Summer Love (1957); The Unknown War (1978); Wild Heritage (1958).

McNEELY, Joel
American composer, conductor and jazz musician who has also written much for television.
FILMS INCLUDE: Gold Diggers – The Secret of Bear Mountain (1995); Iron Will (1994); Radioland Murders (1994); Samantha (1992); Terminal Velocity (1994).
RECORDINGS: Gold Diggers – The Secret of Bear Mountain. Varèse Sarabande VSD5633; Iron Will. Varèse Sarabande VSD5467; Terminal Velocity. Varèse Sarabande VSD5546.

MACONIE, Robin (1942–)
New Zealand composer and writer of music who studied partly with Messiaen in Paris. Returned to New Zealand to work as a film composer (1965–7). Came to Britain in 1969.
FILMS INCLUDE: Runaway (1965).

McPHEE, Colin (1900–1964)
American composer and ethnomusicologist of Canadian origin. Studied partly with Varèse in New York until 1934 when he went to Berlin where he studied music and drama. During World War II McPhee was a music consultant to the Office of War Information and at the end of World War II he was commissioned by the United Nations to compose music for three documentary films.
FILMS INCLUDE: Documentary: H_2O (1931); Mechanical Principles (1931).

MADETOJA, Leevi (1887–1947)
Finnish composer, conductor and teacher. A pupil of Järnefelt and Sibelius, and d'Indy in Paris (1910). Wrote the successful opera Pohjalaisia.
FILMS INCLUDE: Taistelu Heikkilän Talosta (The Fight for Heikkilä's House – Op. 77) (1936).

MAGNE, Michel (1930–1984)
French composer and arranger. Involved in 'musique concrète'. Worked with most of the leading French directors.
FILMS INCLUDE: Two Weeks in September (1967); A Tout Coeur à Tokyo Pour Oss 117 (1966); Angélique Marquise des Anges (1964); Banco a Bangkok Pour Oss 117 (1964); I Bastardi (1968); Les Bricoleurs (1962); The Gentle Art of Seduction (1964); Compartiment Teurs (1965); Coplan FX 18 Casse Tout (1965); Détournement de Mineures (1959); Don Juan 1973 ou Si Don Juan Etait Une Femme (1973); Emmanuelle IV (1984); Fantomas se Déchaine (1965); Furia à Bahia Pour Oss 117 (1965); Galia (1966); Le Gentleman de Cocody (1965); Gigot (1962 – nominated for an Academy Award); Le Gorille a Mordu L'Archevêque (1962); Les Grands Chemins (1962); Les Lâches Vivent d'Espoir (1961); Melodie en Sous-Sol (1962); Merveilleuse Angélique (1964); Néa (1976); Les Pique-Assiette (1960); Quatre Nuits d'un Rêveur (1971); La Ronde (1964); The Sergeant (1968); Un Singe en Hiver (1962); Symphonie pour un Massacre (1963); Les Tontons Flingeurs (1963); Le Vice et la Vertu (1962).

MAJEWSKI, Hans-Martin (1911–1981)
German composer.
FILMS INCLUDE: Der Besuch (The Visit) (1964); Die Brücke (The Bridge) (1959); Double Destin (1955); El Hakim (1957); Labyrinth (1959); Magdelena – Vom Teufel Besessen (Magdalena – Possessed by the Devil) (1974); Question 7 (1961); Die Schachnovelle (Brainwashed) (1960); Sie (1954); Tod Eines Fremden (The Assassination) (1972); Tunnel 28 (Escape from East Berlin) (1961).

MAKLAKIEWICZ, Jan A. (1899–1954)
Polish composer, choral conductor and teacher. Studied partly with Dukas in Paris. Wrote in all genres of composition.

MALLABY, Cedric
British composer.
FILMS INCLUDE: Fanny by Gaslight (1944); The Man in Grey (1943); Man of Evil (1948).

MALOTTE, Albert H. (1895–1964)
American composer who wrote scores for many Disney cartoons.
FILMS INCLUDE: The Big Fisherman (1959); Dr. Cyclops (1940); The Enchanted Forest (1945).

MAMIYA, Michio (1929–)
Japanese composer and pianist who took a particular interest in Japanese folk music, notating tunes and using some of them in compositions.

MANCINIA, Mark (1957–)
American composer who collaborated with Hans Zimmer, including producing some of the songs for his Oscar winning *The Lion King* (1994). Asked by director Jon de Bout to write his first independent scores *Speed* (1994) and *Twister* (1996). Also wrote the score for *Con Air* (1997).
RECORDINGS: Speed. Milan 74321–23465–2.

MANCINI, Henry (1924–1994)
American composer and songwriter. An arranger and pianist with the post-war Glenn Miller orchestra before working at Universal Studios (1952–8). Also worked in television. His best known songs were 'Moon River' (written for *Breakfast at Tiffany's*) and 'Days of Wine and Roses'.
FILMS INCLUDE: Alex and the Gypsy (1976); Arabesque (1966); Bachelor in Paradise (1961); Back Roads (1981); The Benny Goodman Story (1955 – arranger); Blind Date (1987); Breakfast at Tiffany's (1961); A Change of Seasons (1980); Charade (1963); Chicago, Chicago (1969); Condorman (1981); Curse of the Pink Panther (1983); Damn Citizen (1957); Darling Lili (1969); Days of Wine and Roses (1962); Dear Heart (1964); A Fine Mess (1986); Ghost Dad (1990); I Girasoli (Sunflower) (1969); The Glass Menagerie (1987); The Glenn Miller Story (1953 – arranger); The Great Impostor (1960); The Great Mouse Detective (1986); The Great Race (1965); The Great Waldo Pepper (1975); Gunn (1967); Harry and Son (1984); Hatari! (1961); The Hawaiians (1970); Heavy Petting (1988); High Time (1960); House Calls (1978); Jacqueline Susann's Once is not Enough (1974); The Killers (1964); Lifeforce (1985); Little Miss Marker (1980); Man Afraid (1957); The Man Who Loved Women (1983); Man's Favourite Sport (1963); Married to It (1991); Me, Natalie (1969); The Molly Maguires (1969); Moment to Moment (1966); Mommie Dearest (1981); Mr Hobbs takes a Vacation (1962); Nightwing (1979); Oklahoma Crude (1973); The Party (1968); Physical Evidence (1988); The Pink Panther (1963); The Pink Panther Strikes Again (1976); The Pique Poquette of Paris (1966); The Prisoner of Zenda (1979); Return of the Pink Panther (1974); Revenge of the Pink Panther (1978); Rock, Pretty Baby (1957); Salem Come to Supper (1971); Santa Clause (1985); Second Thoughts (1982); A Shot in the Dark (1964); Silver Streak (1976); S.O.B. (1981); Soldier in the Rain (1963); Sometimes a Great Notion (1971); Son of the Pink Panther (1993); Summer Love (1957); Sunflower (1970); Sunset (1988); Switch (1991); That's Dancing! (1985); That's Entertainment (1974); The Thief Who Came to Dinner (1973); Tom and Jerry: The Movie (1992); Touch of Evil (1958); Trail of the Pink Panther (1982); Two for the Road (1966); Victor/Victoria

(1982); Visions of Eight (1973); Voice in the Mirror (1958); W.C. Fields and Me (1976); Wait until Dark (1967); Welcome Home (1989); What Did You Do in the War, Daddy? (1966); White Dawn (1974); Who is Killing the Great Chefs of Europe? (1978); Without a Clue (1988).
RECORDINGS: Breakfast at Tiffany's. Decca 444 460-2DH; The Great Waldo Pepper. Silva Screen SILVAD3001; The Pink Panther. Telearc CD80401; Tom and Jerry: The Movie. MCA MCD10721; The White Dawn. RCA RD60471.

MANDEL, Johnny (1935–)

American composer, trumpeter and trombonist. His song 'The Shadow of Your Smile' (from *The Sandpiper*) won an Oscar in 1965.
FILMS INCLUDE: Agatha (1978); An American Dream (1966); The Americanization of Emily (1964); The Baltimore Bullet (1980); Being There (1979); Brenda Starr (1989); Caddyshack (1980); Deathtrap (1982); Drums of Africa (1963); Escape to Witch Mountain (1974); Freaky Friday (1976); Harper (1966); Heaven with a Gun (1969); I Want to Live! (1958); The Last Detail (1973); The Lawbreakers (1960); Lookin' to Get Out (1982); The Man Who Had Power Over Women (1970); MASH (1969); Point Blank (1967); Pretty Poison (1968); The Russians are Coming, The Russians are Coming (1966); The Sailor Who Fell From Grace With The Sea (1976); The Sandpiper (1965); Some Kind of Nut (1969); Staying Alive (1983); Summer Wishes, Winter Dreams (1973); That Cold Day in the Park (1969); The Verdict (1982); W (Terror is One Letter) (1973).

MANFREDINI, Harry

American composer who wrote music for horror films.
FILMS INCLUDE: Cameron's Closet (1987); The Final Chapter (1984); Friday the 13th (1980); Friday the 13th (Part 2) (1981); Friday the 13th (Part 3) (1982); Friday the 13th: The Final Chapter (1984); Friday the 13th: A New Beginning (1985); Friday the 13th (Part 6) Jason Lives (1986); Friday the 13th (Part 7) The New Blood (1988); Jason Goes to Hell: The Final Friday (1993); Spy Break (1983); Swamp Thing (1982); Through the Looking Glass (1976).

MANN, Barry (1942–)

American composer, songwriter and singer whose songs have featured in many films since the 1970s.
FILMS INCLUDE: An American Tail (1986); Harry and the Hendersons (1987); I Never Sang For My Father (1969); Million Dollar Mystery (1987); National Lampoon's Christmas Vacation (1989); Oliver and Company (1988); Sibling Rivalry (1990); Summer Heart (1987); Wild in the Streets (1968).

MANNE, Shelly (1920–1984)
American composer.

FILMS INCLUDE: Clarence, the Cross-Eyed Lion (1965); The Five Pennies (1959); The Gene Krupa Story (1959); Herman's Herd (1949); I Want to Live! (1958); The Man Who Loved Women (1983); The Murder Men (1962); The Proper Time (1961); T-Bird Gang (1958); Tall Story (1960); Wild and Wonderful (1963); Young Billy Young (1969); The Young Sinner (1965).

MANSFIELD, David
American composer.

FILMS INCLUDE: Ballad of Little Jo (1993); Desperate Hours (1990); Heaven's Gate (1980); Renaldo and Clara (1977); Timerider – The Adventure of Lyle Swann (1982); The Year of the Dragon (1985).

RECORDINGS: The Ballad of Little Jo. Intrada MAF7053D; Heaven's Gate. Silva Screen FILMCD176.

MARLY, Anne
British composer and songwriter. Wrote the song 'Hullalooba' for the Ealing film *Dead of Night* (1945).

MARTELL, Philip (1906–1993)
British composer who wrote scores for many horror films.

FILMS INCLUDE: Adventure in the Hopfields (1954); Albert R.N. (1953); The Anniversary (1967); Another Man's Poison (1951); The Bawdy Adventures of Tom Jones (1975); Blood from the Mummy's Tomb (1971); Boy with a Flute (1964); The Brigand of Kandahar (1965); Can Heironymus Merkin ever Forget Mercy Humphe and find True Happiness? (1969); Captain Clegg (1961); Captain Kronos, Vampire Hunter (1972); Cartouche (1954); Catacombs (1964); A Challenge for Robin Hood (1967); Countess Dracula (1970); Creatures The World Forgot (1970); Crescendo (1969); Cuckoo Patrol (1965); The Curse of the Mummy's Tomb (1964); Danger Route (1967); Dark Places (1973); Dead Man's Evidence (1962); The Deadly Bees (1966); Demons of the Mind (1971); The Devil Rides Out (1967); Doctor Blood's Coffin (1960); Dr Jekyll and Sister Hyde (1971); Dr Terror's House of Horrors (1964); Dracula has Risen from the Grave (1968); Dracula – Prince of Darkness (1965); The Earth Dies Screaming (1964); Emergency (1962); Escapade (1955); The Eyes of Annie Jones (1963); Face in the Night (1956); Fanatic (1965); Fear in the Night (1972); The File of the Golden Goose (1969); Frankenstein and the Monster from Hell (1973); Frankenstein Created Woman (1966); Frankenstein Must Be Destroyed (1969); Freedom to Die (1962); The Ghoul (1975); Hands of the Ripper (1971); Hello London (1958); Home is the Hero (1959); The House in Marsh Road (1960); Hysteria (1964); Innocent Bystanders (1972); Jackpot (1960); The Lady Vanishes (1979); The Last

Remake of Beau Geste (1977); The Legend of the 7 Golden Vampires (1974); Legend of the Werewolf (1974); Lost Continent (1968); Lust for a Vampire (1970); Made in Heaven (1952); Mary had a Little . . . (1961); Master Spy (1963); Mijn Nachten Met Susan, Olga, Albert, Julie, Piet and Sandra (1975); Miss Pilgrim's Progress (1949); Monster of Terror (1965); Moon Zero Two (1969); Mr Drake's Duck (1950); The Mummy's Shroud (1966); Murder at the Windmill (1949); Mutiny on the Buses (1972); The Nanny (1965); Nearest and Dearest (1972); Nothing but the Night (1972); On the Buses (1971); One Million Years B.C. (1966); Out of the Fog (1962); Penny Princess (1952); The Plague of the Zombies (1966); The Price of Silence (1960); The Psychopath (1966); Quatermass and the Pit (1967); Rasputin The Mad Monk (1965); The Reptile (1966); Rising Damp (1980); Run with the Wind (1966); The Satanic Rites of Dracula (1973); The Scars of Dracula (1970); Shatter (1974); She (1965); She Knows y'Know (1962); The Skull (1965); The Small World of Sammy Lee (1962); The Snake Woman (1961); Spaceflight IC-1 (1965); The Spiral Staircase (1975); Straight on till Morning (1972); The Surgeon's Knife (1957); The Sweet and the Bitter (1962); Taste the Blood of Dracula (1969); The Terrornauts (1967); That's Your Funeral (1972); Theatre of Death (1966); They came from beyond Space (1967); The Third Alibi (1961); Three on a Spree (1961); To Sir, with Love (1966); To the Devil a Daughter (1976); Treasure of San Teresa (1959); Twins of Evil (1971); The Uncanny (1977); Vampire Circus (1971); The Vampire Lovers (1970); The Vengeance of She (1967); The Viking Queen (1966); When Dinosaurs Ruled the Earth (1969); Where the Bullets Fly (1966); The Witches (1966); Women of Twilight (1952).

MARTIN, Hugh (1914–   )

American composer and lyricist. Associated with Ralph Blane. Has also written for television e.g. *Hans Brinker* (1955).

FILMS INCLUDE: Athena (1954); Best Foot Forward (1941); The Girl Most Likely (1957); The Girl Rush (1955); Meet Me in St Louis (1944).

RECORDINGS: Best Foot Forward. Nonesuch 7559–79413–2; The Girl Most Likely. Nonesuch 7559–79314–2; Meet Me in St Louis. Nonesuch 7559–79314–2.

MARTINU, Bohuslav (1890–1959)

Czech composer and violinist who studied with Suk in Prague. Also studied with Roussel in Paris (1923). Settled in the USA (1941) where he composed five symphonies. Returned to Europe in 1953. Wrote music in many genres.

FILMS INCLUDE: *Feature*: Melo (1932); Unfaithful Marijka (1935). *Documentary*: City of the Quick Water (1935); Folk Dances and Customs into the Slovacko Region (1922); The Slipper (1935).

MASETTI, Erizio
Italian composer.
FILMS INCLUDE: Attila, Flagello di Dio (1954); Fabiola (1948); Gelosia (1948); Hercules (1959); Hercules Unchained (1960); La Romana (1954); Volcano (1953).

MATHIAS, William (1934–1992)
Welsh composer, conductor and pianist. Well known, especially in the USA, for his church music.
FILMS INCLUDE: *Documentary*: Britannia: A Bridge (1972); Forward to First Principles (1965).

MATHIESON, Muir (1911–1975)
British music director who began to work as assistant musical director for Alexander Korda (1931–9). Was musical director for government film units (1940–45) and then for J. Arthur Rank films. Persuaded many British composers to write for films. Arranged music for many documentary films including *Going Places Fast, Journey – Intercity* (1972); *Operation London Bridge* (1975); *Sing of the Border* (1964).

MATSU, Yama
Japanese composer.
FILMS INCLUDE: Biruma No Tategoto (1956); Taiheiyo Hitoribotchi (1963).

MATZ, Peter (1928–   )
American composer and conductor.
FILMS INCLUDE: Bye Bye Braverman (1968); Funny Lady (1975 – nominated for an Academy Award); The Gumshoe Kid (1989); Lust in the Dust (1985); Marlowe (1969); The Private Eyes (1980); The Prize Fighter (1979); Rivals (1972); Torch Song Trilogy (1988).

MAXWELL, Charles (1892–1962)
American composer and arranger.
FILMS INCLUDE: Calm Yourself (1935); In Old Sacramento (1946); Parole (1936); Romance of the Rio Grande (1941 – with Mockridge); Scotland Yard Investigator (1945); White Fang (1936 – with Lange).

MAY, Brian (1934–1997)
Australian composer who was musical director for the Australian Broadcasting Corporation.
FILMS INCLUDE: Barnaby and Me (1978); Cloak and Dagger (1984); Dangerous Summer (1982); Dead Sleep (1990); Death Before Dishonour (1987); Freddy's Dead: The Final Nightmare (1991); Gallipoli (1981); Harlequin (1980); Hurri-

cane Smith (1990); Mad Max (1979); Mad Max II (1982); Missing in Action II: The Beginning (1984); Nightmare on Elm Street IV (1993); Patrick (1979); Pirates (1986); Steel Dawn (1987); The Survivors (1983); The True Story of Eskimo Nell (1975).

RECORDINGS: Death before Dishonour. Prometheus PCD118; Mad Max. Varèse Sarabande VCD47144; Missing in Action II. Silva Screen SILVAD3001.

MAY, Hans (1886–1958)

Viennese composer and music director who settled in Britain in the early 1930s. He was one of the earliest of film music pioneers, being associated with the 'Kinothek', a catalogued library of music used for the musical accompaniment to silent films, which was originated by Guiseppe Becce in 1919.

FILMS INCLUDE: Backgroom Boy (1942); Bridegroom Widow (1931); Brighton Rock (1947); Candlelight in Algeria (1944); Flame of Love (1930); The Gypsy and the Gentleman (1957); I Killed the Count (1939); The Lisbon Story (1946); Madonna of the Seven Moons (1944); Mayerling (French film with Charles Boyer) (1935); Salute to the Soldier (1945); The Stars Look Down (1939); Thunder Rock (1942); Uncensored (1943); Waltz Time (1945); The Witches Lady (1945).

MAYER, John

British composer.

FILMS INCLUDE: Danger Route (1967).

MAYUZUMI, Toshiro (1929–)

Japanese composer who studied with Ifukube. He has worked extensively in Japanese theatre and written many film scores.

FILMS INCLUDE: Akasen Chitai (Street of Shame) (1956 – the first Japanese film to use electronic music); La Bibbia (Bible in the Beginning . . .) (1966); Reflections in a Golden Eye (1967); Tokyo Orinpikku (Tokyo Olympiad) (1965).

MEDEK, Tilo (1940–)

German composer and musicologist. Has written many scores for the theatre, cinema and television.

MEISEL, Edmund (–1930)

German composer.

FILMS INCLUDE: Berlin – Symphony of a Great City (1927); The Crimson Circle (1929); October (1928); Potemkin (1925); Ten Days That Shook the World (1927).

MELACHRINO, George (1909–1965)
British composer and dance bandleader.
FILMS INCLUDE: Appointment with Crime (1946); April in Portugal (1955); Code of Scotland Yard (1948); Dark Secret (1950); The Gamma People (1955); The Lady Craved Excitement (1950); No Orchids for Miss Blandish (1948); Odango (1956); Stars of Shirley Yorke (1950); Woman to Woman (1947).

MELLE, Gil (1935–)
American composer who has also written for television e.g. *Dynasty*.
FILMS INCLUDE: The Andromeda Strain (1971); Blood Beach (1981); Borderline (1981); Hot Target (1985); The Last Chase (1981); The Organisation (1971); Restless (1986); The Savage is Loose (1974); The Sentinel (1976); Starship Invasion (1978); The Ultimate Warrior (1975); You'll Like My Mother (1972).

MENDOZA, David (1894–)
American composer.
FILMS INCLUDE: Annie Laurie (1927); Ben Hur A Tale of Christ (1925); The Big Parade (1925); Camille (1927); Don Juan (1926); The Duke Steps Out (1929); The Finger Points (1931); The Fire Brigade (1926); The Flying Fleet (1929); The Merry Widow (1925); The Public Enemy (1931); The Scarlet Letter (1926); Slide, Kelly, Slide (1927); White Shadows of the South Seas (1928).

MENDOZA-NAVA, Jaime
FILMS INCLUDE: The Boys in Company C (1977); The Brotherhood of Satan (1971); Fever Heat (1968); The Hard Road (1970); High, Wild and Free (1968); The Legend of Boggy Creek (1972); The Savage Wind (1970); The Talisman (1968); The Witchmaker (1969).

MENKEN, Alan (1949–)
American composer who has worked with lyricist Howard Ashman. Has scored many of the lastest Disney releases.
FILMS INCLUDE: Aladdin (1992 – Academy Award for the music); Beauty and the Beast (1991 – Academy Award for the music); Home Alone II (1992); The Hunchback of Notre Dame (1996); Life with Mikey (1993); The Little Mermaid (1989 – Academy Award for the music); Little Shop of Horrors (1986 – nominated for an Academy Award); Newsies (1992); Pocahontas (1995); Rocky V (1990).
RECORDINGS: Aladdin. Varèse Sarabande VSD5452; Beauty and the Beast. Delos DE3186; The Hunchback of Notre Dame. Walt Disney 60893–7; The Little Mermaid. Varèse Sarabande VSD5452; Pocahontas. Delos DE3186.

MERCER, John (1909–1976)
American composer and lyricist who worked in Hollywood from the early 1930s.
FILMS INCLUDE: The Belle of New York (1951); Bernardine (1957); Breakfast at Tiffany's (1961); Charade (1963); Daddy Long Legs (1955); Dangerous When Wet (1953); Darling Lili (1969); The Harvey Girls (1946 – Academy Award); Here Come the Waves (1944); Hollywood Hotel (1937); Merry Andrew (1957); My Favorite Spy (1951); The Petty Girl (1950); The Pink Panther (1963); Second Chorus (1941); Seven Brides for Seven Brothers (1954 – Academy Award); The Sky's the Limit (1943); That Certain Feeling (1956); Top Banana (1953); You Can't Run Away From It (1956).

MERRILL, Robert (1921–)
American composer and lyricist whose chief film score has been *Funny Girl*.

MEWTON-WOOD, Noel (1922–1953)
Australian concert pianist and composer who wrote the score for *Tawny Pipit* (1944).

MEYER, H. Ernst (1905–1988)
German composer and special sound effects expert who partly studied with Hanns Eisler, famous film music composer, and Paul Hindemith. Came to England in 1933 and entered films in 1937 to work for Cavalcanti at the GPO documentary film unit.
FILMS INCLUDE: *Documentary*: British Made (GPOFU, 1939); Collective Adventure (Jewish Agency for Palestine, 1940); A Few Ounces a Day (1941); Filling the Gap (Realist, 1942); Lambert Walk (British Council and Imperial Airways); Mobilise Your Scrap (MoI, 1941); North Sea (GPOFU, 1938); Oil from the East (Shell Film Unit, 1939); Roadways (GPOFU, 1937); When the Pie was Opened (1941); Work Party (Realist, 1942).

MICHELET, Michel (1899–)
French composer, born in Russia.
FILMS INCLUDE: Captain Sinbad (1963); The Chase (1946); The Diary of a Chambermaid (1945); Fort Algiers (1953); The Hairy Ape (1944); Impact (1949); The Journey (1958); Siren of Atlantis (1946); Der Tiger von Eschnapur (The Tiger of Eschnapur) (1958); Tigress of Bengal (1958); La Venere di Cheronea (Aphrodite Goddess of Love) (1957); Voice in the Wind (1944).

MILHAUD, Darius (1892–1974)
French composer who studied with Widor and D'Indy. A member of 'Les Six', he went to America in 1941. Associated with the cinema from 1924 onwards.
FILMS INCLUDE: *Feature*: Actualités (1928); Days of Hope (1938–45); Dreams

that Money Can Buy (1946); L'Hippocampe (1934 – dir. J. Painlevé); Madame Bovary (1934); Mamz'elle Nitouche (1954); Mollenard (1938); Tartarin de Tarascon (1934); Voix d'enfants (1935 – dir. Reynaud) Vormittagsspuk (1928). *Documentary* Islands: (1939 – dir. Cavalcanti).

MILLS, Charles B. (1914–1982)
American composer and critic who had composition lessons from Aaron Copland, Roger Sessions and Roy Harris.
FILMS INCLUDE: On the Bowery (1957).

MILNER, Cecil
British composer who provided orchestration for about thirty-five films, and composed scores for about twenty, usually in collaboration with others.
FILMS INCLUDE: *Documentary*: Down at the Local (1944); Some Like It Rough (1944).

MINGUS, Charles (1922–1979)
American jazz double bass player and composer.

MIRZOYAN, Eduard M. (1921–)
Armenian composer and teacher whose music has been greatly influenced by the Armenian traditions and the music of Prokofiev, Shostakovich and Bartok.

MISRAKI, Paul (1908–)
French composer, born in Turkey.
FILMS INCLUDE: Ali Baba et les Quarante Voleurs (1954); Alphaville une étrange aventure de Lemmy Caution (1965); Les bonnes femmes (Girls . . . Girls!) (1960); La Châtelaine du Liban (Desert Retour) (1956); Le Chevalier de Pardaillan (Clash of Steel) (1962); Comment qu'elle est! (Women are like that) (1960); Les Cousins (1959); Le Couturier de ces dames (1956); En effeuillant la Marguerite (Mam'selle Striptease) (1956); Escale à Orly (1955); Et Dieu . . . Créa la femme (And God Created Woman) (1956); Faibles Femmes (Women are Weak) (1959); Les Fanatiques (1957); Les Femmes s'en Balancent (Dames don't Care) (1954); La Fievre Monte a El Pao (1959); La Française et L'Amour (Love and The Frenchwoman) (1960); L'Homme de ma Vie (Man in My Life) (1952); Identité Judiciaire (Monsieur Murderer) (1951); Les Jeux Dangereux (1958); Mademoiselle S'Amuse (1947); Maigret tend un piège (1958); Méfiez-vous Fillettes (1957); Un Meurtre est Un Meurtre (1972); Monte Carlo Baby (1952); Montparnasse 19 (1958); La Mort en ce jardin (1956); Mr Arkadin (1954); Nous irons à Paris (Let's go to Paris) (1949); Oasis (1955); Obsession (1954); Pardonnez nos Offenses (1956); La Petite Chocolatière (1949); Port Afrique (1956); Le Rosier de Madame Husson (1950); Sans Famille (1958); Sénéchal le Magnifique (1957).

MITCHELL, Richard G. (1956–   )
British composer who has done much work for television e.g. *Children of the Holocaust, Harry* and *Masterchef*.
FILMS INCLUDE: Across the Lake; Beastly Treatment; Born American; The Bridge (1992); Worlds Beyond.

MIZZY, Vic (1922–   )
American composer.
FILMS INCLUDE: The Busy Body (1967); The Caper of the Golden Bulls (1966); Did You Hear the One About the Travelling Saleslady? (1967); Don't Make Waves (1967); The Ghost and Mr Chicken (1966); The Love God? (1969); The Night Walker (1964); The Perils of Pauline (1967); The Reluctant Astronaut (1967); The Shakiest Gun in the West (1967); The Spirit is Willing (1966); A Very Special Favour (1965).

MOCKRIDGE, Cyril (1896–1979)
British composer and music director who went to the USA in 1921. Entered films in 1932. Also composed for television.
FILMS INCLUDE: The Adventures of Sherlock Holmes (1939); All Hands on Deck (1961); American Guerilla in the Philippines (1950); April Love (1957); The Beautiful Blonde from Bashful Bend (1949); Belles on their Toes (1952); Bus Stop (1956); Captain Eddie (1945); The Dark Corner (1946); Deadline – USA (1952); Desk Set (1957); Everything Happens at Night (1939); The Farmer Takes a Wife (1953); Flaming Star (1960); The Gift of Love (1958); The Girl Next Door (1952); Half Angel (1951); Hot Spot (1941); Hound Dog Man (1959); The Hound of the Baskervilles (1939); How to Be Very, Very Popular (1955); I Was a Male War Bride (1949); The Lieutenant Wore Skirts (1955); The Man Who Shot Liberty Valance (1962); Many Rivers to Cross (1955); Miracle on 34th Street (1947); My Darling Clementine (1946); Night without Sleep (1952); Oh Men! Oh Women! (1957); A Private's Affair (1959); Rally Round the Flag, Boys! (1958); The Solid Gold Cadillac (1956); Tall Story (1960); Thunder in the Sun (1959); Wake Me When It's Over (1960); Will Success Spoil Rock Hunter? (1957); Woman's World (1954).

MOHAUPT, Richard (1904–1957)
German composer, conductor and pianist for a film company. Emigrated to New York in 1939.

MOLE, Charles
British composer who has worked with Kenneth Branagh.
FILMS INCLUDE: Othello (1996).

MONACO, James (1885–1945)
American composer who wrote songs for seven Bing Crosby films.
FILMS INCLUDE: Dr Rhythm (1938); East Side of Heaven (1939); If I Had My Way (1940); Irish Eyes are Smiling (1944); Pin up Girl (1944); Rhythm on the River (1940); Road to Singapore (1940); Sing you Sinners (1938); Stage Door Canteen (1943); The Star Maker (1939); Sweet and Lowdown (1944).
RECORDINGS: Rhythm on the River. Koch International 37906–2.

MONTGOMERY, Bruce (1921–1978)
British composer, conductor and organist who entered films in 1948. Also known for writing detective novels under the name of Edmund Crispen.
FILMS INCLUDE: *Feature*: Carry on Cruising (1962); Carry on Sergeant (1958); Cartouche (1954); Checkpoint (1956); Circus Friends (1956); Doctor at Large (1957); Doctor at Sea (1955); Doctor in Love (1960); The Duke wore Jeans (1958); Escapade (1955); Eyewitness (1956); Guilty? (1956); Heart of a Child (1958); Home is the Hero (1959); Keep it Clean (1955); The Kidnappers (1953); No Kidding (1960); Raising a Riot (1955); Raising the Wind (1961); The Surgeon's Knife (1957); Too Young to Love (1959); The Truth About Women (1957); Twice round the Daffodils (1962); Watch Your Stern (1960); Which Will Ye Have? (1949). *Documentary*: Scottish Highlands (1953).

MOORE, Dudley (1935–)
British composer, pianist and comedian who often teamed with the late Peter Cook.
FILMS INCLUDE: Alice's Adventures in Wonderland (1972); Arthur (1981); Arthur 2: On the Rocks (1988); The Bed Sitting Room (1969); Bedazzled (1967); Best Defence (1984); Crazy People (1990); Fatal Instinct (1993); Foul Play (1978); The Hound of the Baskervilles (1977); Inadmissible Evidence (1968); Like Father Like Son (1987); Lovesick (1983); Micki and Maude (1984); The Most (1962); The Pickle (1993); Quei Temerari Sulle Loro Pazze, Scatenate, Scalcinate Carriole (1969); Romantic Comedy (1983); Santa Claus – The Movie (1985); Six Weeks (1982); Staircase (1969); Thirty is a Dangerous Age (1967); To Russia ... With Elton (1979); Unfaithfully Yours (1983); Wholly Moses! (1980); The Wrong Box (1966).

MORAN, Mike
Composer who has also written for television.
FILMS INCLUDE: Betrayal (1982); The Bitch (1979); Bloodbath at the House of Death (1983); Body Parts (1991); Death Wish 3 (1985); The Missionary (1981); Time Bandits (1981); Water (1985).

MORAWECK, Lucien (–1973)
American composer.

FILMS INCLUDE: Dreaming Out Loud (1940); International Lady (1941); The Man in the Iron Mask (1939); Strange Voyage (1946).

MORODER, Giorgio (1940–   )
Italian composer, resident in the USA, who is a specialist in synthesizers. Wrote the score for the reconstructed 1984 version of Fritz Lang's 1926 classic *Metropolis*.

FILMS INCLUDE: American Gigolo (1980); Cat People (1982); D.C. Cab (1983); Electric Dreams (1984); Fair Game (1988); Flashdance (1983); Foxes (1979); Let It Ride (1989); Metropolis (1984); Midnight Express (1978 – awarded an Academy Award); Over the Top (1987); Scarface (1983); Die Unendliche Geschichte (The Neverending Story) (1984).

RECORDINGS: Flashdance. Telearc CD80243; Over the Top. Silva Screen FILMCD139.

MOROSS, Jerome (1913–1983)
American composer and pianist who wrote the famous score for *The Big Country* (1988).

FILMS INCLUDE: The Adventures of Huckleberry Finn (1960); The Big Country (1958); The Bishop's Wife (1947); The Cardinal (1963); Close Up (1948); Five Finger Exercise (1962); Hail, Hero! (1969); The Mask of Dimitrios (1944); The Mountain Road (1960); Northern Pursuit (1943); The Proud Rebel (1958); Rachel, Rachel (A Jest of God) (1968); Seven Wonders of the World (1955); The Sharkfighters (1956); The Valley of Gwangi (1968); The War Lord (1965); When I Grow Up (1951).

RECORDINGS: The Adventures of Huckleberry Finn. Silva Screen FILMCD161; The Big Country. Silva Screen SILVAD3002; The Cardinal. Preamble PRCD1778; The Valley of Gwangi. Silva Screen FILMCD161; The War Lord. Silva Screen FILMXCD187.

MORRICONE, Enrico (1928–   )
Italian composer and arranger who is associated with the films of Sergio Leone. Starting with *A Fistful of Dollars* in 1964, he scored all of the director's later films. He won a British Academy Award for *The Mission* which was also nominated for an Oscar.

FILMS INCLUDE: Ad Ogni Costo (Grand Slam) (1967); Addio, Fratello Crudele (1971); Agent 505 – Todesfalle Beirut (1965); Allonsanfan (1974); Amanti D'Oltretomba (1965); L'Anticristo (1974); L'Assoluto Naturale (1969); L'Attentat (1972); Autostop Rosso Sangue (1976); Barbe-Bleu (1972); La Bataille de San Sebastian (1968); La Battaglia di Algeri (1965); Bloodline (1979); Il Buono, Il Brutto, Il Cattivo (The Good, The Bad and the Ugly) (1966);

Butterfly (1981); La Cage aux Folles (1978); La Cage aux Folles: Elles se marient (1985); La Cage aux Folles II (1980); I Cannibali (1969); Le Casse (1971); C'Era Una Volta Il West (1968); La Chiave (1983); Città Violenta (1970); Le Clan des Siciliens (1968); I Crudeli (1966); Da Uomo a Uomo (Death Rides a Horse) (1967); Dalle Ardenne All'Inferno (1967); Days of Heaven (1978); Il Decamerone (The Decameron) (1970); Diabolik (1967); El Greco (1965); L'Envers du Decor: Portrait de Pierre Guffroy (1992); L'Eredita Ferramonti (1976); Escalation (1968); Un Esercito di Cinque Uomini (1969); Exorcist II The Heretic (1977); Faccia a Faccia (1967); Fatti di Gente Perbene (1974); Il Fiore Delle Mille e Una Notte (1974); Forza G (1971); Le Foto Priobite di Una Signora per Bene (1970); Fräulein Doktor (1968); Galileo (1968); Il Gatto a Nove Code (1971); Genesis: The Creature and the Flood (1994); Giornata Nera Per L'Ariete (1971); Il Giorno del Giudizio (1971); Giù la Testa (1971); Grazie Zia (1968); Holocaust 2000 (1977); Hornets' Nest (1969); The 'Human' Factor (1975); Hundra (1983); Ilona und Kurti – Du Sprechen Deutsch (1991); In the Line of Fire (1993); Indagine su un Cittadino al di Spora di Ogni Sospetto (1970); Gli Intoccabili (1968); The Island (1980); Jona Che Visse Nella Balena (1993); Kommando Leopard (1985); Una Lucertola Con la Pelle Di Donna (1971); Il Maestro e Margherita (1972); Matchless (1966); Il Mercenario (1968); Metello (1970); Metti, Una Sera a Cena (1968); Mio Caro Dr Gräsler (1990); Il Mio Nome è Nessuno (My Name is Nobody) (1973); The Mission (1986); La Monaca Di Monza (1969); Mose (Moses) (1975); Nana (1982); Navajo Joe (1966); The Night and the Moment (1994); Nuovo Cinema Paradiso (1988); O.K. Connery (1967); Once Upon a Time in America (1983); Orca . . . Killer Whale (1977); Order of Death (1983); Partner (1968); Per Pochi Dollari Ancora (1967); Per Qualche Dollaro in Più (For a Few Dollars More) (1965); Per Un Pugno Di Dollari (Fistful of Dollars) (1964); Peur Sur La Ville (1975); Una Pistola per Ringo (1965); Prima Della Rivoluzione (1964); I Pugni in Tasca (1965); I Racconti di Canterbury (1971); La Ragazza E Il Generale (1967); Rappresaglia (1973); Red Sonja (1985); La Resa Dei Conti (The Big Gundown) (1967); Il Ritorno Di Ringo (The Return of Ringo) (1965); Roma Come Chicago (Bandits in Rome) (1968); Ruba Al Prossimo Tuo (1968); Sahara (1983); Salo O Le Centoventi Giornate Di Sodoma (1975); La Scorta (1993); Le Secret (1974); Le Serpent (1973); Sette Pistole Per I MacGregor (Seven Guns for the MacGregors) (1966); So Fine (1981); Il Sorriso Del Grande Tentatore (1973); Storie Di Vita E Malavita (1975); La Tarantola Dal Ventre Nero (1972); Tempi Di Uccidere (1989); La Tenda Rossa (1969); Teorema (1968); The Thing (1982); La Tragedia Di Un Uomo Ridicolo (1981); Un Tranquillo Posto in Campagna (1968); Treasure of the Four Crowns (1982); Le Trio Infernal (1974); Two Mules for Sister Sara (1969); L'Uccello Dalle Piume Di Cristallo (The Bird with the Crystal Plumage) (1969); L'Umanoide (1979); Un Uomo Da Rispettare (1972); Vaarwel (The Romantic Agony) (1973); Vamos a Matar,

Companeros! (Companeros) (1970); La Villa Del Venerdì (1991); White Dog (1981).
RECORDINGS: Casualties of War. Silva Screen FILMCD148; A Fistful of Dollars. Silva Screen FILMCD138; The Good, The Bad and The Ugly. Silva Screen FILMCD138; The Mission. Silva Screen FILMCD148; Two Mules for Sister Sara. Silva Screen FILMCD138.

MORRIS, John (1926–)

American composer who has scored many of Mel Brooks' films including *Blazing Saddles* (1974).
FILMS INCLUDE: The Adventure of Sherlock Holmes' Smarter Brother (1975); The Bank Shot (1974); Blazing Saddles (1974); Clue (1985); The Doctor and The Devils (1985); The Elephant Man (1980); Haunted Honeymoon (1986); High Anxiety (1977); History of the World Part One (1981); In God We Trust (1980); The In-Laws (1979); Iron Weed (1967); Johnny Dangerously (1984); The Last Remake of Beau Geste (1977); Life Stinks (1991); The Producers (1967); Second Sight (1989); Silent Movie (1976); Spaceballs (1987); Stella (1990); Table for Five (1983); To be or Not to be (1983); The Twelve Chairs (1970); The Wash (1988); The Woman in Red (1984); The World's Greatest Lover (1977); Young Frankenstein (1974).
RECORDINGS: The Elephant Man. Milan 74321 19986–2.

MORTON, Arthur

American composer who worked for Columbia and Universal.
FILMS INCLUDE: The Day the Bookies Wept (1939); Father is a Bachelor (1950); Fit for a King (1937); Millie's Daughter (1947); Night Life of the Gods (1935); Pick a Star (1937 – with Hatley); The Walking Hills (1949).

MUL, Jan (1911–1971)

Dutch composer and music editor.

MULDOWNEY, Dominic (1952–)

British composer who has written scores for television e.g. *Sharpe*.
FILMS INCLUDE: Betrayal (1982); 1984 (1984); The Ploughman's Lunch (1983 – dir. Richard Eyre).

MUNROW, David (1942–1976)

British composer and recorder, crumhorn player, etc. Specialist in early music and instruments. Also wrote for television e.g. *Elizabeth R*.
FILMS INCLUDE: The Devils (1971 – part); Henry VIII and His Six Wives (1972); Zardoz (1973).

MURADELI, Vano (1908–1976)
Georgian composer who wrote a considerable amount of theatre music.
During World War II he composed the music to the films *Hatred* and *Retribution*.
FILMS INCLUDE: The Ferghana Canal.

MURRAY, Lyn (1909–1989)
American composer who has also written for television e.g. *The Magic Carpet* – 1971.
FILMS INCLUDE: The Bridges at Toko-Ri (1954); Come Fly with Me (1962); D-Day The Sixth of June (1956); Daniel Boone – Frontier Trail Rider (1966); Don't Push, I'll Charge When I'm Ready (1969); Escape from Zahrain (1961); On the Threshold of Space (1956); Period of Adjustment (1962); Promise Her Anything (1965); Rosie! (1967); The Sea Gypsies (1978); Signpost to Murder (1964); Slaughter Trail (1951); Snow White and the Three Stooges (1961); Son of Paleface (1952); Strategy of Terror (1964); To Catch a Thief (1954); Wives and Lovers (1963).
RECORDINGS: To Catch a Thief. Silva Screen FILMCD159.

MURRILL, Herbert (1909–1952)
British composer, organist and administrator. Director of music at the BBC (1950–52).
FILMS INCLUDE: *Documentary*: And So to Work; The Daily Round.

MYERS, Stanley (1930–1993)
British composer who originally worked in the theatre. Famous for his 'Cavatina' which was used in *The Deer Hunter* (1978).
FILMS INCLUDE: Absolution (1978); Age of Consent (1969); The Apprenticeship of Duddy Kravitz (1974); Beverley Hills (1989); Blind Date (1983); The Blockhouse (1973); The Boost (1988); Caravan to Vaccares (1974); The Chain (1984); The Class of Miss MacMichael (1978); Cold Heaven (1992); The Comeback (1977); Conduct Unbecoming (1975); The Deer Hunter (1978); The Devil's Widow (1971); Dreamchild (1985); Eureka (1982); Der Fangschuss (1976); Frightmare (1974); The Greek Tycoon (1978); Herzube (1972); The Honorary Consul (1983); House of Mortal Sin (1975); House of Whipcord (1974); Incubus (1981); Insignificance (1985); Iron Maze (1991); It's a 2'6" Above the Ground World (1972); Janice (1973); Kaleidoscope (1966); Lady Chatterley's Lover (1981); The Lightship (1985); Little Malcolm and his Struggle against the Eunuchs (1974); Michael Kohlhaas – Der Reell (1968); Murder Reported (1957); My Beautiful Launderette (1985); The Night of the Following Day (1968); No Way to Treat a Lady (1967); Otley (1968); Percy

(1971); A Portrait of the Artist as a Young Man (1977); The Raging Moon (1970); Road to Saint Tropez (1966); Schizo (1976); Separation (1967); Serafina! (1992); A Severed Head (1970); Sitting Target (1972); Success is the Best Revenge (1984); Torrents of Spring (1989); Tropic of Cancer (1969); Ulysses (1967); Underground (1970); Voyager (1991); The Walking Stick (1970); The Watcher in the Woods (1980); The Wilby Conspiracy (1974); Wish You Were Here (1987); The Witches (1989); Yesterday's Hero (1979); Zee and Co. (1971).

RECORDINGS: Cold Heaven. Intrada MAF7048D; The Deer Hunter. RCA 09026 61326–2.

MYROW, Fred (1939–   )
American composer.
FILMS INCLUDE: Bundle of Joy (1956); The French Line (1953); Leo the Last (1970); Love Melvin (1952); Phantasm (1979); Phantasm II (1988); The Steagle (1971); Wabash Avenue (1950); When My Baby Smiles at Me (1948).
RECORDINGS: Phantasm. Silva Screen FILMCD071; Phantasm II. Silva Screen FILMCD071.

NASCIMBENE, Mario (1916–   )
Italian composer and conductor. Also became the Italian table-tennis champion. Associated with epic costume films, e.g. *Alexander the Great* (1956) and *The Vikings* (1958).
FILMS INCLUDE: Agostino D'Ippona (1972); Alexander The Great (1955); Angela (1954); Anno Uno (1974); L'Arciere Delle Mille E Una Notte (1963); Barabba (Barabbas) (1961); The Barefoot Contessa (1954); Blaise Pascal (1971); Cartagine in Fiamme (Carthage in Flames) (1959); Child in the House (1956); Costantino Il Grande – In Hoc Signo Vinces (Constantine The Great) (1960); Creatures The World Forgot (1970); Doctor Faustus (1967); L'Età Dell'Amore (1953); A Farewell to Arms (1957); Francis of Assisi (1961); Giuseppe Venduto Dai Fratelli (Joseph and His Brethren) (1960); The Happy Thieves (1961); I Lancieri Neri (1961); Light in the Piazza (1961); El Mumia (1970); O.K. Nerone (1951); One Million Years B.C. (1966); The Quiet American (1957); Ragazza Con La Valigia (1960); Romanoff and Juliet (1960); Room at the Top (1958); Scent of Mystery (1960); Se Tutte Le Donne Del Mondo (1966); Le Sette Folgori Di Assur (1962); Solomon and Sheba (1959); Lo Spadaccino di Siena (1962); Subway in the Sky (1958); That Night (1957); The Vengeance of She (1967); The Vikings (1958); Villa Borghese (1953); When Dinosaurs Ruled The Earth (1969); Where the Spies Are (1965).
RECORDINGS: The Vikings. Silva Screen FILMXCD187.

NAUSHAD (1919–)
Indian composer.
FILMS INCLUDE: Aan (1952); Gunga Jumna (1960); A Handful of Grain (1959); Mughal-e-Azam (1952); Rharat Mata (1957).

NELSON, Oliver (1932–1975)
American composer, arranger, jazz saxophonist and bandleader.
FILMS INCLUDE: Death of a Gunfighter (1967); Inside Job (1973); Last Tango in Paris (1973); Skullduggery (1969); Zigzag (1970).

NEWBORN, Ira (1949–)
American composer.
FILMS INCLUDE: Ace Ventura, Pet Detective (1994); All Night Long (1981); The Blues Brothers (1980); Brain Donors (1992); Dragnet (1987); Ferris Bueller's Day Off (1986); The Final Insult (1994); My Blue Heaven (1990); The Naked Gun: From the Files of Police Squad (1988); Naked Gun 2½: The Smell of Fear (1991); Naked Gun 33⅓: The Final Insult (1994); Planes, Trains and Automobiles (1987); Short Time (1990); Sixteen Candles (1984); Uncle Buck (1989); Weird Science (1985); Wise Guys (1986).

NEWLEY, Anthony (1931–)
British actor, composer and singer.
FILMS INCLUDE: Above us the Waves (1955 – part); The Bandit of Zhobe (1959); A Boy, A Girl and a Bike (1949); Can Heironymus Merkin ever Forget Mercy Humphe and Find True Happiness? (1969); The Cockleshell Heroes (1955 – part); Doctor Dolittle (1967); The Garbage Pail Kids Movie (1987); Goldfinger (1964); The Good Companions (1956); The Heart of a Man (1959); How to Murder a Rich Uncle (1957); Idle on Parade (1958); In the Nick (1959); It Seemed Like a Good Idea at the Time (1974); Jazzboat (1959); Killers of Kilimanjaro (1959); The Lady is a Square (1958); Let's Get Married (1960); The Man Inside (1958); Mister Quilp (1974); No Time to Die (1958); Oliver Twist (1948); The Small World of Sammy Lee (1962); Stop the World I Want to Get Off (1966); Summertree (1971); Sweet November (1968); Top of the Form (1953); Vice Versa (1947); Willy Wonka and The Chocolate Factory (1971); X The Unknown (1956).

NEWMAN, Alfred (1900–1970)
American composer, conductor, pianist and music director. Went to Hollywood in 1930 where he was associated with some two hundred films, mostly for Twentieth Century Fox, and won nine Academy Awards. Composed for Twentieth Century Fox (1935, revised 1954) and the Selznick International Pictures fanfares.
FILMS INCLUDE: The Affairs of Cellini (1934); Airport (1969); All About Eve

(1950); Anastasia (1956); April Love (1957); Arrowsmith (1932); Ball of Fire (1941); Beau Geste (1939); The Best of Everything (1959); Boomerang! (1947); Broadway Melody of 1940 (1940); Bulldog Drummond Strikes Back (1934); Bus Stop (1956); The Call of the Wild (1935); Camelot (1967); Carousel (1956); A Certain Smile (1958); The Counterfeit Traitor (1961); Cynara (1932); Daddy Long Legs (1955); Dancing in the Dark (1949); David and Bathsheba (1951); Dead End (1937); Demetrius and the Gladiators (1954); The Devil to Pay (1931); The Diary of Anne Frank (1959); Dodsworth (1936); The Egyptian (1954 – with Bernard Herrmann); Firecreek (1967); Flowerdrum Song (1961); Foreign Correspondent (1940); Gallant Lady (1934); The Gang's All Here (1943); The Goldwyn Follies (1938); The Great American Broadcast (1941); The Greatest Story Ever Told (1965); Half Angel (1951); Holiday for Lovers (1959); How Green was my Valley (1941); How the West was Won (1962); The Hurricane (1937); Indiscreet (1931); Kiki (1931); Love is a Many Splendored Thing (1955); A Man Called Peter (1955); The Mark of Zorro (1940); The Masquerader (1933); Miracle on 34th Street (1947); My Blue Heaven (1950); My Darling Clementine (1946); Nana (1934); Night without Sleep (1952); O. Henry's Full House (1952); Oh You Beautiful Doll (1949); The Pleasure of his Company (1961); Prince of Foxes (1949); The Prisoner of Zenda (1937)(1952); The Rains Came (1939); Reaching for the Moon (1931); The Real Glory (1939); The Robe (1953); Roxie Hart (1942); Secrets (1933); The Seven Year Itch (1955); Sky Devils (1931); Song of Bernadette (1943); The Star Maker (1939); Stars and Stripes Forever (1952); State Affair (1962); Street Scene (1931); There's No Business like Show Business (1954); These Three (1936); Thieves' Highway (1949); Tin Pan Alley (1940); Tonight We Sing (1953); Transatlantic Merry Go Round (1934); Vigil in the Night (1939); The Wedding Night (1935); Wee Willie Winkie (1937); The Westerner (1940); What Price Glory (1952); When My Baby Smiles at Me (1948); Whoopee (1930); With a Song in my Heart (1952); Wuthering Heights (1939); You Only Live Once (1937); Young Mr Lincoln (1939); You're my Everything (1949);

RECORDINGS; All About Eve. RCA GD80183; How Green Was My Valley. FOX 07822 11008–2; How The West Was Won. Silva Screen FILMCD173; The Prisoner of Zenda. Koch 373762–2; The Robe. Varèse Sarabande VSD5295; Wuthering Heights. Koch 373762–2.

NEWMAN, David (1954–   )
American composer and conductor. Son of Alfred Newman. In 1987 he became the music director of Robert Redford's Sundance Institute which aims to encourage young talent and to preserve and reconstruct old film music for performance by orchestras.
FILMS INCLUDE: The Brave Little Toaster (1987); Coneheads (1993); Critters (1986); Don't Tell Mom the Babysitter's Dead (1991); The Flintstones (1994);

Malone (1987); Throw Momma from The Train (1987); Undercover Blues (1993); The War of the Roses (1989).
RECORDINGS: Critters. Intrada MAF7044D.

NEWMAN, Emil
American composer. Brother of Alfred and Lionel Newman.
FILMS INCLUDE: Beachhead (1954); The Best Years of Our Lives (1946); The Bishop's Wife (1947); Body and Soul (1947); Captain Eddie (1945); Castle in the Desert (1942); Charlie Chan at the Wax Museum (1940); Charlie Chan in Rio (1941); Chicago Confidential (1957); Cry Danger (1951); The Dark Corner (1946); Dead Men Tell (1941); Death in Small Doses (1957); Down Argentine Way (1940); The Great Sioux Massacre (1965); Hello Frisco, Hello (1943); Hondo (1953); The House on 92nd Street (1945); The Iron Sheriff (1957); Japanese War Bride (1951); Journey into Light (1951); Just for You (1952); Laura (1944); Lifeboat (1944); The Lodger (1944); The Mad Magician (1954); The Magnificent Dope (1942); Murder over New York (1941); The Naked Street (1955); Ring of Fear (1954); The San Francisco Story (1952); Seven Wonders of the World (1955); Somebody Loves Me (1952); A Song is Born (1948); The Steel Lady (1953); The Undying Monster (1942); Unwed Mother (1958); Wing and a Prayer (1944); Woman on the Run (1950).

NEWMAN, Lionel (1916–1989)
American composer who received eleven Oscar nominations for writing various film scores. In charge of music at Twentieth Century Fox and supervised and orchestrated more than two hundred and fifty. Won an Academy Award for *Hello Dolly!*
FILMS INCLUDE: Alien (1979); American Guerilla in the Philippines (1950); At Long Last Love (1975); Bernardine (1957); The Best Things in Life are Free (1956); Bloodhounds of Broadway (1952); The Boston Strangler (1968); Boy on a Dolphin (1957); The Bravados (1958); Breaking Away (1979); Cleopatra (1963); Compulsion (1959); Cross Creek (1983); Desk Set (1957); Do Not Disturb (1965); Doctor Dolittle (1967); The Final Conflict (Omen III) (1981); Flaming Star (1960); A Flea in Her Ear (1968); The Gambler from Natchez (1954); Gentlemen Prefer Blondes (1953); The Girl Can't Help It (1956); The Girl Next Door (1952); Golden Girl (1951); The Great White Hope (1970); Hello, Dolly! (1969); Hound Dog Man (1959); I Deal in Danger (1966); The I Don't Care Girl (1953); I Was a Male War Bride (1949); I'll Get By (1950); Kiss Them for Me (1957); The Last Wagon (1956); Let's Make Love (1960); Love Me Tender (1956); Lydia Bailey (1952); Man in the Attic (1953); Mardi Gras (1958); Meet Me After the Show (1951); Move Over, Darling (1963); Myra Breckinridge (1970); North to Alaska (1960); The Pleasure Seekers (1964); Powder River (1953); A Private's Affair (1959); The Proud Ones (1956); River of No Return (1954); The Salzburg Connection (1972); The

Sand Pebbles (1966); Say One for Me (1959); Sing Boy Sing (1958); The St Valentine's Day Massacre (1967); Star Trek The Motion Picture (1979); Swingin' Along (1961); There's No Business Like Show Business (1954); Thieves' Highway (1949); Unfaithfully Yours (1983); The Way to the Gold (1957); When the Legends Die (1972).

NEWMAN, Randy (1943–)
American composer and singer. Son of Irving Newman and nephew of Alfred and Lionel Newman. Won an Emmy Award for his music for the television series *Cop Rock* in 1991.
FILMS INCLUDE: April Fool's Day (1986); Avalon (1990); Awakenings (1990); Cold Turkey (1970); Cover Me Babe (1969); The Lively Set (1964); Maverick (1994); The Natural (1984); Parenthood (1989); Performance (1970); The Pursuit of Happiness (1970); Ragtime (1981).
RECORDINGS: Maverick. Varèse Sarabande VSD5531.

NEWMAN, Thomas
American composer. Youngest son of Alfred Newman and brother of David Newman. Became involved in film scoring in 1984 with *Reckless*. *Desperately Seeking Susan* (1985) was his first major success. In 1994 he received two Academy Award nominations for *Little Women* and *The Shawshank Redemption*.
FILMS INCLUDE: Desperately Seeking Susan (1985); Flesh and Bone (1993); Fried Green Tomatoes (1991); Josh and S.A.M. (1993); Little Women (1994); The Linguini Incident (1992); The Player (1992); Real Genius (1985); Scent of a Woman (1992); The Shawshank Redemption (1994); The War (1994); Whispers in the Dark (1992).
RECORDINGS: Desperately Seeking Susan. Varèse Sarabande VSD47291; Flesh and Bone. Varèse Sarabande VSD5460; Little Women. Sony SK66922; The Shawshank Redemption. Epic 478332–2.

NICOLAI, Bruno (–1991)
Italian composer.
FILMS INCLUDE: Ad Ogni Costo (1967); Addio, Fratello Crudele (1971); Allonsanfan (1974); America Così Nuda Così Violenta (1970); And Then There Were None (1974); L'Anticristo (1974); I Cannibali (1969); Le Casse (1971); Città Violenta (1970); Le Clan des Siciliens (1968); El Conde Dracula (1970); Da Berlino L'Apocalisse (1966); Dalle Ardenne All'Inferno (1967); Dio Perdona... Io No! (God Forgives... I Don't) (1967); Django Spara Per Primo (1966); Escalation (1968); Escondido (1967); Un Esercito di Cinque Uomini (1969); Fräulein Doktor (1968); Il Gatto a Nove Code (1971); Indagine su Un Cittadini Al di Sopra di Ogni Sospetto (1970); Indio Black, Sai Che Ti Dico: Sei Un Gran Figlio Di... (1970); Io, Io, Io... E Gli Altri

(1965); Land Raiders (1969); Matchless (1966); Il Mio Nome E Shanghai Joe (1973); Il Natale Che Quasi Non Fu (1966); Una Nuvola Di Polvere . . . un Grido Di Morte . . . Arriva Sartana (Gunman in Town) (1970); O.K. Connery (1967); Il Pelo Nel Mondo (1964); Perche Quelle Strane Gocce Di Sangue sul Corpo Di Jennifer? (1972); Rappresaglia (1973); La Resa Dei Conti (The Big Gundown) (1967); Roma Come Chicago (Bandits in Rome) (1968); Ruba al Prossimo Tuo (1968); Salon Kitty (1976); Serafino (1968); Le Serpent (1973); Lo Straniero (1967); Il Tuo Vizio E Una Stanza Chiusa E Solo Io Ne Ho La Chiave (1972); Uomo Avvisato Mezzo Ammazzato . . . Parola Di Spirito Santo (Blazing Guns) (1972); Vamos A Matar, Companeros! (1970).

NIEHAUS, Lenni (1929–)
American composer and jazz alto-saxophone player, noted for his playing in the Stan Kenton orchestra in the 1950s.
FILMS INCLUDE: Black Heart (1990); City Heat (1984); Heartbreak Ridge (1986); Lush Life (1993); Never Too Young to Die (1986); Pale Rider (1985); A Perfect World (1993); Ratboy (1986); Tightrope (1984); Unforgiven (1992 – 'Claudia's Theme' written by Clint Eastwood).
RECORDINGS: Unforgiven. Varèse Sarabande VSD5380.

NITZSCHE, Jack (1937–)
American composer.
FILMS INCLUDE: Blue Collar (1978); Breathless (1983); Cannery Row (1982); Cruising (1980); Cutter and Bone (1981); 8½ Weeks (1986); The Exorcist (1973); Greaser's Palace (1972); Hardcore (1978); Heart Beat (1979); Heroes (1977); The Indian Runner (1991); The Jewel of the Nile (1985); The Last of the Finest (1990); Next of Kin (1989); Nine Weeks (1985); An Officer and a Gentleman (1981); One Flew Over The Cuckoo's Nest (1975); Performance (1970); Personal Best (1982); Revenge (1989); The Seventh Sign (1988); Stand by Me (1986); Starman (1984); Sticks and Bones (1973); Streets of Gold (1986); When You Comin' Back, Red Ryder (1979); The Whoopee Boys (1986); Without a Trace (1983).
RECORDINGS: Revenge. Silva Screen SILVAD3001; Starman. Varèse Sarabande VCD47220.

NORDGREN, Erik (1913–)
Swedish composer, associated with the early films of Ingmar Bergman.
FILMS INCLUDE: All These Women (1964); Eva (1948); Kvinna Utan Ansikte (1947); Kvinnors Väntan (Secret of Women) (1952); The Magician (1958); Manika (1952); Pleasure Garden (1961); The Seventh Seal (1957); Törst (Three Strange Loves) (1949); The Virgin Spring (1960); Wild Strawberries (1957).

NORMAN, Monty (1928–   )

British composer, associated with the Bond films.

FILMS INCLUDE: Call Me Bwana (1963); Dr No (1962); For Your Eyes Only (1981); From Russia With Love (1963); Live and Let Die (1973); Octopussy (1983); On Her Majesty's Secret Service (1969); The Spy Who Loved Me (1977); The Two Faces of Dr Jekyll (1960).

RECORDINGS: Dr No. Silva Screen FILMCD007.

NORTH, Alex (1910–1991)

American composer who was awarded an honorary Oscar in 1986. In 1934 he went to the Moscow Conservatory and became the only American member of the Union of Soviet Composers. Later studied with Ernst Toch and Aaron Copland. Wrote several documentaries for the Office of War Information during World War II. His commissioned score for Kubrick's film *2001: A Space Odyssey* was not used and became the basis of his 3rd Symphony.

FILMS INCLUDE: The Agony and The Ecstasy (1965); All Fall Down (1961); The Bachelor Party (1956); The Bad Seed (1956); Bite the Bullet (1975); Carny (1980); Cheyenne Autumn (1964); The Children's Hour (1961); Cinerama South Seas Adventure (1958); Cleopatra (1963); Daddy Long Legs (1955); The Dead (1987); Desirée (1954); The Devil's Brigade (1968); Dragonslayer (1981); A Dream of Kings (1969); Four Girls in Town (1956); Go Man Go (1954); Hard Contract (1969); Hot Spell (1957); I'll Cry Tomorrow (1955); The King and Four Queens (1956); The Long, Hot Summer (1958); Les Misérables (1952); The Misfits (1961); The Outrage (1964); Pocket Money (1972); Prizzi's Honor (1985); The Racers (1955); The Rainmaker (1956); Rich Man, Poor Man (1976); The Rose Tattoo (1955); Sanctuary (1961); The Shoes of the Fisherman (1968); Somebody Killed Her Husband (1978); The Sound and The Fury (1959); Spartacus (1960); Stage Struck (1958); A Streetcar Named Desire (1951 – the first major jazz-based score to be written in Hollywood); Unchained (1954); Under the Volcano (1984); Viva Zapata! (1952); Who's Afraid of Virginia Woolf? (1966); Willard (1970); Wise Blood (1979); The Wonderful Country (1959).

RECORDINGS: 2001: A Space Odyssey (not used in the completed film). Varèse Sarabande VSD5400; Dragon Slayer. Silva Screen SILVAD3003; Spartacus. Varèse Sarabande VSD5500; Who's Afraid of Virginia Woolf? Varèse Sarabande VSD5207.

NYMAN, Michael (1944–   )

British composer who has worked with director Peter Greenaway. Has composed five operas.

FILMS INCLUDE: Brimstone and Treacle (1982); Carrington (1995); The Cook, The Thief, His Wife and Her Lover (1989); The Draughtsman's Contract (1982); Drowning by Numbers (1988); The Falls (1980); Frozen Music (1983);

The Man Who Mistook His Wife for a Hat: A Neurological Opera (1987); The Piano (1993); The Pledge (1981); Prospero's Book (1991); Twenty-six Bathrooms (1986); Vertical Features Remake (1978); A Walk Through H (The Reincarnation of an Ornithologist) (1978); A Zed and Two Noughts (1985). RECORDINGS: Carrington. Argo 444 873-2ZH; The Piano. Virgin COVE919; Prospero's Book. Unicorn-Kanshana DKPCD9160; A Zed and Two Noughts. Argo 436 820-2ZH.

OHANA, Maurice (1914–1992)
French composer and pianist of British origin who partly studied with Casella in Italy after World War II.
FILMS INCLUDE: Les Dents du Singe (1960); Goha (1956).

OLIVER, Stephen (1950–1992)
British composer who studied electronic music with Robert Sherlaw Johnson. Wrote operas and music for the theatre as well as scores for television e.g. *The Life and Adventures of Nicholas Nickleby.*

O'RIADA, Sean (1931–1971)
Irish composer who studied under Aloys Fleischmann at University College, Cork. Music director of the Abbey Theatre, Dublin.
FILMS INCLUDE: Miss Eire, Saoirse? (1961); Young Cassidy (1964).

ORNADEL, Cyril (1924–)
British composer who has also written for television e.g. *Brief Encounter* (1975); *Edward VII* (1976); *The Strauss Family* and the musical theatre e.g. *Pickwick* (1963).
FILMS INCLUDE: Die Screaming Marianne (1971); The Flesh and Blood Show (1972); Man of Violence (1970); Not Now Darling (1972); Some May Love (1967); Subterfuge (1968); Tiffany Jones (1973).

ORR, Buxton (1924–)
Scottish composer who originally studied medicine. Studied with Benjamin Frankel (1952–55).
FILMS INCLUDE: Corridors of Blood (1958); Doctor Blood's Coffin (1960); The Eyes of Annie Jones (1963); Fiend without a Face (1957); How to Undress in Public Without Undue Embarrassment (1965); The Snake Woman (1961); Suddenly, Last Summer (1959).
RECORDINGS: Corridors of Blood. Silva Screen FILMCD175; Fiend Without a Face. Silva Screen FILMCD175.

ORREGO-SALAS, Juan (1919–)

Chilean composer and musicologist who partly studied with Virgil Thompson and Aaron Copland in the USA. Founded and directed the Latin American Music Centre at Indiana University (from 1961) which aimed to promote Latin American music through festivals, broadcasts, etc.

FILMS INCLUDE: La Caleta Olvidada (1959); La Veta Del Diablo (1953).

ORTOLANI, Riz (1925–)

Italian composer.

FILMS INCLUDE: The Adventures of Gerard (1970); Africa Addio (1966); The Biggest Bundle of Them All (1967); The Bliss of Mrs Blossom (1968); Buona Sera, Mrs Campbell (1968); O Cangaceiro (1969); Casanova and Company (1977); La Cattura (1969); Cavalca e Uccidi (1963); Ciak Mull, L'Uomo Della Vendetta (1969); Confessione Di Un Commissario Di Polizia Al Procuratore Della Repubblica (1971); Il Consigliori (1973); De L'Enfer à La Victoire (1979); La Donna Nel Mondo (1962); Enigma Rosso (1978); Gli Eroi (1972); Fangio (1971); Flying Clipper (1962); Das Geheimnis Der Drei Dschunken (1965); I Giorno Dell'Ira (1967); Il Giorno Del Furore (1973); The Glory Guys (1965); Le Guerriere Dal Seno Nuda (1973); The Hunting Party (1971); Joe Valachi: I Segreti Di Cosa Nostra (1972); Lady Hamilton (1968); Mal D'Africa (1967); Maya (1965); The McKenzie Break (1970); Mondo Cane (1963); Operazione Goldman (1965); La Ragazza Di Nome Giulio (1970); La Ragazza Di Trieste (1983); Say Hello to Yesterday (1970); Lo Sbarco Di Anzio (1968); Sequestro Di Persona (1968); Si Può Essere Più Bastardi Dell'Ispettore Cliff? (1973); The Spy with a Cold Nose (1966); The Statue (1970); Tenderly (1968); Le Vergine Di Norimberga (1963); Woman Times Seven (1967); The Yellow Rolls Royce (1964); Zio Tom (1971).

RECORDINGS; Mondo Cane. RCA 09026 61326–2.

OTTMAN, John

American composer and film editor. Associated with director Bryan Singer.

FILMS INCLUDE: Public Access (1993); The Usual Suspects (1995).

RECORDINGS: The Usual Suspects. Milan 74321 30107–2.

OVCHINNIKOV, Vlacheslav (1934–)

Russian composer.

FILMS INCLUDE: Andrei Rublev (1966); Arsenal (1929); Dvorianskoe Gnezdo (1969); Ivanovo Detstvo (1962); Katok I Skripka (1961); Voina I Mir I (1966); Voina I Mir II (1966); Voina I Mir III (1967); Voina I Mir IV (1967); War and Peace (1968).

PANUFNIK, Andrzej (Sir Andrzej Panufnik) (1914–1991)
Polish-born composer and conductor (British citizen 1961 and knighted 1991).
Wrote ten symphonies and many other orchestral works. His works up to
1944 were destroyed during the Warsaw uprising of that year.
FILMS INCLUDE: *Documentary*: Altar Masterpiece (1952).

PARAMOR, Norri (1913–1979)
British composer and band leader.
FILMS INCLUDE: Doctor in Distress (1964); Expresso Bongo (1959); The Fright-
ened City (1962); My Lover, My Son (1970); Play it Cool (1963); Young and
Willing (1964).

PARKER, Clifton (1905–1989)
British composer and orchestral player. Wrote an opera and incidental music.
FILMS INCLUDE: *Feature*: Acacia Avenue (1945); The Big Day (1960); The
Birthday Present (1957); Blanche Fury (1947); Campbell's Kingdom (1957);
Circle of Deception (1960); Diamond City (1949); The Feminine Touch
(1956); The Gift Horse (1952); Girl on Approval (1961); HMS Defiant (1962);
Harry Black (1958); The Hellfire Club (1960); The House of the Seven Hawks
(1959); The Informers (1963); Johnny Frenchman (1945); The Man Within
(1947); Mystery Submarine (1962); Night of the Demon (1957); Passage
Home (1955); Perfect Strangers (1945); Sea of Sand (1958); The Secret Place
(1957); The Silver Darlings (1947); Sink the Bismarck! (1960); Snowball
(1960); The Story of Robin Hood and His Merrie Men (1952); Tarzan and
the Lost Safari (1956); Taste of Fear (1961); The Teckman Mystery (1954);
The Thirty-Nine Steps (1958); Treasure Island (1950); The Treasure of Monte
Cristo (1960); Virgin Island (1958); The Wooden Horse (1950); The Yellow
Canary (1943). *Documentary*: Battle is our Business (1944); Beyond the Pylons
(1945); Blue Pullman (1960); Children on Trial (CFU, 1946); Conversation
Piece; Elizabethan Express (1952); Jungle Patrol; The Long Night Haul (1956);
Mine Gapping, Steam (1945); Ocean Terminal (1951); Towards the Offensive;
Two Fathers (CFU, 1945); Western Approaches (CFU, 1944).
RECORDINGS: Night of the Demon. Silva Screen FILMCD175; Sink the
Bismarck. Silva Screen FILMCD151; Western Approaches. EMI CDGO 2059.

PARKS, Gordon (1925–   )
American director, novelist and composer.
FILMS INCLUDE: Aaron Loves Angela (1985); Leadbelly (1976); The Learning
Tree (1968); Moments without Proper Names (1986); Shaft (1971); Shaft's
Big Score! (1972); The Super Cops (1973).

PARKS, Van Dyke (1941–)
American composer and singer.
FILMS INCLUDE: Casual Sex? (1988); Cub Paradise (1986); Goin' South (1978); Popeye (1980); Rented Lips (1988); The Two Jakes (1990).

PARR-DAVIES, Harry (1914–1955)
Welsh composer and songwriter who wrote songs to many of Gracie Fields' films and other British musicals of the 1930s and 1940s. His big wartime hit was 'Pedro the Fisherman' from his stage show *The Lisbon Story*, later filmed in 1949.
FILMS INCLUDE: It's in the Air (1938); Keep Smiling (1938); The Lisbon Story (1946); Maytime in Mayfair (1949); Queen of Hearts (1936); Sing as We Go (1934); This Week of Grace (1933); We're Going to be Rich (1938).

PARYS, George van (1902–1971)
French composer.
FILMS INCLUDE: L'Affaire Manet (1950); L'Affaire Maurizius (1954); Les Années Folles (1960); La Bonne Tisane (1958); Un Caprice de Caroline Cherie (1953); Les Carnets du Major Thompson (1955); C'est Arrivé à Aden (1956); Charmants Garçons (1957); Comme un Cheveu Sur La Soupe (1957); Coplan Prend Des Risques (1964); Les Diaboliques (1955); Le Dortoir des Grandes (1953); L'Ecole des Cocottes (1958); Fanfan la Tulipe (1952); Faut Pas Prendre Les Enfants Du Bon Dieu Pour Des Canards Sauvages (1968); Les Fêtes Galantes (1965); French Cancan (1955); Le Grand Jeu (1954); Les Grandes Manoeuvres (1955); The Happy Road (1956); L'Homme à L'Impermeable (1957); Lady Paname (1950); Madame Du Barry (1954); Les Magiciennes (1960); Mamz'elle Nitouche (1954); Le Million (1931); The Millionairess (1960); Le Mouton à Cinq pattes (1954); Mr Topaze (1961); Nana (1955); Nathalie (1957); Papa, Maman, La Bonne et Moi (1954); Paris Canaille (1956); Les Petits Matins (1962); Rue de L'Estrapade (1953); Scandale (1948); Si Tous Les Gars Du Monde (1956); Signé: Arsène Lupin (1959); Tendre et Violente Élisabeth (1960); Tout L'Or du Monde (1961); Les Truands (1956).

PATACHICH, Iván (1922–)
Hungarian composer and conductor. Pioneered electronic music in Hungary, and his electronic score for the film *Immortality* won first prize at the San Francisco Film Festival.
FILMS INCLUDE: Szivdobogas (1961); Tihany (1955).

PATTERSON, Rick
American composer.
FILMS INCLUDE: The Cold Eye (1980); Slow Burn (1989); Young Giants (1983).

PEARSON, Johnny
British composer and arranger who has also written for television.
FILMS INCLUDE: The Jokers (1967).

PEASLEE, Richard (1930–)
American composer.
FILMS INCLUDE: The Marat/Sade (1966); Tell me Lies (1967).

PENDERECKI, Krzysztof (1933–)
Polish composer and conductor of his own compositions.
FILMS INCLUDE: A Fratricide (1981); Les Gauloises Bleues (1968); I Love You, I Love You (1968); The Saragossa Manuscript (1964).

PETERSON, Oscar (1925–)
Canadian jazz pianist and composer.
FILMS INCLUDE: The Silent Partner (1978); Les Tricheurs (1958).

PETIT, Jean-Claude (1943–)
French composer.
FILMS INCLUDE: L'Addition (1984); Coupable D'Innocence (1992); Cyrano de Bergerac (1989); Foreign Student (1994); Le Grand Crimonial (1968); Le Hussard sur le Toit (1995); Jean de Florette (1987); Mayrig (1991); The Playboys (1992); Return of the Musketeers (1989); Rue du Bac (1990); Tawk al Hamama al Mafkoud (1991); Toujours Seuls (1991); La Veritable Histoire D'Artaud Le Momo (1993); Le Zèbre (1992).
RECORDINGS: Cyrano de Bergerac. Colosseum CST34 8046; Jean de Florette. Virgin CDV2774.

PETRASSI, Goffredo (1904–)
Italian composer. Wrote eight concertos for orchestra between 1933/4 and 1970/2.
FILMS INCLUDE: Bitter Rice (1949); Family Diary (1963); A Geometry Lesson (1947); Under the Olive Tree (1951).

PETROV, Andrei P. (1930–)
Russian composer and editor. Composed much light music and film scores, besides serious works.
FILMS INCLUDE: Banked Fires (1972); The Blue Bird (1976).

PETROVICS, Emil (1930–)
Hungarian composer who has written operas and chamber music, together with incidental music for the theatre, cinema, radio and television.

FILMS INCLUDE: The Legend about the Death and Resurrection of Two Young Men (1972).

PHELOUNG, Barrington (1954–   )

Australian composer and conductor, now resident in Britain. Has written forty-eight commissioned scores for ballet and dance companies in Britain and Europe. Musical advisor to the London contemporary Dance Theatre. Has composed much for television including *Boon* (1985), *Daziel and Pascoe*, *Morse*, *The Politician's Wife*, *Portrait of a Marriage* and *Trip Trap* (BBC Wales).
FILMS INCLUDE: Truly, Madly, Deeply.

PHILLIPS, Stu

American composer.
FILMS INCLUDE: Angels from Hell (1968); Battlestar Galactica (1978); Beyond the Valley of the Dolls (1970); Buck Rogers in the 25th Century (1979); Conquest of the Earth (1980); Curious Female (1969); Dead Heat on a Merry-go-Round (1966); Fast Charlie – The Moonbeam Rider (1978); Follow Me (1969); The Gay Deceivers (1969); The Losers (1970); Macon County Line (1973); Mad Dog Coll (1960); The Man from the Diners' Club (1963); Mission Galactica: The Cylon Attack (1979); Pickup on 101 (1972); Ride the Wild Surf (1964); Run, Angel, Run! (1969); The Seven Minutes (1971); Simon, King of the Witches (1971); Spider-man Strikes Back (1978).

PICCIONI, Piero

Italian composer.
FILMS INCLUDE: Addio, Alexandra! (1969); Adua e le Compagne (1960); L'Avare (1990); Belle ma Povere (1957); Cadaveri Eccellenti (1975); Camille 2000 (1969); Il Caso Mattei (1972); Cattive Ragazze (1992); C'Èra Una Volta (1967); La Commare Secca (1962); Congo Vivo (1961); Cristo Si È Fermato A Eboli (Christ Stopped at Eboli) (1979); La Decima Vittima (1965); I Dolci Inganni (1960); Fighting Back (1982); Il Gobbo (1960); L'Imprévu (1961); Inghilterra Nuda (1969); The Light at the Edge of the World (1971); Lucky Luciano (1973); Le Mani Sulla Città (1963); Matchless (1966); Il Momento Della Verita (1964); Le Monache Di Sant'Arcangelo (1973); Il Mondo Di Notte (1959); Il Mondo Di Notte N.2 (1961); El Ojo Del Huracan (1971); Puppet on a Chain (1970); Racconti D'Estate (1958); Romolo E Remo (1961); Salvatore Giuliano (1962); Senilità (1961); La Spina Dorsale Del Diavolo (1970); Lo Straniero (1967); La Tempesta (1958); Travolti Da Un Insolito Destino Nell'Azzurro Mare D'Agosto (1975); Tre Fratelli (1980); La Viaccia (1961).

PINKHAM, Daniel (1923–)
American composer, organist and conductor who has written a symphony, two violin concertos and a chamber opera.
FILMS INCLUDE: *Documentary*: Land of White Alice (1959).

PIOVANI, Nicola (1946–)
Italian composer.
FILMS INCLUDE: Amok (1993); Caro Diario (1993); Flavia La Monaca Musulmana (1974); Ginger e Fred (1986); Good Morning, Babilonia (1986); Huevos De Oro (193); Het Meisje Met Het Rode Haar (1981); Nel Nome Delpadre (1971); De Schorpioen (1984); Soleil Des Hyènes (1977).

PIPKOV, Lyubomir (1904–1974)
Bulgarian composer and pianist who studied partly with Paul Dukas in Paris.

PIZZETTI, Ildebrando (1880–1968)
Italian composer, conductor and critic who wrote eleven operas.
FILMS INCLUDE: Il Mulino del Po (1948).

PLENIZIO, Gianfranco
Italian composer.
FILMS INCLUDE: Alfredo Alfredo (1971); Cipolla Colt (1975); La Città Delle Donne (1980); ... Continuavano A Chiamarlo Trinità (1971); Una Donna Di Notte (1979); Dramma Della Gelosia (1970); E La Nave Va (1983); L'Infermiera (1975); Joe E Margherito (1974); Killer Fish (1978); La Moglie Di Mio Padre (1976); Più Forte Ragazzi (1972).

PLUMB, Edward (1907–1958)
American composer who worked for Disney.
FILMS INCLUDE: Bambi (1942 – with Churchill); The Best of Walt Disney's True-Life Adventures (1975); The Woman Who Came Back (1945).

PODÉŠŤ Ludvík (1921–1968)
Czech composer and administrator who directed music for Czech television from 1958.

POLEDOURIS, Basil (1945–)
American composer who studied music under David Raksin.
FILMS INCLUDE: Big Wednesday (1978); The Blue Lagoon (1980); Conan the Barbarian (1981); Conan the Destroyer (1984); Defiance (1979); Extreme Close-Up (1972); Flesh and Blood (1985); The Flight of the Intruder (1990); Free Willy (1993); The Hunt for Red October (1990); Intruder (1990); The Iron Eagle (1985); The Jungle Book (1994); Lassie (1994); Lonesome Dove

(1990); Making the Grade (1984); Protocol (1984); Red Dawn (1984); Robocop (1987); Robocop 3 (1993); Serial Mom (1994); Tintorera (1977); Wired (1989).

RECORDINGS: The Blue Lagoon. Southern Cross SCCD1018; Conan the Barbarian. Telearc CD80342; The Hunt for Red October. Telearc CD80342; Lonesome Dove. Silva Screen FILMCD176; Robocop. TER Classics CDTER1146.

POLOVINKIN, Leonid (1894–1949)
Russian composer and teacher. Music director of the Moscow Central Children's Theatre.

POPOV, Todor (1921–   )
Bulgarian composer who was, from 1946–49, composer to the folk song and dance ensemble of the Ministry of the Interior. Also a composer to the Bulgarian Army.

PORTER, Cole (1892–1964)
American songwriter and composer.

FILMS INCLUDE: Anything Goes (1955); The Battle of Paris (1929); The Boys in the Band (1970); Born to Dance (1936); Broadway Melody of 1940 (1940); Can-Can (1960); Dubarry was a Lady (1943); Evil Under the Sun (1981); High Society (1956); Kiss Me Kate (1953); Les Girls (1957); Night and Day (1946); The Pirate (1948); Rosalie (1937); Silk Stockings (1957); Something for the Boys (1944); You'll Never get Rich (1941).

RECORDINGS: High Society. EMI CDC5 55050–2; Kiss Me Kate. Silva Screen SILKTVCD2.

PORTER, Quincy (1897–1966)
American composer and string player who partly studied in Paris with D'Indy.

PORTMAN, Rachel (1962–   )
British composer now based in Hollywood. Received a BAFTA award nomination for her TV work on Oranges are not the only Fruit (1990) and The Woman in Black.

FILMS INCLUDE: Benny and Joon (1993); Emma (1996); Joy Luck Club (1993); Only You (1994); The Road to Wellville (1994); Sirens (1994); Used People (1992); War of the Buttons (1994).

POSFORD, George (1906–1976)
British composer who wrote for music for radio production and subsequently composed for the stage and for films.

FILMS INCLUDE: Café Colette (1936); Goodbye Vienna (1932).

POULENC, Francis (1899–1963)
French composer and member of 'Les Six'. Well known for his ballets, operas and religious works.
FILMS INCLUDE: Le Belle au Bois Dormant (1935); La Duchesse de Langeais (1942); Le Voyage en Amérique (1951); Le Voyageur Sans Bagages (1944).

POWELL, Mel (1923–   )
American composer and teacher who studied with Hindemith. Arranger for Benny Goodman and Glenn Miller. Later became interested in electronic music.
FILMS INCLUDE: *Documentary*: American Frontier (1953); New York University (1952); There is a Season (1953).

PRATELLA, Francesco B. (1880–1955)
Italian composer who had a few compositon lessons from Mascagni.

PREISNER, Zbigniew (1955–   )
Polish composer
FILMS INCLUDE: At Play in the Fields of the Lord (1991); Damage (1992); Europa Europa (1991); The Secret Garden (1993); Trois Couleurs Bleu (1993); When a Man Loves a Woman (1994).
RECORDINGS: Damage. Varèse Sarabande VSD5046; The Secret Garden. Varèse Sarabande VSD5443.

PREVIN, André (Sir André Previn) (1929–   )
American composer and conductor of German origin. Pupil of Marcel Dupré in Paris. Went to the USA in 1939 and worked as a jazz pianist, and later as a composer and arranger of film music in Hollywood. Made his debut as a conductor in 1962. Conductor in Chief of The London Symphony Orchestra (1968–79) where he championed English music. Received honorary knighthood in 1996 for his 'outstanding contribution to Anglo-American cultural relations and the musical life of Britain'.
FILMS INCLUDE: All in a Night's Work (1960); Bad Day at Black Rock (1954); Bells are Ringing (1960); Benny Goodman – Let's Dance – A Musical Tribute (1986); Border Incident (1949); The Catered Affair (1956); Dead Ringer (1964); Designing Woman (1957); Elmer Gantry (1960); The Fastest Gun Alive (1956); The Fortune Cookie (1966); The Four Horsemen of the Apocalypse (1961); Gigi (1957); The Girl who had Everything (1952); Give a Girl a Break (1953); Goodbye Charlie (1964); Harper (1966); House of Numbers (1957); Inside Daisy Clover (1965); Invitation to the Dance (1954); Irma La Douce (1963); It's Always Fair Weather (1955); Jesus Christ Superstar (1973); Kim (1950); Kismet (1955); Kiss Me Kate (1953); Kiss Me, Stupid (1964); Long Day's Journey into Night (1962); The Music Lovers (1970); My Fair

Lady (1964); One, Two, Three (1961); Paint Your Wagon (1969); Pepe (1960); Porgy and Bess (1959); Rollerball (1975); Romeo and Juliet (1990); Scene of the Crime (1949); Silk Stockings (1957); Small Town Girl (1952); The Subterraneans (1960); The Sun Comes Up (1948); The Swinger (1966); Tall Story (1960); Thoroughly Modern Millie (1967); Three Little Words (1950); Two For the Seesaw (1962); Valley of the Dolls (1967); The Way West (1967); Who Was That Lady? (1959).
RECORDINGS: It's Always Fair Weather. EMI CDODEON21.

PREVIN, Charles (1888–1973)
American composer of German birth. Great uncle of André Previn and musical director for Universal Studios in Hollywood.
FILMS INCLUDE: And Then There Were None (1945); Between us Girls (1942); Broadway (1942); Charlie McCarthy, Detective (1939); Danger on the Air (1938); Destry Rides Again (1939); East Side of Heaven (1939); The Flame of New Orleans (1941); The Ghost of Frankenstein (1942); Hellzapoppin' (1941); Hired Wife (1940); If I Had My Way (1940); Invisible Man Returns (1940); The Invisible Woman (1940); It Started With Eve (1941); Letter of Introduction (1938); Mad About Music (1938); My Man Godfrey (1936); Nice Girl? (1941); One Hundred Men and A Girl (1937); Reign of Terror (1949); Saboteur (1942); Seven Sinners (1940); Shadow of Doubt (1943); Sherlock Holmes and the Secret Weapon (1942); Sherlock Holmes and the Voice of Terror (1942); Sherlock Holmes in Washington (1942); Son of Frankenstein (1939); State Police (1938); Two Sisters from Boston (1946); When Tomorrow Comes (1939); The Wolf Man (1941).

PRICE, Alan (1942–)
British composer, singer and pianist. Founder member of the 1960s pop group The Animals.
FILMS INCLUDE: Alfie Darling (1975); Britannia Hospital (1982); The Dance Goes On (1980); Don't Look Back (1967); O Lucky Man (1973); The Whales of August (1987).

PRIGOZHIN, Lyutsian A. (1926–)
Soviet composer and teacher who has written oratorios and symphonic works, together with music for the theatre, cinema and radio.

PRINCE, Robert (1929–)
American composer.
FILMS INCLUDE: A Great Big Thing (1968); Strangers in the City (1962); You're a Big Boy Now (1966).

PRODROMIDÈS, Jean
French composer.
FILMS INCLUDE: Archimede le Clochard (1959); Le Baron de L'Cluse (1960); Danton (1982); ... et Mourir de Plaisir (1960); Histoires Extraordinaires (1967); Vingt-Quatre Heures de la Vie D'Une Femme (1968); Le Voyage en Ballon (1960).

PROKOFIEV, Serge (1891–1953)
Russian composer, born in the Ukraine. After the Russian Revolution he spent much of his time either in the USA or Paris, but from 1936 settled permanently in Moscow. Studied film music techniques during a visit to Hollywood with a view to applying them to Soviet films.
FILMS INCLUDE: Alexander Nevsky (1938); The Czar Wants to Sleep (1934); Ivan the Terrible – Part I (1944); Ivan the Terrible – Part II (1946); Lermontov (1943); Lieutenant Kijé (1934).
RECORDINGS: Alexander Nevsky. RCA 09026 61926–2; Ivan the Terrible. Chandros CHAN 8977; Lieutenant Kijé. Chandos CHAN 8806.

RABAUD, Henri (1873–1949)
French composer and conductor who studied composition with Massenet.
FILMS INCLUDE: Jouer d'échecs (1925); Le Miracle des Loups (1924).

RABINOWITZ, Harry (1916–)
South African composer and conductor, resident in Britain, who has also written for television e.g. *Reilly, Ace of Spies*.
FILMS INCLUDE: The Bostonians (1984); Chariots of Fire (1981); Electric Dreams (1984); F/X (1985); The Four Seasons (1979); Funeral in Berlin (1966); Goldengirl (1979); The Greek Tycoon (1978); Hanover Street (1979); Heat and Dust (1982); Inside Out (1975); Lady Jane (1985); The Missionary (1981); Ninety Years On (1964); Puppet on a Chain (1970); Return to Oz (1985); Revolution (1985); Seven Nights in Japan (1976); The Sign of Four (1983); Time Bandits (1981).

RAGLAND, Robert O. (1931–)
American composer.
FILMS INCLUDE: Abby (1974); Assassination (1986); The Babysitter (1969); The Day of the Locust (1974); Grizzly (1976); Hysterical (1982); Jaguar Lives (1979); Mansion of the Doomed (1975); Return to Macon County (1975); Seven Alone (1974); Sharks' Treasure (1974); 10 To Midnight (1983); The Thing with Two Heads (1972); Tracks (1976); The Winged Serpent (1982).

RAKSIN, David (1912–   )
American composer who worked in Hollywood from the mid-1930s. Arranged Chaplin's score for *Modern Times* (1936). Has also written for television.
FILMS INCLUDE: Al Capone (1959); The Bad and The Beautiful (1952); A Big Hand for the Little Lady (1966); Bigger Than Life (1956); Force of Evil (1948 – started as a concert piece under Schoenberg's influence); Forever Amber (1947); The Gang's All Here (1943); The Girl in White (1952); Glass Houses (1972); Gunsight Ridge (1957); Hilda Crane (1956); Invitation to a Gunfighter (1964); It's a Big Country (1950); Jubal (1956); Lady in a Corner (1989); A Lady without Passport (1950); Laura (1944); Love Has Many Faces (1964); Man on Fire (1957); Night Tide (1961); Pat and Mike (1952); The Patsy (1964); Pay or Die (1960); Separate Tables (1958); Seven Wonders of the World (1955); Sylvia (1964); Too Late Blues (1961); Two Weeks in Another Town (1962); The Undying Monster (1942); Until They Sail (1957); The Vintage (1957); What's the Matter with Helen? (1971); Whirlpool (1950); Will Penny (1967).
RECORDINGS: Laura. Phillips 454 647–2PH.

RALSTON, Alfred
British composer.
FILMS INCLUDE: Jerusalem's Army (1982); Oh! What a Lovely War (1969); Young Winston (1972).

RAPÉE, Erno (1891–1945)
American composer. Compiled an encyclopaedia of music for pictures which was published in 1922.
FILMS INCLUDE: A Connecticut Yankee (1931); Fazil (1928); Four Devils (1929); Four Sons (1928); The Iron Horse (1924); The Last Man on Earth (1924); Little Ceasar (1930); Old English (1930); Seventh Heaven (1926); Waltzertraum (1925); What Price Glory? (1926).

RATHBURN, Eldon
Canadian composer.
FILMS INCLUDE: Circle of the Sun (1960); City of Gold (1957); Creative Process: Norman McLaren (1990); La Grand Rock (1969); It's a Crime (1957); Morning on the Lievre (1961); Nobody Waved Goodbye (1964); The Shepherd (1955); Waiting for Caroline (1967).

RAWSTHORNE, Alan (1905–1971)
British composer who trained as a dentist before studying music with Egon Petri.
FILMS INCLUDE: *Feature*: The Captive Heart (1946); The Cruel Sea (1952); Floods of Fear (1958); Lease of Life (1954); The Man Who Never Was (1955);

Pandora and the Flying Dutchman (1950); Saraband for Dead Lovers (1948); School for Secrets (1946); Uncle Silas (1947); West of Zanzibar (1953); Where no Vultures Fly (1951). *Documentary*: Broken Dykes (MoI, 1945); Burma Victory (AFU, 1945); Cargo for Ardrossen (1939); The City (GPOFU, 1939); The Dancing Fleece (CFU, 1950); The Drawings of Leonardo da Vinci (Leonardo Film Committee, 1953); The Legend of the Good Beasts (Bear Films, 1956); Messenger of the Mountains (Countryman Films, 1964); The Port of London (Greenpark, 1959); Power Unit (Shell Film Unit, c.1937); Street Fighting (AFU, 1942); Sweat without Tears (Kuwait Oil Co, 1960); Tank Tactics (AFU, 1942); USA – The Land and the People (War Office, 1945); The Waters of Time (Port of London Authority, 1951); X-100 (Shell Mex, 1948).
RECORDINGS: The Captive Heart; The Cruel Sea; Sarabande for Dead Lovers. Silva Screen FILMCD 177.

RAY, Satyajit (1921–1992)
Indian director who was awarded an honorary Oscar in 1992. Also wrote scores for some of his productions from the early 1960s.
FILMS INCLUDE: Abhijan (1962); The Adversary (1971); Days and Nights in the Forest (1970); Kanchehkungha (1966); Nayak (1966); Shakespeare Wallah (1966).

RAYBOULD, Clarence (1886–1972)
British composer, conductor and pianist. Joined the BBC in 1936. Founded the National Youth Orchestra of Wales (1945) which he conducted until 1966. One of the first composers to write original scores for British documentary films.
FILMS INCLUDE: *Documentary*: Contact (Imperial Airways, 1935); Flight to India (1933); Rising Tide (Empire Marketing Board Film Unit, 1933); Where the Road Begins (1933).

READE, Paul (1943–1997)
British composer who wrote music for television. Wrote more than 80 songs for *Play School* besides other music for children's television programmes such as *Crystal Tipps and Alistair*, *Ludwig* and *The Flumps*. Also composed many theme tunes, including those for *The Antiques Road Show* and the *Victorian Kitchen Garden* series, together with incidental music for *Great Expectations* and *Jane Eyre*.

REED, Les (1935–)
British composer and conductor. Was a member of the John Barry Seven.
FILMS INCLUDE: Les Bicyclettes de Belsize (1969); Creepshow 2 (1987); Girl on

a Motorcycle (1968); The Lady Vanishes (1979); One More Time (1969); Play Misty For Me (1971).

REED, William L. (1910–)
English composer who studied with Herbert Howells and Constant Lambert. Later spent time in the USA.

REICH, Steve (1936–)
American composer who studied with Milhaud and Berio.

REILLY, Tommy (1919–)
British composer and harmonica player of Canadian birth. Has composed incidental music for radio and television as well as film scores.
FILMS INCLUDE: The Navy Lark (1959).

REIZENSTEIN, Franz (1911–1968)
English composer and pianist of German birth who studied with Hindemith. Came to London in 1934 where he studied composition with Ralph Vaughan Williams at the Royal College of Music. Scored British horror films from 1951.
FILMS INCLUDE: Circus of Horrors (1960); Jessy (1960); The Mummy (1959); The White Trap (1959).

REMAL, Gary S.
Composer.
FILMS INCLUDE: Breakin' (Breakdance) (1984); Dark Circle (1982); Maria's Lovers (1984).

REVEL, Harry (1905–1958)
British composer who went to Hollywood.
FILMS INCLUDE: Are You With It? (1948); The Big Broadcast of 1936 (1935); Here We Go Again (1942); Minstrel Man (1944); Not Wanted (1949); The Old Fashioned Way (1934); Sitting Pretty (1933).

REVELL, Graeme (1955–)
New Zealand composer who came to Europe in 1979.
FILMS INCLUDE: Body of Evidence (1992); Boxing Helena (1993); Child's Play 2 (1990); The Craft (1996); The Crow (1994); Dead Calm (1989); The Hand that Rocks the Cradle (1992); Hard Target (1993); Hear No Evil (1993); No Escape (1994); Streetfighter (1994).
RECORDINGS: Body of Evidence. Milan 12720–2; The Craft. Varèse Sarabande VSD5732; Streetfighter. Varèse Sarabande VSD5560.

REYNDERS, John (1888–)
British composer and music director who worked at Elstree Studios as Director of British International Pictures Ltd. Wrote music for travel and interest films.
FILMS INCLUDE: Bassetsbury Manor (1936); The Dragon of Wales (1936); Elephant City (1936); Facts and Figures (1935); Father Thames (1935); Fire Fighters (1936); Grey Seal (1937); Happy Hampstead (1936); High Hazard (1935); In Search of Gold (1936); The Seventh Day (1936).

RICHARDSON, Chris (1909–)
British composer and arranger of light music and pianist. Went to the USA in 1936 where he wrote incidental music for films and plays.
FILMS INCLUDE: Alf's Button Afloat (1938); Convict 99 (1938); Miss London Ltd (1943); Oh! Mr Porter (1937); Sailing Along (1938); Strange Boarders (1938); Those Were The Days (1934); Two For Danger.

RIDDLE, Nelson (1921–1985)
American composer who has also written music for television.
FILMS INCLUDE: Batman (1966); Can-Can (1960); Come Blow Your Horn (1962); El Dorado (1966); Flame of the Islands (1955); The Great Bank Robbery (1969); The Great Gatsby (1974 – Academy Award); Happy Anniversary and Goodbye (1974); Hell's Bloody Devils (1968); Hey Boy! Hey Girl! (1959); A Hole in the Head (1959); How to Succeed in Business Without Really Trying (1966); A Kiss Before Dying (1955); Li'l Abner (1959); Lisbon (1956); Lolita (1961); Marriage on the Rocks (1965); The November Plan (1976); Ocean's Eleven (1960); On a Clear Day You Can See Forever (1970); Paint Your Wagon (1969); The Pajama Game (1957); Pal Joey (1957); Paris When it Sizzles (1964); A Rage to Live (1965); Red Line 7000 (1965); Robin and the Seven Hoods (1964); Rough Cut (1980); St Louis Blues (1958); That's Entertainment Part II (1976); What a Way to Go! (1964).

RIEDL, Josef A. (1927–)
German composer who studied with Carl Orff. Composed many electronic works.
FILMS INCLUDE: Adam II (1968); Geschwindigkeit (1963); Impuls Unserer Zeit (1959); Kummunikation (1961); Sekundenfilme (1968); Stunde X (1959); Thunder Over Mexico (1966); Unendliche Fahrt (1965).

RIESENFELD, Hugo (1879–1939)
American composer.
FILMS INCLUDE: Abraham Lincoln (1930); Alibi (1929); The Awakening (1928); The Bad One (1930); The Battle of the Sexes (1928); Be Yourself! (1930); The Cavalier (1928); The Covered Wagon (1923); Eternal Love (1929); Evangeline

(1929); Hell's Angels (1930); Make a Wish (1937); Tarzan's Revenge (1938); The Toilers (1928).

ROBBINS, Richard
American composer.
FILMS INCLUDE: The Ballad of the Sad Café (1990); The Bostonians (1984); The Europeans (1979); Heat and Dust (1982); Howard's End (1992); Jane Austen in Manhattan (1980); Jefferson in the Park (1995); Maurice (1987); Quarter (1981); Remains of the Day (1993); A Room with a View (1985); Surviving Picasso (1996); Sweet Sounds (1976).
RECORDINGS: Howard's End. EMI CMS5 65220–2; A Room with a View. EMI CMS5 65220–2.

ROBERTSON, Robbie (1943–   )
Canadian composer, songwriter and guitarist.
FILMS INCLUDE: Carny (1980); The Colour of Money (1986); Jimmy Hollywood (1994); The King of Comedy (1982); The Last Waltz (1978).

RODGERS, Richard (1902–1979)
American composer of musicals who worked with lyricists Lorenz Hart and Oscar Hammerstein II. Also wrote for television (e.g. *Victory at Sea* and *Winston Churchill (The Valiant Years)*).
FILMS INCLUDE: Babes in Arms (1939); Carousel (1956); Flower Drum Song (1961); Follow Thru (1930); Hallelujah I'm a Bum (1933); I Married an Angel (1942); Jumbo (1962); The King and I (1956); Love Me Tonight (1932); Main Street to Broadway (1953); Nana (1934); Oklahoma! (1955); Pal Joey (1957); Slaughter on Tenth Avenue (1957); The Sound of Music (1965); South Pacific (1958); State Fair (1962); Too Many Girls (1940).
RECORDINGS: Love Me Tonight. Phillips 422 401–2PH.

ROEMHELD, Heinz (1901–1985)
German composer who lived in Hollywood.
FILMS INCLUDE: Blues in the Night (1941); British Intelligence (1940); Captain of The Guard (1930); A Child is Born (1940); Christmas Eve (1947); Decision at Sundown (1957); Dracula's Daughter (1936); Golden Harvest (1933); Imitation of Life (1934); The Invisible Man (1933); Jack and the Beanstalk (1951); Lad: A Dog (1961); The Lady from Shanghai (1948); The Man Who Talked Too Much (1940); The Monster That Challenged The World (1957); O.S.S. (1946); Ride Lonesome (1959); Rogues of Sherwood Forest (1950); Ruby Gentry (1953); The Square Jungle (1955); The Strawberry Blonde (1941); Thank Your Lucky Stars (1943); Valentino (1951).

ROGERS, Eric (died 1981)
British composer, associated with many of the Carry On films.
FILMS INCLUDE: All Coppers Are (1971); Assault (1970); The Best House in London (1968); The Big Job (1965); Bless This House (1972); Carry On Abroad (1972); Carry On Again Doctor (1969); Carry On at Your Convenience (1971); Carry On Behind (1975); Carry On Cabby (1963); Carry On Camping (1969); Carry On Cleo (1964); Carry On Cowboy (1965); Carry On Dick (1974); Carry On Doctor (1967); Carry On Emmanuelle (1978); Carry On Girls (1973); Carry On Henry (1971); Carry On Jack (1964); Carry On Loving (1970); Carry On Matron (1972); Carry On Screaming (1966); Carry On Spying (1964); Carry On Up The Jungle (1970); Carry on . . . Up The Khyber (1968); Caught in the Net (1960); Countdown to Danger (1967); Davy (1957); Doctor in Trouble (1970); Don't Lose Your Head (1966); Escape from the Sea (1968); Follow That Camel (1967); The Horse Without a Head (1963); The Iron Maiden (1963); Masters of Venus (1962); No Sex Please – We're British (1973); Nurse on Wheels (1963); Quest for Love (1971); Revenge (1971); That's Carry On (1977); This is My Street (1963); Three Cases of Murder (1954); Three Hats for Lisa (1965); A Woman of Paris (1923).

ROGERS, Shorty (1924–1994)
American jazz composer, arranger and trumpet player. Associated with Woody Herman (1945–51) as an arranger and then became increasingly involved with the cinema. Continued to play and record jazz in the 1950s and 1960s.
FILMS INCLUDE: The Best Little Whorehouse in Texas (1982); Blues Pattern (1956); Dr Minx (1975); Fools (1970); Heart Beat (1979); Private Hell 36 (1954); The Specialist (1975); Tafty and the Jungle Hunter (1965); Tarzan, The Ape Man (1959); The Teacher (1974); The Tiger Makes Out (1967); The Wild One (1954); Young Dillinger (1965).

ROLAND-MANUEL, Alexis (1891–1966)
French composer and writer on music. Studied with Roussel and Ravel about whom he wrote three books.
FILMS INCLUDE: Le Ciel est à Vous: L'Étrange Monsieur Victor: Lumière d'été; Remorques.

ROLLINS, Sonny
British composer and saxophone player.
FILMS INCLUDE: Alfie (1965); Saxophone Colossus (1986).

ROMBERG, Sigmund (1887–1951)
Hungarian composer who wrote much light music. Many of his stage operettas were later made into films.

FILMS INCLUDE: Balalaika (1939); Deep in My Heart (1954); The Desert Song (1929, 1943 and 1953); Foolish Wives (1922); Maytime (1937); New Moon (1931 and 1940); The Night is Young (1935); The Student Prince (1954). RECORDINGS: The Night is Young. RCA 09026 62681–2.

ROSE, David (1910–1990)

British composer and pianist who lived in America from 1914. He also worked in television from the 1950s and wrote the themes for such series as *Bonanza*, *The High Chaparral* and *The Little House on the Prairie*. Scored several TV films in the 1970s and 1980s. Married to Judy Garland (1941–45).

FILMS INCLUDE: The Clown (1953); Everything I Have is Yours (1952); Hombre (1966); Jupiter's Darling (1954); Never Too Late (1965); Operation Petticoat (1959); Please Don't Eat the Daisies (1960); The Princess and The Pirate (1944 – nominated for an Academy Award); Public Pigeon No. 1 (1956); Quick, Before It Melts (1964); Ride the Wind (1967); Sam's Son (1984); The Underworld Story (1950); Winged Victory (1944).

ROSEN, Milton (1906–1994)

American composer who worked for Universal.

FILMS INCLUDE: Cuban Pete (1946); Daniel in the Lion's Den (1948); Enter Arsene Lupin (1944); The Milkman (1950); Sudan (1945); Swing Out, Sister (1945); White Tie and Tails (1946).

ROSENBERG, Hilding (1892–1985)

Swedish composer and conductor who wrote seven operas and eight Symphonies. During a stay in Germany and Austria, he was very much influenced by Schoenberg. Wrote music for many theatrical productions, including Greek dramas and modern plays.

ROSENMAN, Leonard (1924–   )

American composer who originally wanted to become a painter. Studied composition with Schoenberg, Roger Sessions and Dallapicola. Scored Elia Kazan's first film, *East of Eden.* (1954). During the early 1960s he lived and worked in Rome after which he returned to Hollywood where he wrote some of his avante-garde scores, e.g. *Fantastic Voyage* (1966) and *Beneath the Planet of the Apes* (1970).

FILMS INCLUDE: Ambition (1991); Barry Lyndon (1975); Battle for the Planet of the Apes (1973); Beneath the Planet of the Apes (1969); The Big Land (1957); Bomber B-52 (1957); Bound for Glory (1976 – awarded an Academy Award as musical director); The Bramble Bush (1959); The Car (1977); The Chapman Report (1962); The Cobweb (1955); Countdown (1967); A Covenant with Death (1967); Cross Creek (1983); The Crowded Sky (1960); East of Eden (1954); Edge of the City (1956); An Enemy of the People (1977);

Fantastic Voyage (1966); Heart of the Story (1984); Hell is for Heroes (1961); Hellfighters (1968); Hide in Plain Sight (1980); James Dean – The First American Teenager (1975); The Jazz Singer (1980); Keeper of the City (1991); Lafayette Escadrille (1957); Lord of the Rings (1978); Making Love (1982); A Man called Horse (1970); The Outsider (1961); The Plunderers (1960); Pork Chop Hill (1959); Prophecy (1979); Promise in the Dark (1979); Race with the Devil (1975); Rebel Without a Cause (1955); Reprieve (1962); The Rise and Fall of Legs Diamond (1960); Robocop 2 (1990); The Savage Eye (1959); Silvia (1984); Star Trek IV – The Voyage Home (1986); The Todd Killings (1970).
RECORDING: Beneath the Planet of the Apes. Silva Screen FILMCD146; Countdown. Silva Screen FILMCD146; East of Eden. Chesky CD71; Fantastic Voyage. Silva Screen FILMCD146; The Lord of The Rings. Intrada FMT8003D; Rebel Without a Cause. Edelweiss CIN2206-2; Robocop 2. Varèse Sarabande VSD5271; Star Trek IV. Telarc CD80146.

ROSENTHAL, Laurence (1926–)
American composer and conductor who also writes for television. Studied composition with Howard Hanson and then travelled to Europe to receive further training in Paris from Nadia Boulangar. During the Korean War, as composer for the American Air Force's film unit, he wrote music for a documentary about Russia which was narrated by Henry Fonda. Scored his first success with *The Miracle Worker* in 1962.
FILMS INCLUDE: The African Elephant (1971); Becket (1964); Brass Target (1978); Clash of the Titans (1981); The Comedians (1967); Easy Money (1983); A Gunfight (1970); Heart Like a Wheel (1983); Hotel Paradiso (1966); The Island of Dr Moreau (1977); Man of La Mancha (1972); Meetings with Remarkable Men (1978); Meteor (1979); Naked in the Sun (1956); The Power and the Glory (1961); A Raisin in the Sun (1956); Requiem for a Heavy Weight (1962); The Return of a Man Called Horse (1976); Rooster Cogburn (1975); Three (1969); The Water Party (1974); Who'll Stop the Rain (1978); The Wild Party (1974); Yellowneck (1954).
RECORDINGS: Clash of the Titans. Telarc CD80342; The Island of Dr Moreau. Silva Screen FILM CD156; The Return of a Man Called Horse. Silva Screen FILM CD136.

ROSSELLINI, Renzo (1908–1982)
Italian composer.
FILMS INCLUDE: L'Amore (1948); Angst (1954); La Donna Del Lago (1965); La Donna Più Bella Del Mondo (1955); Il Figlio Dell'Uomo (1954); Il Generale Della Rovere (1959); Le Legioni di Cleopatra (1959); La Macchina Ammazza-cattivi (1948); Madama Butterfly (1954); Noi Vivi (1942); Paisa (1946); La Ragazza Del Palio (1957); Il Segno di Venere (1955); Stromboli, Terra di Dio

(1949); I Tartari (1960); Teodora, Imperatrice di Bisanzio (1953); Tosca (1956); Viaggio in Italia (1953).

ROSTANG, Hubert
French composer.
FILMS INCLUDE: Candide ou L'Optimisme au XXe Siècle (1960); César et Rosalie (1972); Cette Sacrée Gamine (1956); Le Désir Mene Les Hommes (1958); Le Juge Fayard Dit le Sheriff (1976); Le Locataire (1976); Moments de la Vie D'Une Femme (1979); Une Parisienne (1957); Les Saintes Nitouches (1962); L'Ultima Donna (1976); La Vie à Deux (1958); La Vie Devant Soi (1977); Where is Parsifal? (1983).

ROTA, Nino (1911–1979)
Italian composer who wrote oratorio at the age of eleven and opera at fourteen. Studied with Pizzetti and Casella. Wrote ten operas, three symphonies and various concertos, as well as 145 film scores for various directors including Fellini, de Filippo, Visconti and Zeffirelli.
FILMS INCLUDE: The Abdication (1974); L'Amante di Paride (Face That Launched a Thousand Ships) (1953); Amarcord (1973); Amici per la Pelle (1955); Anna (1951); Il Bidone (1955); Boccaccio'70 (1962); Il Casanova di Federico Fellini (1976); I Clowns (1970); Daniele Cortis (1946); Death on the Nile (1978); La Diga Sul Pacifico (1957); La Dolce Vita (1960); I Due Nemici (1961); L'Ennemi Public No 1 (1954); Fantasmi a Roma (1961); Fellini Satyricon (1969); Il Gattopardo (The Leopard) (1962); Giulietta Degli Spiriti (1965); The Godfather (1972); The Godfather Part II (1974); The Godfather Part III (1990); Her Favourite Husband (1950); Hurricane (1979); Londra Chiama Polo Nord (1955); Mambo (1954); Plein Soleil (1960); Prova D'Orchestra (1978); The Reluctant Saint (1962); Rocco e I Suoi Fratelli (1960); Roma (1972); Romeo and Juliet (1968); I Setti Dell'Orsa Maggiore (1952); Sotto Dieci Bandiere (1960); The Taming of the Shrew (1966); Valley of Eagles (1951); War and Peace (1956); Waterloo (1970); Zaza (1943).
RECORDINGS: Amaracard. Silva Screen FILMCD129; Il Bidone. Silva Screen FILMCD129; Death on the Nile. Cloud Nine CN55007; La Dolce Vita. Silva Screen FILMCD129; The Godfather Part II. Silva Screen FILMCD077; The Godfather Part III. Epic 467813–2; Waterloo. EMI CDC7 54528–2.

ROZSA, Miklos (1907–1995)
Hungarian composer who lived in Britain and the USA. Studied at Leipzig Conservatory, and went to Paris in 1931 (Honegger introduced him to writing film music) and London in 1935. Scored his first film *Knight Without Armour* in 1936 and became closely associated with Alexander Korda and his films at Denham Studios. Went to the USA in 1941 to score *Lady Hamilton* and *Jungle Book*, both made by Korda in Hollywood. Remained in Hollywood,

scoring many American films. Won Academy Awards for *Spellbound* (1945), *A Double Life* (1947) and *Ben-Hur* (1959). Introduced the theremin, an electronic instrument, to Hollywood, and used it to great effect in some of his scores.

FILMS INCLUDE: All the Brothers were Valiant (1953); Because of Him (1946); Ben-Hur (1959: Rozsa was involved in the film from the beginning, and went to Rome for the recording); Bhowani Junction (1955); Blood on the Sun (1945); Crisis (1950); Dead Men Don't Wear Plaid (1981); Diane (1955); Divorce of Lady X (1937); Double Indemnity (1944); A Double Life (1947); El Cid (1961 – used 250 Spanish cantigas in this score); Eye of the Needle (1981); Fedora (1978); Five Graves to Cairo (1943); Four Dark Hours (1937); The Four Feathers (1939); The Golden Voyage of Sinbad (1973); The Green Berets (1968); Green Fire (1954); The Hour before the Dawn (1944); Ivanhoe (1952); Julius Caesar (1953 – stereophonic sound was used in the recording of the music); Jungle Book (1942); The Killers (1946); King of Kings (1961 – serialism used in this score); The King's Thief (1955); Knight Without Armour (1936); The Knights of the Round Table (1953); Lady Hamilton (1941); Lady on a Train (1945); Last Embrace (1979); The Lost Weekend (1946); Lust for Life (1956); Madame Bovary (1949); The Man in Half Moon Street (1944); Moonfleet (1955); The Naked City (1948); The Power (1967); The Private Lives of Sherlock Holmes (1970); Providence (1977); Quo Vadis (1951); Sahara (1943); The Seventh Sin (1957); Sodom and Gomorrah (1961); Something of Value (1957); Spellbound (1945 – he later transferred some of the music into his Spellbound Piano Concerto); The Spy in Black (1939); The Squeaker (1937); The Story of Three Loves (1952); Sundown (1941); The Thief of Bagdad (1940); Time After Time (1979); A Time to Love and a Time to Die (1958); Tip on a Dead Jockey (1957); Tribute to a Bad Man (1955); U Boat 29 (1939); The V.I.Ps (1963); The World, the Flesh and The Devil (1958); Young Bess (1953).

RECORDINGS: All the Brothers were Valiant. Silva Screen FILMCD170; Ben-Hur. EMI CDODEON18; Double Indemnity Koch 37375–2; El Cid. Koch 37340–2; Ivanhoe. Intrada MAF7055D; Julius Caesar. Intrada MAF7056D; King of Kings. Silva Screen FILMCD170; The Lost Weekend. Koch 37375–2; Lust for Life. Varèse Sarabande VSD5405; Quo Vadis. Silva Screen FILMCD170; The Thief of Bagdad. Silva Screen FILMXCD 187; Young Bess. Prometheus PCD133–2.

RUBENSTEIN, B. Arthur
American composer.
FILMS INCLUDE: Another Stakeout (1993); Blue Thunder (1982); Deal of the Century (1983); Lost in America (1985); Nick of Time (1996); Wargames (1983).
RECORDINGS: Nick of Time. Milan 74321 34864–2.

RUBENSTEIN, John (1946–)

American actor and occasional composer. Son of Arthur Rubenstein.
FILMS INCLUDE: The Boys from Brazil (1978); The Candidate (1972); The Car (1977); The Catwalk Killer; Corey: For the People; Daniel (1983); Getting Straight (1970); The Gift of the Magi (1978); I Take These Men (1983); In Search of the Historic Jesus (1980); Jeremiah Johnson (1972); Kid Blue (1973); The Killer Inside Me (1975); Liberace (1988); Paddy (1969); The Sandpit Generals (1971); Someone to Watch Over Me (1987); The Trouble with Girls (1969); Zachariah (1970).

RUGOLO, Pete (1915–)

American composer and jazz band leader.
FILMS INCLUDE: The Challengers (1968); Jack the Ripper (1960); The Sweet Ride (1967); Underground Acres (1980); Where the Boys Are (1960).

RUSSELL, Kennedy (1883–)

British composer, pianist and musical director who studied in Brussels.
FILMS INCLUDE: Asking for Trouble (1941); The Common Touch (1941); Crooks (1940); Dreaming (1944); The Dummy Talks (1943); Give Me the Stars (1944); Heaven is Round the Corner (1943); Let the People Sing (1942); Old Mother Riley, Detective (1943); Old Mother Riley's Circus (1941); Old Mother Riley's Ghosts (1941); Salute John Citizen (1942); Shipbuildings (1943); Stepping Toes (1938); Theatre Royal (1943); Those Kids from Town (1941).

RUSTICHELLI, Carlo (1916–)

Italian composer.
FILMS INCLUDE: Accattone (1961); Alfredo Alfredo (1971); Annibale (1959); Antinea, L'Amante Della Città Sepolta (1961); Arrivano I Titani (1961); Avanti! (1972); La Battaglia Di El Alamein (1968); Le Beaujolais Nouveau est Arrivé (1978); Black 13 (1953); Boccaccio (1972); Buffalo Bill L'Eroe del West (1963); The Call of the Wild (1972); Claretta and Ben (1983); Il Colpo Segreto di D'Argtagnan (1962); La Commare Secca (The Grim Reaper) (1963); Coriolano, Eroe Senza Patria (1963); Detenuto in Attesa di Giudizio (1971); Divorzio All'Italiana (Divorce – Italian Style) (1961); E Venne Il Giorno Dei Limoni Neri (1970); Escondido (1967); Il Ferroviere (1956); La Frusta e Il Corpo (1963); Le Gang (1976); I Giganti Della Tessaglia (1960); Gioventù Perduta (1947); Gordon Il Pirata Neo (1961); In Nome Della Legge (1949); Io, Io, Io . . . E Gli Altri (1965); L'Isola Di Arturo (Arturo's Island) (1962); Kapo (1960); Il Leone di San Marco (1963); I Lunghi Capelli Della Morte (1964); Maciste Alla Corte Dello Zar (1964); Un Maledetto Imbroglio (1959); Mamma Roma (1962); Meglio Vedova (1968); I Misteri Della Giungla Nera (1964); Nefertite Regina Del Nilo (1961); Operazione Paura (1966); Persiane

Chiuse (1950); I Predoni Della Steppa (1964); I Quattro Dell'Ave Maria (1968); Le Quattro Giornate Di Napoli (1962); La Ragazza di Bube (1963); Rosmunda e Alboino (1961); The Secret War of Harry Frigg (1967); Sedotta e Abbandonata (1963); Serafino (1968); Signore E Signori (1965); Lo Spadaccino di Siena (1962); Stuntman (1968); Teseo Contro Il Minotauro (1960); La Tigre Dei Sette Mari (1962); La Venere Dei Pirati (1960); Zanna Bianca (1973).
RECORDINGS: Alfredo Alfredo. CAM CSE107.

SAFAN, Craig
American composer who has also written many scores for television.
FILMS INCLUDE: Angel (1983); The Bad News Bears in Breaking Training (1977); Corvette Summer (1978); Enid is Sleeping (1990); Fade to Black (1980); Good Guys Wear Black (1977); The Great Texas Dynamite Chase (1976); The Last Starfighter (1984); The Legend of Billie Jean (1985); A Nightmare on Elm Street Part 4 (1988); Nightmares (1983); Remo Williams: The Adventure Begins (1985); Stand and Deliver (1988); Thief (1981).
RECORDINGS: Angel. Intrada MAF7051D; The Last Starfighter. Intrada MAF7066; A Nightmare on Elm Street Part 4. Varèse Sarabande VSD5203.

SAINT-SAËNS, Camille (1835–1921)
French composer, pianist, organist and writer. Wrote thirteen operas. The first established composer to write film music for *L'Assassinat du Duc de Guise* (Op.128) in 1908. The film was directed by Henri Lavedan and first shown in Paris at the Salle Charras on 16 November 1908.
RECORDINGS: L'Assassinat du Duc de Guise. Harmonia Mundi HMTT90 1472.

SAKAMOTO, Ryiuchi (1952–)
Japanese composer, rock musician and leader of the Yellow Magic Orchestra.
FILMS INCLUDE: Emily Bronte's Wuthering Heights (1992); The Handmaid's Tale (1990); The Last Emperor (1987); Little Buddha (1993); Marathon (1993); Merry Christmas Mr Lawrence (1982); The Sheltering Sky (1990); Tacones Lejanos (1991).
RECORDINGS: The Handmaid's Tale. GNPD8020; The Sheltering Sky. Virgin CDV2774.

SALTER, Hans J. (1896–1994)
Austrian composer who went to Hollywood in 1937 and was hired by Charles Previn at Universal Studios in 1938. Became associated with horror films e.g. Dracula, Wolfman and Frankenstein. Wrote scores for television in addition to the cinema.
FILMS INCLUDE: Autumn Leaves (1956); Beau Geste (1966); Bedtime Story

(1963); The Black Cat (1941); Call a Messenger (1939); Come September (1961); Creature from the Black Lagoon (1954); The Far Horizons (1954); The Female Animal (1957); Follow that Dream (1962); Frankenstein Meets the Wolfman (1943); The Ghost of Frankenstein (1942); The Gunfight at Dodge City (1958); Gunpoint (1965); His Butler's Sister (1943); Hitler (1961); Hold Back the Night (1956); Hold That Ghost (1941); The House of Frankenstein (1944); The Human Jungle (1954); If a Man Answers (1962); Incident at Phantom Hill (1965); The Incredible Shrinking Man (1957); Invisible Agent (1942); Invisible Man Returns (1940); The Invisible Man's Revenge (1944); It Started with Eve (1941); The Man in the Net (1959); Man-made Monster (1941); The Mummy's Hand (1940); Navy Wife (1956); The Oklahoman (1956); Phantom Lady (1944); Raw Wind in Eden (1958); Red Sundown (1955); Scarlet Street (1945); Seven Sinners (1940); Sherlock Holmes Faces Death (1943); Showdown (1963); Sign of the Pagan (1954); So Goes My Love (1946); The Tall Stranger (1957); Three Brave Men (1957); Wichita (1955); The Wild and the Innocent (1959).
RECORDINGS: Creature from the Black Lagoon. Intrada MAF7054D; The House of Frankenstein. Marco Polo 8.223748; The Invisible Man Returns. Marco Polo 8.223747.

SALZEDO, Leonard (1921–)
British composer who wrote much for Hammer films.
FILMS INCLUDE: Before I Wake (1955); The Glass Cage (1955); The Revenge of Frankenstein (1958); Shadow of Fear (1956); Sporting Life (1958); The Steel Bayonet (1958); Women without Men (1956).

SARDE, Philippe (1945–)
French composer.
FILMS INCLUDE: La Cage (1974); César et Rosalie (1972); Le Chat (1971); Les Choses de La Vie (1969); Ciao Maschio (1978); Coup de Torchon (1981); Le Diable Probablement (1977); Une Dimanche à La Campagne (1984); L'Envers Du Décor: Portrait de Pierre Guffroy (1992); L'Etoile du Nord (1982); La Fille de D'Artagnan (1994); Fort Saganne (1984); Ghost Story (1981); La Grande Bouffe (1973); Hellé (1972); L'Horloger de Saint-Paul (1973); Le Juge Fayard dit le Sheriff (1976); Lancelot du Lac (1974); Liza (1972); Le Locataire (1976); Lord of the Flies (1990); Loulou (1980); Lovesick (1983); Lung Ta – Les Cavaliers du Vent (1990); Ma Saison Préférée (1993); La Petite Apocalypse (1993); Pirates (1986); Poisson Lune (1993); Quest for Fire (1981); Rendez-vous (1985); Storie di Ordinaria Follia (1981); Tess (1979); L'Ultima Donna (1976); Undiscovered (1994); La Vie Devant Soi (1977); Violette and François (1977).
RECORDINGS: La Fille de D'Artagnan. Sony SK66364; Lord of the Flies. Silva Screen FILMCD067.

SATO, Masaru (1928–)

Japanese composer.

FILMS INCLUDE: *Feature*: Ebirah, Horror of the Deep (1968); Godzilla vs Mecha-Godzilla (1976); The Hidden Fortress (1958); Kozoku (1971); The Lower Depths (1957); Red Beard (1965); Sanjuro (1962); Sensei the Teacher (1983); Shogun's Shadow (1989); Throne of Blood (1957); The Wolves (1972); The Yellow Handkerchief of Happiness (1978); Yojimbo (1961). *Documentary*: Sapporo Winter Olympics (1972).

SAUGET, Henri (1901–1989)

French composer who studied with Canteloube and Koechlin. Best known for his eight operas and twenty-five ballets. Also composed music for television and plays, including some incidental music for Giraudoux's *Ondine*.

FILMS INCLUDE: *Feature*: Les Amoureux sont seuls au Monde (1947); Le Charron (1943); Le Cirque Enchanté (1943); Clochemerle (1947); Entre Onze Heures et Minuit (1949); L'Épivier (1933); Farrebique (1946); La Fortune Enchantée (1935); L'Honorable Catherine (1942); Julie de Carneilhan (1950); Le Part de L'Enfant (1943); Pêches de Jeunesse (1941); Premier de Cordée (1944); Sur les Chemins de Lamartine (1941); Symphonie en Blanc (1942); Terre Sauvage (1947); Le Tonnelier (1942). *Documentary*: Ouvrages de Fer (1949).

SAUNDERS, Max

New Zealand composer and arranger, who came to England in 1932.

FILMS INCLUDE: *Feature*: Five Clues to Fortune (1956); Mystery in the Mine (1959). *Documentary*: Battle of Britain (MoI, 1944 – with Hubert Clifford).

SAVINA, Carlo (1919–)

Italian composer and conductor.

FILMS INCLUDE: Amarcord (1973); An-Nasar Salah Ad-Din (1963); Le Caldi Notti di Caligola (1977); Carnalità (1974); La Casa Dell'Escorcismo (1975); Il Casanova di Federico Fellini (1976); I Clowns (1970); Comin' at Ya! (1981); Ercole Sfida Sansone (1964); Erode Il Grande (1959); L'Etoile du Nord (1982); Europa di Notte (1959); Eva (Eve) (1962); Finalmente . . . Le Mille e Una Notte (1972); Il Futuro e Donna (1984); Il Giardino dei Finzi-Contini (1970); Giuditta e Oloferne (1958); The Godfather (1972); Io Amo, Tu Ami (1961); L'Ira di Achille (1962); It Started in Naples (1960); Johnny Oro (1966); Jours Tranquilles à Clichy (1990); Le Locataire (1976); Maciste Nell'Inferno di Gengis Khan (1964); Ming, Ragazzi! (1973); La Notte dei Dannati (1971); La Nuora Giovane (1975); Pochi Dollari per Django (1966); Prova D'Orchestra (1978); Roma (1972); Rosmunda e Alboino (1961); Sfida Al Re Di Castiglia (1963); Spartacus E I Dieci Gladiatori (1964); Le Spie Uccidono a Beirut

(1965); Stavisky . . . (1974); The Taming of the Shrew (1966); Tess (1979); Il Trionfo Dei Dieci Gladiatori (1965); Ultime Grida Dalla Savana (1975); L'Uomo Che Ride (1965); Zorro e I Tre Moschettieri (1962).

SAWTELL, Paul (1906–1971)
Polish-born composer who went to work in America. Associated with the Tarzan films.
FILMS INCLUDE: Africa Adventure (1954); Ambush at Cimarron Pass (1957); Animal World (1956); Below the Sahara (1953); The Big Circus (1959); The Big Show (1961); The Black Scorpion (1957); Born to Kill (1947); The Bubble (1966); Cage of Evil (1960); Cattle Empire (1958); The Christine Jorgensen Story (1970); The Cosmic Man (1958); Counterplot (1959); Criminal Court (1946); A Date with the Falcon (1941); The Deerslayer (1957); The Desperados are in Town (1956); Desperate (1947); Dick Tracy Meets Gruesome (1947); A Dog of Flanders (1959); A Dog's Best Friend (1959); Down Three Dark Streets (1954); The Falcon in San Francisco (1945); The Falcon's Adventure (1947); Faster, Pussycat! Kill! Kill! (1965); Five Guns to Tombstone (1960); Five Steps to Danger (1956); Five Weeks in a Balloon (1962); The Fly (1958); Frontier Uprising (1961); The Gay Falcon (1941); Ghost Diver (1957); Gun Duel in Durango (1957); Harbor Lights (1963); Hell Ship Mutiny (1957); Hong Kong Confidential (1958); The House of Fear (1944); The Hunters (1958); Island of the Blue Dolphins (1964); It! The Terror from beyond Space (1958); Jack the Giant Killer (1961); Kronos (1957); The Last Man on Earth (1964); Last of the Bad Men (1957); A Lawless Street (1955); The Living Swamp (1955); The Long Rope (1960); The Lost World (1960); Machete (1958); The Maurauders (1955); Los Marcados (1971); The Miracle of the Hills (1959); Misty (1961); Monkey on My Back (1957); The Mummy's Curse (1944); The Music Box Kid (1960); Mystery in Mexico (1948); Noose for a Gunman (1960); Operation Bottleneck (1960); Pale Arrow (1957); The Pearl of Death (1944); Pirates of Tortuga (1961); Pop Always Pays (1940); Rage at Dawn (1955); Return of the Fly (1959); The Sad Horse (1959); Scandal Inc (1956); She Devil (1957); Sky Full of Moon (1952); Stopover Tokyo (1957); The Story of Mankind (1957); Tall Man Riding (1954); Tarzan and the Amazons (1945); Tarzan and the Huntress (1947); Tarzan and the Leopard Woman (1945); Tarzan and the She-Devil (1953); Tarzan Triumphs (1943); Tarzan's Desert Mystery (1943); Tarzan's Hidden Jungle (1955); Ten Wanted Men (1954); Tess of the Storm Country (1960); Texas Lady (1955); They Rode West (1954); Three Came to Kill (1960); Three Hours to Kill (1954); Thunder Island (1963); Villa!! (1958); Voyage to the Bottom of the Sea (1961); The Walking Target (1960); Wild Harvest (1961); Young Guns of Texas (1962).

SCHÄFFER, Boguslaw (1929–)
Polish compose, theorist and teacher. Composed the first Polish twelve-note work for orchestra (1953).

SCHARF, Walter (1910–)
American composer and musical director.
FILMS INCLUDE: Are You With It? (1948); Artists and Models (1955); The Bellboy (1960); Ben (1972); The Birds and the Bees (1956); Chatterbox (1943); The Cheyenne Social Club (1970); Cinderfella (1960); The Countess of Monte Cristo (1948); Dakota (1945); Deported (1950); Don't Give Up the Ship (1959); The Errand Boy (1961); Funny Girl (1968); The Geisha Boy (1958); Guns of Diablo (1964); Hans Christian Andersen (1952); Honeymoon Hotel (1964); If It's Tuesday, This Must Be Belgium (1969); It'$ Only Money (1962); The Joker is Wild (1957); Journey Back to Oz (1971); Kicma (1975); King Creole (1958); The Ladies' Man (1961); Loving You (1957); My Six Loves (1962); The Nutty Professor (1963); Part 2 Walking Tall (1975); Pendulum (1968); Pocketful of Miracles (1961); Rock-a-Bye Baby (1958); The Sad Sack (1957); The Saxon Charm (1948); Sylvia (1964); This is Elvis (1981); Tickle Me (1965); Timetable (1955); Twilight Time (1983); Walking Tall (1973); Where Love Has Gone (1964); Willy Wonka and the Chocolate Factory (1971); Yes Sir, That's My Baby (1949).

SCHERTZINGER, Victor (1880–1941)
American director who was a concert violinist. Wrote the music score for *Civilisation* (1915). Also the part scores, usually songs, for many of his other films.
FILMS INCLUDE: Fashions in Love (1929); The Fleets In (1942); Heads Up (1930); Kiss the Boys Goodbye (1941); Let's Live Tonight (1935); The Music Goes Round (1936); Rhythm on the River (1940); Road to Singapore (1940); Something to Sing About (1937); The Wheel of Life (1929).
RECORDINGS: Kiss the Boys Goodbye. Koch 37906–2; Rhythm on the River. Koch 37906–2.

SCHIFRIN, Lalo (1932–)
Argentinian composer who studied classical music and jazz in Paris, partly with Messiaen. Settled in Hollywood (1964) where he started to write for the cinema and television e.g. *Mission Impossible*.
FILMS INCLUDE: The Amityville Horror (1979); Amityville II: The Possession (1982); The Beguiled (1970); The Big Brawl (1980); Black Moon Rising (1985); Blindfold (1965); Boulevard Nights (1979); The Brotherhood (1968); Brubaker (1980); Buddy Buddy (1981); Bullitt (1968); The Cat from Outer Space (1978); Caveman (1981); Charley Varrick (1973); Che! (1969); The Cincinatto Kid (1965); Class of 1984 (1981); The Competition(1980); The

Concorde – Airport '79 (1979); Coogan's Bluff (1968); Cool Hand Luke (1967); Dark Intruder (1965); Day of the Animals (1976); The Dead Pool (1988); Dirty Harry (1971); Don Quixote (1993); The Doomsday Flight (1966); The Eagle has Landed (1976); Enter the Dragon (1973); Escape to Athena (1979); Eye of the Cat (1969); Fast-Walking (1981); The Four Musketeers (1974); The Fourth Protocol (1987); The Fox (1967); Golden Needles (1974); Harry in your Pocket (1973); Hell in the Pacific (1968); The Helstrom Chronicle (1971); Hit (1973); I Deal in Danger (1966); I Love my Wife (1970); Joe Kidd (1972); Kelly's Heroes (1970); The Liquidator (1965); Loophole (1980); Love and Bullets (1978); Magnum Force (1973); The Manitou (1978); The Master Gunfighter (1975); The Mean Season (1985); Mission Impossible vs. The Mob (1969); Mrs Pollifax – Spy (1970); Murderers' Row (1966); Naked Tango (1990); The Neptune Factor An Undersea Odyssey (1973); The Nude Bomb (1980); Once a Thief (1964); The Osterman Weekend (1983); The President's Analyst (1967); Pretty Maids all in a Row (1971); Prime Cut (1972); Pussycat, Pussycat, I Love you (1970); Return from Witch Mountain (1978); Rhino! (1963); Rollercoaster (1977); Sky Riders (1976); Sol Madrid (1967); Special Delivery (1976); St Ives (1976); Sting II (1983); Sudden Impact (1983); Sullivan's Empire (1967); Tank (1984); Telefon (1977); THX 1138 (1970); The Venetian Affair (1966); Voyage of the Damned (1976); Way Way Out (1966); When Time Ran Out (1980); Where Angels Go Trouble Follows! (1967); Who's Minding the Mint? (1966); The Wrath of God (1972); WUSA (1970).

RECORDINGS: The Competition. Telearc CD80243; Magnum Force. Silva Screen FILMCD136; Sudden Impact. Silva Screen FILMCD138.

SCHMIDT-GENTNER, W.
German composer.
FILMS INCLUDE: The Angel with the Trumpet (1949); Cabaret (1957); Casta Diva (1935); Circus of Love (1958); Frau in Mond (1929); Das Lied Einer Nacht (1932); Operette (1940); Rendezvous in Wien (1936); Der Verlorene (1951); The Woman on the Moon (1928); The Wonder Kid (1951); Die Wunderbare Lüge der Nina Petrowna (1929).

SCHMITT, Florent (1870–1958)
French composer who studied harmony with Dubois, Massenet and Fauré. Wrote music in many genres including ballets, choral works and chamber music.
FILMS INCLUDE: *Feature*: Salammbô (1925). *Documentary*: Essais de Locomotives (1943).

SCHNITTKE, Alfred (1934–   )
Soviet composer and theorist who has worked in the Experimental Studio of
Electronic Music in Moscow. He has written music for many film and stage
productions.
FILMS INCLUDE: Uncle Vanya (1971).

SCHUMAN, William (1910–1992)
American composer.
FILMS INCLUDE: Africa Screams (1949); Buck Privates Come Home (1947);
Dragnet (1954); The Night of the Hunter (1955); The Noose Hangs High
(1948); The Wistful Widow of Wagon Gap (1947).

SCHURMANN, Gerard (1928–   )
Dutch composer and conductor who has worked in British films since the late
1940s. Was introduced to film scoring by Alex Rawsthorne and helped him
with his films e.g. *The Cruel Sea* (1952). Also orchestrated the scores for
Exodus (1960), *Lawrence of Arabia* (1962) and *The Vikings* (1958).
FILMS INCLUDE: Attack on the Iron Coast (1967); The Bedford Incident (1965);
But Not in Vain (1948); The Camp on Blood Island (1957); The Ceremony
(1963); Cave of Silence (1960); Cross of Iron (1977); Day In Day Out (1965);
Dr Syn Alias The Scarecrow (1963); The Headless Ghost (1959); The Horrors
of the Black Museum (1959); Konga (1960); The Long Arm (1956); The Lost
Continent (1968); Man in the Sky (1956); The Third Key (1957); The Two-
Headed Spy (1958).
RECORDINGS: Attack on the Iron Cross. Cloud Nine CNS 5005; The Bedford
Incident. Cloud Nine CNS 5005; Horrors of the Black Museum. Cloud Nine
CNS 5005; The Lost Continent. Cloud Nine CNS 5005; Man in the Sky. Silva
Screen FILMCD 177.

SCHWARZ, Arthur (1900–1984)
American composer and producer who was formerly a lawyer.
FILMS INCLUDE: The Band Wagon (1953); Dancing in the Dark (1949);
Dangerous When Wet (1953); Excuse my Dust (1951); Follow the Leader
(1930); Thank Your Lucky Stars (1936); You're Never Too Young (1955).
RECORDINGS: The Band Wagon. EMI CDODEON19.

SCOTT, John (1930–   )
British composer and conductor who arranged for the Ted Heath Band. Also
conducted and arranged for such artists as Tom Jones, Cilla Black and The
Hollies.
FILMS INCLUDE: *Feature*: Antony and Cleopatra (1972); Becoming Colette
(1992); Billy Two Hats (1973); Birds and Planes (1964); Craze (1973); The
Deceivers (1988); Doctor in Clover (1966); Dog Tags (1990); Doomwatch

(1972); England Made Me (1972); The Final Countdown (1980); Girl Stroke Boy (1971); Greystoke: The Legend of Tarzan The Lord of the Apes (1984); Hennessy (1975); Inseminoid (1980); The Jerusalem File (1971); King of the Wind (1989); Lionheart (1990); Man on Fire (1987); North Dallas Forty (1979); Outback (1971); Penny Gold (1973); The People That Time Forgot (1977); Prayer for the Dying (1987); Satan's Slave (1976); Shoot to Kill (1988); The Shooting Party (1984); Spys (1974); A Study in Terror (1965); Sumuru (1967); Symptoms (1974); That Lucky Touch (1975); To the End of the Earth (1984); Trog (1970); Twinky (1969); Winter People (1989). *Documentary*: Has scored many of Jacques Cousteau's nautical documentaries including Amazon I and II; The First 75 Years; The Warm Blooded Sea; Papua New Guinea; Saint Lawrence/Australia. Others include: Give your Car a Holiday (BTF, 1967).

RECORDINGS: Antony and Cleopatra. JOS JSCD114; King of the Wind. JOS JSCD109; Prayer for the Dying. JOS JSCD102; Winter People. JOS JSCD102.

SCOTT, Patrick
British composer.
FILMS INCLUDE: Amsterdam Affair (1968); Berserk! (1967); Crooks and Coronets (1969); Jules Verne's Rocket to the Moon (1967); The Long Duel (1967); Loving Feeling (1968); Stranger in the House (1967); The Violent Enemy (1969).

SCOTT, Tom (1948–   )
American composer.
FILMS INCLUDE: Amadeus (1984); Class (1983); Conquest of the Planet of the Apes (1972); The Culpepper Cattle Company (1972); Fallout (1993); Fast Forward (1984); A Force of One (1978); Hanky Panky (1982); Heaven Help Us (1984); Koyaanisqatsi (1983); The No Mercy Man (1973); The Plague Dogs (1982); The Right Stuff (1983); Sidecar Racers (1974); The Slags Kaerlighed (1970); Soul to Soul (1971); Stir Crazy (1980); The Sure Thing (1985); The Titan Find (1984); Uptown Saturday Night (1974).

SCOTTO, Vincent (1876–1952)
French composer.
FILMS INCLUDE: Algiers (1938); Domino (1943); La Fille du Puisatier (1940); L'Ingénue Libertine (1950); Jofroi (1933); Marinella, Pepe le Moko (1936); Le Roman de Renard (1941).

SCULTHORPE, Peter (1929–   )
Australian composer who studied at Oxford University with Rubbra and Wellesz. Later visiting Professor of Music at Sussex University. Has written an opera, and scores for radio productions.
FILMS INCLUDE: They Found a Cave (1962).

SEARLE, Humphrey (1915–1982)
British composer and writer who studied music at the Royal College of Music
with R.O. Morris and John Ireland, and in Vienna with Webern. Wrote five
symphonies and two piano concertos.
FILMS INCLUDE: *Feature*: The Abominable Snowman (1957); Action of the Tiger
(1957); The Baby and the Battleship (1956); Beyond Mombasa (1956); The
Haunting (1963); Law and Disorder (1958); Left, Right and Centre (1959);
The Passionate Stranger (1956). *Documentary*: Coasts of Clyde (1959); Com-
monwealth Games (1958); Greek Sculpture (1959); Holiday in Norway
(1955); Mountains and Fjords (1955); Woodland Harvest (1977).
RECORDINGS: The Abominable Snowman. Silva Screen FILMCD175; The
Haunting. Silva Screen FILMCD175.

SEGALL, Bernardo (1911–)
American composer.
FILMS INCLUDE: Custer of the West (1966); The Great St Louis Bank Robbery
(1958); Hallucination Generation (1966); Homebodies (1973); The Jesus Trip
(1971); Loving (1970); The Luck of Ginger Coffey (1964).

SEIBER, Matyas (1905–1960)
Hungarian composer who studied with Zoltan Kodaly. Came to England in
1935. Specialised in cartoon and short films and worked as composer to the
Halaas-Batchelor British Cartoon Unit.
FILMS INCLUDE: *Feature*: Chase a Crooked Shadow (1957); For Better, For
Worse (1954); Malaga (1954); The Mark of the Hawk (1958); Robbery Under
Arms (1957); A Town Like Alice (1956). *Documentary*: Abu Zeid and the
Dungeon (1943); Abu Zeid and the Poisoned Wall (1943); Abu Zeid Builds
a Dam (1944); Abu Zeid's Harvest (1943); Animal Farm (1955); The Big Top
(1945); Coupon Hearers (1943); The Diamond Wizard (1954); The Figure-
head (1952); Good King Wenceslas (1944); Job for the Future (1945); The
Magic Canvas (1949); Old Wives' Tale (1945); Paper People Land (1938);
Six Little Jungle Boys (1944).

SENIA, Jean-Marie (1947–)
Algerian-French composer.
FILMS INCLUDE: Céline et Julie en Bateau (1974); Jonas Qui Aura 25 ans en
L'an 2000 (1976); Swing Troubadour (1990); Tendres Cousines (1980).

SERRA, Eric (1959–)
French composer.
FILMS INCLUDE: Atlantis (1991); The Big Blue (1988); Le Dernier Combat
(1983); Nikita (1990); Subway (1985).

SHAIMAN, Marc

American composer and arranger who was a member of Bette Midler's band. Also associated with Billy Crystal.

FILMS INCLUDE: The Addams Family (1991); Addams Family Values (Addams Family II) (1993); Big Business (1988); City Slickers (1991); A Dangerous Woman (1994); Divine Madness (1980); Misery (1990); Mr Saturday Night (1992); North (1994); Scenes From a Mall (1991); Sister Act (1992); Sleepless in Seattle (1993); When Harry met Sally (1989).

RECORDINGS: The Addams Family. Silva Screen FILMCD156; Addams Family Values. Varèse Sarabande VSD5456; City Slickers. Varèse Sarabande VSD5321.

SHAKESPEARE, John

British composer.

FILMS INCLUDE: Avalanche (1975); Can I Come Too (1979); Connecting Rooms (1969); Fly Away (1972); Girls Come First (1975); The Great McGonagall (1974); Heading for Glory (1975); Killer's Moon (1978); Metal in Harmony (1962); The Over-Amorous Artist (1974); Secrets of a Door-to-door Salesman (1973); Secrets of a Superstud (1975); Side by Side (1975); Son of the Sahara (1966); Swedish Wildcats (1974); Under the Bed (1976); World at Their Feet (1970); The Young Duke: Wayne Before Stagecoach (1989); You're Driving Me Crazy (1978).

SHANKAR, Ravi (1920–)

Indian instrumentalist and composer.

FILMS INCLUDE: Aparajito (The Unvanquished) (1956); Apau Sansar (World of Apu) (1958); A Chairy Tale (1957); Chappaqua (1966); Charly (1968); The Concert for Bangladesh (1972); En Djungelsaga (The Enchanted Leopard) (1957); Gandhi (1982 – part nominated for an Academy Award); Monterey Pop (1968); Pather Panchali (1955); Raga (1971); The Sword and the Flute (1959).

SHAPORIN, Yuri (1887–1966)

Russian composer and teacher. Wrote an opera, oratorios and cantatas. Wrote about eighty scores for the theatre and many film scores.

FILMS INCLUDE: Tri Pesni O Lenine (Three Songs About Lenin) (1934).

SCHEDRIN, Rodion K. (1932–)

Soviet composer who studied composition with Shaporin. Attracted public attention while still a student with his performance of the First Piano Concerto.

SHEBALIN, Vissarion (1902–1963)
Russian composer and teacher who wrote operas, musical comedy and ballets, together with incidental music for the theatre (35), the cinema (22) and radio (12).

SHEFTER, Bert (1904–)
American composer, born in Russia.
FILMS INCLUDE: The Big Circus (1959); Cattle Empire (1957); The Christine Jorgensen Story (1970); Curse of the Fly (1985); Danger Zone (1951); Jack the Giant Killer (1962); Kronos (1957); The Last Shot You Hear (1969); The Lost World (1960); No Escape (1953).

SHERMAN, Richard (1928–) and **Robert** (1925–)
American songwriting team who have worked for Disney. Won an Oscar for 'Chim Chim Cheree' (*Mary Poppins* – 1964).
FILMS INCLUDE: The Adventures of Bullwhip Griffin (1965); Bedknobs and Broomsticks (1970); Big Red (1962); Charlotte's Web (1972); Escapade in Florence (1962); Follow Me, Boys! (1966); The Gnome-Mobile (1966); The Happiest Millionaire (1967); The Horse Without a Head (1963); Huckleberry Finn (1974); In Search of the Castaways (1962); The Jungle Book (1967); The Magic of Lassie (1978); Mary Poppins (1964); The Million Dollar Collar (1963); Miracle of the White Stallions (1962); The Misadventures of Merlin Jones (1963); Monkeys Go Home (1966); The Monkey's Uncle (1964); Moon Pilot (1961); The Parent Trap (1961); The Slipper and the Rose – The Story of Cinderella (1976); Snoopy, Come Home (1972); Summer Magic (1963); The Sword in the Stone (1963); The Tenderfoot (1964); That Darn Cat (1965); Tom Sawyer (1973); Winnie the Pooh and the Blustery Day (1968); Winnie the Pooh and the Honey Tree (1965); Winnie the Pooh and Tigger Too (1974).
RECORDINGS: Mary Poppins. EMI CDC5 56177–2.

SHERWIN, Manning (1903–1974)
American composer who worked for Paramount Studios during the 1930s after which he came to Britain to write for films and the theatre, including many London musicals and revues.
FILMS INCLUDE: Bees in Paradise (1944); Blossom on Broadway (1937); A Girl Must Live (1939); He Found A Star (1941); Hi, Gang! (1941); I'll Be Your Sweetheart (1945); King Arthur Was a Gentleman (1942); Miss London Ltd. (1943); Stolen Holiday (1937); Swing, Teacher, Swing (1938); Vogues of 1938 (1937).

SHIRE, David (1937–   )
American composer.
FILMS INCLUDE: All the President's Men (1976); Backfire (1987); The Big Bus (1976); Class of '44 (1973); The Conversation (1974); Drive, He Said (1970); Farewell My Lovely (1975); Fast Break (1979); The Fortune (1974); Harry and Walter go to New York (1976); The Hindenburg (1975); Monkey Shines (1988); Mother (1986); The Night the Lights Went Out in Georgia (1981); Norma Rae (1979); Old Boy Friends (1978); One More Train to Rob (1970); Only When I Laugh (1981); Paternity (1981); The Promise (1978); Return to Oz (1985); Saturday Night Fever (1977); Short Circuit (1986); Showdown (1972); Skin Game (1971); Steelyard Blues (1972); Straight Time (1977); Summertree (1971); The Taking Of Pelham One, Two, Three (1974); To Find A Man (1971); 2010: Odyssey 2 (1984); Vice Versa (1988); The World According to Garp (1982).
RECORDINGS: 2010. Silva Screen FILMCD146; Monkey Shines. Silva Screen FILMCD156.

SHORE, Howard (1946–   )
Canadian composer who has written for television. Heavily influenced by jazz.
FILMS INCLUDE: After Hours (1985); Big (1988); The Brood (1979); The Client (1994); Ed Wood (1994); The Fly (1986); M. Butterfly (1993); Mrs Doubtfire (1993); Naked Lunch (1991); Philadelphia (1993); Places in the Heart (1984); Prelude to a Kiss (1992); Ransome (1997); Scanners (1980); She-Devils (1989); Silence of the Lambs (1991); Silkwood (1983); Sliver (1993); Videodrome (1982).
RECORDINGS: Big. Varèse Sarabonde VSD5208; The Brood. Silva Screen FILMCD115; The Fly. Varèse Sarabonde VCD47272; Mrs Doubtfire. Fox 07822 11015–2; The Silence of the Lambs. MCA MCAD10194.

SHOSTAKOVICH, Dmitri (1906–1975)
Russian composer and pianist. Wrote operas, ballets and fifteen symphonies. Visited England in 1958 and 1974 where he meet Britten.
FILMS INCLUDE: The Adventures of Korzinkina (1940); Alone (1930–31); The Godfly (1955); Hamlet (1964); Katerina Ismailova (Lady Macbeth of Mtsensk) (1966); Khovanshchina (1959); Korol Lir (King Lear) (1970); Michurin (1948); Novyi Babilon (1928); I Sequestrati di Altona (1962); The Unforgetable Year 1919 (1951); War and Peace (1964); The Young Guard (1947–48); The Youth of Maxim (1934–35); Zoya (1944).
RECORDINGS: The Adventures of Korzinkina. Olympic OCD194; The Godfly. Decca 452 597–2DH; King Lear. Koch International 37274–2; Novyi Babilon. Capriccio 10 341/2.

SHUKEN, Leo (1906–1976)
American orchestrator who received an Oscar for the score of *Stagecoach* (1939).
FILMS INCLUDE: Camelot (1967); The Comancheros (1961); The Fabulous Dorseys (1948); The Flying Deuces (1939); The Greatest Story Ever Told (1965); Gun Crazy (1949); John and Mary (1969); The Lady Eve (1941); Lost Horizon (1972); The Miracle of Morgan's Creek (1943); Seven Alone (1974); Stagecoach (1939); Sullivan's Travels (1941); Those Redheads from Seattle (1953); Waikiki Wedding (1937).

SICA, Manuel de
Italian composer
FILMS INCLUDE: Amanti (1968); L'Età di Cosimo de' Medici (1972); Folies Bourgeoises (1976); Il Giardino dei Finzi-Contini (1970); Sette Scialli di Seta Gialla (1972).

SILVERS, Louis (1889–1954)
American composer and musical director
FILMS INCLUDE: The Barker (1928); The Baroness and the Butler (1938); The Black Room (1935); Dancing Lady (1933); Disraeli (1929); The Doorway to Hell (1930); Heidi (1937); Hollywood Cavalcade (1939); Hot Stuff (1979); In Old Chicago (1937); Isn't Life Wonderful (1924); It Happened One Night (1934); The Jazz Singer (1927); Little Miss Broadway (1938); A Message to Garcia (1936); Noah's Ark (1928); One Night of Love (1934 – Academy Award); The Prisoner of Shark Island (1936); Stanley and Livingstone (1939); Stowaway (1936); Suez (1938); Way Down East (1920).

SILVESTRI, Alan (1950–   )
American composer who has worked in television.
FILMS INCLUDE: The Abyss (1989); Back to the Future (1985); Back to the Future II (1989); Back to the Future III (1990); Blown Away (1994); Cat's Eye (1984); The Clan of the Cave Bear (1985); Clean Slate (1994); Cop and a Half (1993); The Delta Force (1986); The Doberman Gang (1972); Driving Me Crazy (1991); Fandango (1984); Father of the Bride (1991); Forrest Gump (1994); Grumpy Old Men (1993); Judge Dredd (1995); Judgement Night (1993); Predator (1987); Predator II (1989); The Quick and the Dead (1995); Romancing the Stone (1984); Sidekicks (1993); Stop! Or My Mom Will Shoot (1992); Who Framed Roger Rabbit? (1988).
RECORDINGS: The Abyss. Varèse Sarabande VSD5235; Back to the Future. Telarc CD809146; Forrest Gump. Epic 477369–2; The Quick and the Dead. Varèse Sarabande VSD5595; Who Framed Roger Rabbit. Varèse Sarabande VSD5208.

SIMON, Carly (1945–   )

American composer and singer

FILMS INCLUDE: Heartburn (1986); Postcard From the Edge (1990); This Is My Life (1992).

SIMON, Paul (1941–   )

American lyricist and singer as part of Simon and Garfunkel. Remembered for the music backing to *The Graduate* (1967).

ŠKERJANC, Lucijan M. (1900–1973)

Yugoslav composer, conductor and pianist.

SKILES, Marlin (1906–   )

American composer, arranger and musical director.

FILMS INCLUDE: Annapolis Story (1955); Battle Flame (1959); The Beast of Budapest (1958); Calling Homicide (1956); Canyon River (1956); Chain of Evidence (1956); Dayton's Devils (1968); The Deadly Companions (1961); Dial Red O (1955); The Disembodied (1957); Fighter Attack (1953); Fort Massacre (1958); The Golden Idol (1954); Gunfight At Comanche Creek (1963); High Society (1955); The Hypnotic Eye (1960); In the Money (1958); Indian Paint (1965); The Jail Busters (1955); Killer Leopard (1954); King of the Wild Stallions (1958); Looking for Danger (1957); Man From God's Country (1958); My Gun is Quick (1957); Quantrill's Raiders (1958); Queen of Outer Space (1958); The Resurrection of Zachary Wheeler (1971); Skabenka (1955); Spooks Chasers (1957); Spy Chasers (1955); The Stranglers (1963); Sudden Danger (1955); Up in Smoke (1957).

SKINNER, Frank (1897–1968)

American composer.

FILMS INCLUDE: The Appaloosa (1966); Away all Boats (1956); Bagdad (1949); Battle Hymn (1957); Black Angel (1946); Black Bart (1948); Broadway (1942); Bud Abbot and Lou Costello Meet Frankenstein (1948); Bullet for a Badman (1964); Captain Newman, M.D. (1963); Charlie McCarthy, Detective (1939); Destry Rides Again (1939); Double Crossbones (1950); Dressed to Kill (1946); East Side of Heaven (1939); The Flame Of New Orleans (1941); Foxfire (1955); The Gal Who Took the West (1949); The Great Ziegfeld (1936); Harvey (1950); Hellzapoppin' (1941); Hired Wife (1940); If I Had My Way (1940); Imitation of Life (1958); Interlude (1957); Invisible Man Returns (1940); Mad About Music (1938); Madame X (1965); Magnificent Obsession (1954); Man of a Thousand Faces (1957); Mark of the Renegade (1951); Midnight Lace (1960); The Mississippi Gambler (1953); My Man Godfrey (1957); The Naked City (1948); Never Say Goodbye (1955); Nice Girl? (1941); The Perfect Furlough (1958); Portrait in Black (1960); The Restless

Years (1958); Saboteur (1942); Seven Sinners (1940); Shenandoah (1965); Sherlock Holmes and the Secret Weapon (1942); Sherlock Holmes and the Voice of Terror (1942); Sherlock Holmes in Washington (1942); The Shrike (1955); Son Of Frankenstein (1939); Star in the Dust (1956); The Sword of Ali Baba (1964); Tammy and The Bachelor (1957); Tammy and the Doctor (1963); The Tattered Dress (1957); This Happy Feeling (1958); The Ugly American (1963); The Wolf Man (1941); Written on the Wind (1956).
RECORDINGS: Dressed to Kill. Varèse Sarabande VSD5692; The Wolf Man. Marco Polo 8.223747.

SLANEY, Ivor (1921–)
British composer.
FILMS INCLUDE: Face the Music (1954); Five Days (1954); The Gambler and the Lady (1953); The House across the Lake (1954); Murder by Proxy (1955); The Saints Return (1953); Spaceway (1953); The Stranger Came Home (1954); Terror (1979).

SMALL, Michael (1939–)
American composer.
FILMS INCLUDE: Audrey Rose (1977); Black Widow (1987); Child's Play (1972); Comes a Horseman (1978); Continental Divide (1981); Dream Lover (1986); The Driver (1978); The Drowning Pool (1975); Girl Friends (1978); Jaws: The Revenge (1987); Jenny (1969); Klute (1971); Love and Pain and the Whole Damn Thing (1972); Marathon Man (1976); Mountains of the Moon (1990); Night Moves (1975); The Parallax View (1974); The Postman Always Rings Twice (1981); Pumping Iron (1976); Puzzle of a Downfall Child (1970); The Revolutionary (1970); Rollover (1981); See You in the Morning (1989); Star Chamber (1983); The Stepford Wives (1974); Target (1985).

SMEATON, Bruce
Australian composer.
FILMS INCLUDE: Barbarosa (1982); The Cars That Ate Paris (1974); The Chant of Jimmy Blacksmith (1978); A Cry in the Dark (1988); The Devil's Playground (1976); Eleni (1985); Iceman (1984); Libido (1973); Monkey Grip (1981); The Naked Country (1984); Picnic at Hanging Rock (1975); Plenty (1985); Roxanne (1987); The Silent Flute (1978); Undercover (1983).

SMITH, Paul (1906–1985)
American composer who worked for Disney.
FILMS INCLUDE: The Best of Walt Disney's True-Life Adventures (1975); Bon Voyage (1962); Chico, The Misunderstood Coyote (1961); The Great Locomotive Chase (1956); The Light in the Forest (1958); Love Happy (1949); Miracle of the White Stallions (1962); Moon Pilot (1961); The Parent Trap

(1961); Perri (1957); The Pigeon that Worked a Miracle (1958); Pinocchio (1939 – awarded Academy Award); Pollyanna (1960); Secrets of Life (1956); The Shaggy Dog (1959); Snow White and the Seven Dwarfs (1937); So Dear to my Heart (1948); Song of the South (1946); The Three Lives of Thomasina (1963); Twenty Thousand Leagues under the Sea (1954).

SNELL, David (1897–1967)
American composer.
FILMS INCLUDE: Alias a Gentleman (1948); Bad Bascomb (1946); Keep Your Powder Dry (1945); The Lady in the Lake (1947); Love Crazy (1941); Madame X (1937); The Man from Down Under (1943); Merton of the Movies (1947); Pacific Rendezvous (1942); Twenty Mule Teams (1940); Young Doctor Kildare (1938).

SNOW, Mark (1946–   )
American composer who went to Los Angeles in 1974 to begin composing for the cinema and television. Has written music for *Cagney and Lacey*, *Crazy Like a Fox*, *Hart to Hart* and the *X-Files*.
FILMS INCLUDE: Born to Be Wild (1995); Ernest Saves Christmas (1988); The Oldest Living Confederate Widow Tells All (1994).

SOBEL, Curt
American composer.
FILMS INCLUDE: Against All Odds (1984); Bloody Birthday (1980); Cannery Row (1982); Cast a Deadly Spell (1991); Cutter and Bone (1981); Defenceless (1991); The Escape Artist (1982); The Flamingo Kid (1984); The Money Pit (1985); An Officer and a Gentleman (1981); Personal Best (1982); Risky Business (1983); Starman (1984); Sweet Liberty (1985); Tarzan and the Apeman (1981); Under the Cherry Moon (1986); White Nights (1985); Without a Trace (1983); Young Sherlock Holmes (1985).

SONDHEIM, Stephen (1930–   )
American composer.
FILMS INCLUDE: A Funny Thing Happened on the Way to the Forum (1966); Gypsy (1962); The Last of Sheila (1973); A Little Night Music (1977); Reds (1981); Stavisky . . . (1974).

SOURIS, André (1890–1970)
Belgian composer, conductor and musicologist. Beginning with *Le Monde de Paul Delvaux* (1946), he established himself as a notable composer for the cinema.
FILMS INCLUDE: Babuka (1952); La Belgique Nouvelle (1937); Calligraphie Japonaise (1957); De Renoir à Picasso (1950); Elle Sera Appelée Femme

(1953); Le Froid (1950); Le Monde de Paul Delvaux (1946); Perséphone (1951); Sur les Routes de l'été (1936); Visite à Picasso (1950).

SPEAR, Eric
British composer who also wrote for television e.g. *Coronation Street* (1960). FILMS INCLUDE: *Feature*: Bang your Dead (1953); The Big Chance (1957); Fabian of the Yard (1954); Flight from Folly (1944); Ghost Ship (1953); Handcuffs, London (1955); The Limping Man (1953); Men Against the Sun (1953); Stranglehold (1962); Street of Shadows (1953); The Switch (1963); Too Hot To Handle (1960); The Vulture (1966). *Documentary* The Mosquito (Merton Park Films, 1945).

SPEDDING, Frank
Scottish composer.
FILMS INCLUDE: *Documentary*: The Architecture of Frank Lloyd Wright (1983); The Big Catch (1968); Charles Rennie Mackintosh (1968); Glasgow Belongs to Me (1966); The Heart of Scotland (1961); Space and Light (1972).

SPOLIANSKY, Mischa (1898–1985)
Russian composer who lived in Germany from 1930 and in Britain from 1934.
FILMS INCLUDE: The Battle of the Villa Fiorita (1965); The Best House in London (1968); Don Juan (1934); The Ghost Goes West (1936); The Happiest Days of Your Life (1950); Happy Go Lovely (1951); Hitler: The Last Ten Days (1973); King Solomon's Mines (1937); Das Lied Einer Nacht (1932); North West Frontier (1959); Saint Joan (1957); Sanders of the River (1935); Trouble in Store (1953); The Whole Truth (1958).

STALLING, Carl
American composer who wrote and arranged music for about 1200 Disney and Warner Brothers cartoons in the 1930s, 40s and 50s. A silent film pianist and conductor, he became Disney's musical director in 1928, moving to Warner in 1936 and finally returning in 1958.

STEIN, Herman (1915–)
American composer who worked at Universal.
FILMS INCLUDE: Abbot and Costello Meet Dr Jekyll and Mr Hyde (1953); Back at the Front (1952); The Black Shield of Falworth (1954); The Creature from the Black Lagoon (1954); Destry (1954); Drums across the River (1954); The Fair Country (1955); The Glenn Miller Story (1953); Has Anybody Seen My Gal? (1952); The Incredible Shrinking Man (1957); The Intruder (1961); Last of the Fast Guns (1958); No Name on the Bullet (1959); So This is Paris (1954); This Island Earth (1955).

STEIN, Ronald (1930–1985)

American composer.

FILMS INCLUDE: Apache Woman (1955); Atlas (1960); Attack of the 50 Foot Woman (1958); The Bounty Killer (1965); Cannibal Orgy, or The Maddest Story Ever Told (1965); Dementia 13 (1963); Diary of a High School Bride (1959); Getting Straight (1970); The Ghost of Dragstrip Hollow (1959); The Girl in Lover's Lane (1959); The Haunted Palace (1963); High School Hellcats (1958); Hot Rod Gang (1958); It Conquered the World (1956); Jet Attack (1958); The Legend of Tom Dooley (1959); The Littlest Hobo (1958); Not of This Earth (1956); Paratroop Command (1958); The Premature Burial (1962); The Prisoners (1973); Psych-Out (1968); The Rain People (1969); Raymir (1960); Requiem for a Gunfighter (1965); The She-Creature (1956); She-Gods of Shark Reef (1956); Suicide Battalion (1958); The Terror (1963); Too Soon to Love (1960); The Underwater City (1962); War is Hell (1961); The Young and the Brave (1963).

RECORDINGS: Dementia 13. Varèse Sarabande VSD5634; The Terror. Varèse Sarabande VSD5634.

STEINER, Fred (1923–   )

American composer who also scores television films.

FILMS INCLUDE: The Color Purple (1985 – nominated for an Academy Award); The Man from Del Rio (1956); Robinson Crusoe on Mars (1964); Run for the Sun (1956); The St Valentine's Day Massacre (1967); The Sea Gypsies (1978); Time Limit (1957).

STEINER, Max (1888–1971)

American composer and conductor, born in Austria (his godfather was Richard Strauss). One of Hollywood's most prolific writers of film music, he wrote more than two hundred scores until forced to retire in 1965. At RKO Radio Pictures (1929–36) and Warner Brothers (1936–65) where he composed the familiar Warner Brothers fanfare.

FILMS INCLUDE: Ace of Aces (1933); The Adventures of Don Juan (1949); Alice Adams (1935); The Amazing Dr Clitterhouse (1938); Angels with Dirty Faces (1938); Arsenic and Old Lace (1944); Band of Angels (1957); Battle Cry (1954); The Beast with Five Fingers (1946); Bed of Roses (1933); Before Dawn (1933); The Big Sleep (1946); A Bill of Divorcement (1932); The Bride Came C.O.D. (1941); By the Light of the Silvery Moon (1953); Casablanca (1943); Cash McCall (1959); The Charge of the Light Brigade (1936); Christopher Strong (1933); Cimarron (1931); City for Conquest (1940); Come Next Spring (1955); The Conquerors (1932); The Conspirators (1944); The Corn is Green (1945); Darby's Rangers (1957); The Dark at the Top of the Stairs (1960); The Dawn Patrol (1938); Death of a Scoundrel (1956); The Desert Song (1952); A Distant Trumpet (1964); Dixiana (1930); Down to their Last Yacht (1934); Escapade in Japan (1957); FBI Code 98 (1962); The FBI Story (1959); Flying Devils (1933); Fort Dobbs (1958); Friends and Lovers (1931); Gone with the Wind (1939 – which was written and scored in three weeks. Steiner did a great deal of research, collecting dances, Southern songs and military music); The Half Naked Truth (1932); The Hanging Tree (1959); Hat, Coat and Glove (1934); Headline Shooter (1933); Helen of Troy (1955); Hell on Frisco Bay (1955); Hell's Highway (1932); Ice Palace (1960); Illegal (1955); In This Our Life (1942); The Informer (1935 – Academy Award); Jezebel (1938); John Paul Jones (1959); Keep 'em Rolling (1934); Key Largo (1948); King Kong (1933); Lady with a Past (1932); The Last Command (1955); The Letter (1940); Life with Father (1947); The Little Minister (1934); Long Lost Father (1934); Lost Horizon (1937); The Lost Patrol (1934); A Majority of One (1961); Majorie Morningstar (1958); Mara Maru (1952); The McConnell Story (1955); Mildred Pierce (1945); Mission to Moscow (1943); Morning Glory (1933); The Most Dangerous Game (1932); Murder on the Blackboard (1934); My Reputation (1946); No Marriage Ties (1933); No Other Woman (1933); Now Voyager (1942 – Academy Award); Our Betters (1933); Parrish (1960); Passage to Marseille (1944); The Phantom of Crestwood (1932); Portrait of a Mobster (1961); Pursued (1947); Rhapsody in Blue (1945); The Richest Girl in the World (1934); Roar of the Dragon (1932); Rome Adventure (1962); Santa Fe Trail (1940); The Searchers (1956); She (1935); Since You Went Away (1944 – Academy Award); Sing and Like It (1934); The Sins of Rachel Cade (1960); So This is Love (1953); Son of Kong (1933); Spencer's Mountain (1963); A Star is Born (1937); Star of Midnight (1935); A Stolen Life (1946); Strictly Dynamite (1934); A Summer Place (1959); Susan Slade (1961); Sweepings (1933); Symphony of Six Million (1932); Their Big Moment (1934); They Died with their Boots On (1941); They Made Me A Criminal (1939); This Man is Mine (1934); Those Calloways (1964); Tovarich (1937); The Treasure of Sierra Madre (1948); Trouble Along the Way (1953); Two Alone (1934); Two on a Guillotine (1964); The Unfaithful (1947); The Violent Men (1954); What Price Hollywood? (1932); White Heat (1949); The Woman in White (1947); Youngblood Hawke (1963). RECORDINGS: The Beast with Five Fingers. Marco Polo 8.223870; The Big Sleep. RCA GD80136; Casablanca. Silva Screen FILMCD144; Gone with the Wind. Silva Screen FILMCD144; Key Largo. RCA GD80422; A Summer Place. Silva Screen FILMCD144.

STEVENS, Bernard (1916–1983)
British composer who studied with Dent and Rootham at Cambridge University. Attracted public attention with his 'Symphony of Liberation' (1946).
FILMS INCLUDE: The Mark of Cain (1947); Once a Jolly Swagman (1948); The Upturned Glass (1947).
RECORDINGS: The Mark of Cain. Chandos CHAN7008.

STEVENS, James
British composer.
FILMS INCLUDE: The Baby and the Battleship (1956); The Desperate Man (1959); Feelings (1975); The Fourth Square (1961); Portrait of Queenie (1964); Ring Around the Earth (1964); Sparrows Can't Sing (1962); They Came From Beyond Space (1967); The Traveller (1989); Two of a Kind (1983); The Weapon (1956).

STEVENS, Leith (1909–1970)
American composer and arranger who also worked in television.
FILMS INCLUDE: The Bob Mathias Story (1954); Bullwhip (1958); But not for Me (1959); The Careless Years (1957); Chuka (1967); Crashout (1955); Destination Moon (1950); Eighteen and Anxious (1957); The Five Pennies (1959); The Garment Jungle (1957); The Gene Krupa Story (1959); The Glass Wall (1953); The Great Rupert (1949); The Green-Eyed Blonde (1957); The Gun Runners (1958); Hell to Eternity (1960); The Interns (1962); It Happened at the World's Fair (1962); The James Dean Story (1957); Julie (1956); Lizzie (1957); Mad at the World (1954); Man-Trap (1961); Navajo (1951); A New Kind of Love (1963); The Night of the Grizzly (1966); Not Wanted (1949); On The Double (1961); Private Hell 36 (1954); Ride Out for Revenge (1957); Scared Stiff (1952); The Scarlet Hour (1955); Seven Guns to Mesa (1958); The Treasure of Pancho Villa (1955); Violent Road (1958); War of the Worlds (1953); When Worlds Collide (1951); The Wild One (1954); World Without End (1955).
RECORDINGS: Destination Moon. Klavier STC77101.

STOLL, George (1905–1985)
American musical director who worked with MGM from 1945.
FILMS INCLUDE: Anchors Away (1945 – Academy Award); Athena (1954); Babes in Arms (1939); Cabin in the Sky (1943); The Courtship of Eddie's Father (1962); Dangerous When Wet (1953); Duchess of Idaho (1950); Easy to Love (1953); Girl Crazy (1943); The Girl from Scotland Yard (1937); Girl Happy (1964); Glory Alley (1952); Go West (1940); Hit the Deck (1954); The Horizontal Lieutenant (1962); I Love Melvin (1952); In the Good Old Summertime (1949); Jumbo (1962); Lady be Good (1941); Latin Lovers (1953); Looking for Love (1964); Love Me or Leave Me (1955); Luxury Liner (1948); Made in Paris (1965); Music for Millions (1944); Nancy Goes to Rio (1949); Neptune's Daughter (1949); On an Island with You (1948); The Opposite Sex (1956); Rose Marie (1954); Seven Hills of Rome (1957); Skirts Ahoy! (1952); Spinout (1965); The Strip (1951); The Student Prince (1954); Swing Banditry (1936); Ten Thousand Bedrooms (1956); This Could be the Night (1957); A Ticklish Affair (1963); The Toast of New Orleans (1950); Viva Las Vegas (1964); Where the Boys Are (1960); The Wizard of Oz (1939); Ziegfeld Girl (1941).

STOLOFF, Morris (1894–1980)
American music director who worked in Hollywood from 1936.
FILMS INCLUDE: Affair in Trinidad (1952); All Ashore (1952); All the King's Men (1949); Bring Your Smile Along (1955); The Eddy Duchin Story (1955); Fanny (1960); Gidget (1959); Holiday (1938); I Married Adventure (1940); In a Lonely Place (1950); The Jolson Story (1946); The Lady from Shanghai (1948); Let's Do it Again (1953); The Long Gray Line (1954); Lost Horizon (1937); Man on a String (1960); Miss Sadie Thompson (1953); The Mountain Road (1960); My Sister Eileen (1955); The Naked Run (1967); None But the Brave (1965); Pal Joey (1957); Penny Serenade (1941); Senior Prom (1958); Song Without End (1960); Sound Off (1952); The Talk of the Town (1942); Three for the Show (1954); Together Again (1944); The Undercover Man (1949); You Can't Run Away From It (1956); You Can't Take it With You (1938); You'll Never Get Rich (1941).

STOLZ, Robert (1880–1975)
Austrian composer, pianist and conductor who partly studied with Humperdinck. Lived in Paris (1938–40) and the USA (1940–46) returning to Austria (1946–50).
FILMS INCLUDE: Die Frauenparadies (1936); It Happened Tomorrow (1944); My Heart is Calling (1934); Spring Parade (1940); Zirkus Saran (1935).

STOREY, Michael
British composer.
FILMS INCLUDE: Another Country (1984); The Bloody Chamber (1983); Every Picture Tells a Story (1984); Hidden City (1987); Just Like a Woman (1992); Mark Gertler Fragments of a Biography (1981).

STOTHART, Herbert (1885–1949)
American composer who worked for MGM.
FILMS INCLUDE: After the Thin Man (1936); Anna Karenina (1935); Camille (1936); The Cat and the Fiddle (1933); China Seas (1935); David Copperfield (1935); Devil-May-Care (1929); Dynamite (1929); Edison, The Man (1940); The Florodora Girl (1930); The Girl of the Golden West (1938); I Married an Angel (1942); Idiot's Delight (1939); Madam Satan (1930); Mrs Miniver (1942); Mutiny on the Bounty (1935); Northwest Passage (1940); The Picture of Dorian Gray (1945); Queen Christina (1933); Rasputin and the Empress (1933); The Rogue Song (1929); Rose Marie (1954); San Francisco (1936); A Tale of Two Cities (1935); They Were Expendable (1945); The Three Musketeers (1948); Treasure Island (1934); The Wizard of Oz (1939); Ziegfeld Girl (1941).
RECORDINGS: The Rogue Song. Nimbus N17881.

STOTT, Wally (1925–)
British composer whose name changed to Angela Morley.
FILMS INCLUDE: The Brinks Job (1978); Captain Nemo and the Underwater City (1969); Equus (1977); Fire and Ice (1982); The Heart of a Man (1959); It's Never Too Late (1956); The Lady is a Square (1958); The Little Prince (1974); The Looking Glass War (1970); Peeping Tom (1959); The Slipper and the Rose – The Story of Cinderella (1976); When Eight Bells Toll (1971).

STRAUS, Oscar (1870–1954)
Austrian operetta composer who provided film music.
FILMS INCLUDE: Land Without Music (1936); Madame De (1952); One Hour With You (1932); La Ronde (1950); The Smiling Lieutenant (1931).

STREISAND, Barbra (1942–)
American singer, actress and director who won an Oscar in 1977 for composing the song 'Evergreen' for the film *A Star is Born*.
FILMS INCLUDE: The Prince of Tides (1991); A Star is Born (1976); Yentl (1983).

STROUSE, Charles (1928–)
American composer, mainly for musicals.
FILMS INCLUDE: Annie (1981); Bonnie and Clyde (1967); Bye Bye Birdie (1963); The Night they Raided Minsky's (1968); Replay (1970); There was a Crooked Man (1970).

STRUMMER, Joe (1952–)
British composer and former member of The Clash.
FILMS INCLUDE: Love Kills (1986); Permanent Record (1988); Rude Boy (1980); Sid and Nancy (1986); Walker (1987); When Pigs Fly (1993).

STYNE, Julie (1905–1994)
British born composer, pianist and conductor, who went to the USA when a child. Songs include 'Give me Five Minutes More', 'It's Magic', 'There Goes that Song Again' and 'Three Coins in the Fountain'.
FILMS INCLUDE: Bells are Ringing (1960); Funny Girl (1968); Gentlemen Prefer Blondes (1953); Gypsy (1962); It's a Great Feeling (1949); Living It Up (1954); Meet Me After the Show (1951); My Sister Eileen (1955); Step Lively (1944); Three Coins in the Fountain (1954); Two Guys from Texas (1948); The West Point Story (1950); What a Way to Go! (1964).
RECORDINGS: Three Coins in the Fountain. Chesky CD71.

SUKMAN, Harry (1912–1984)
American composer.
FILMS INCLUDE: Around the World Under the Sea (1965); Battle Taxi (1954);

A Bullet for Joey (1955); The Crimson Kimono (1959); Fanny (1960); Forty Guns (1957); Guns of Diablo (1964); The Hangman (1959); If He Hollers, Let Him Go! (1968); Madison Avenue (1961); The Naked Runner (1967); The Phoenix City Story (1955); The Singing Nun (1966); Song Without End (1960); A Thunder of Drums (1961); Underwater Warrior (1957); Underworld U.S.A. (1960); Verboten! (1958); Welcome to Hard Times (1966).

TAKEMITSU, Toru (1930–1996)

Japanese composer whose work has been admired as cross-cultural.

FILMS INCLUDE: A1 (1962); Ai No Borei (Empire of Passion) (1978); L'Amour à Vingt ans (1962); Bad Boys (1960); Black Rain (1989); Dodes' Ka-Den (1970); Gishiki (1971); Himatsuri (1984); Juvenile Passions (1958); Kaidan (1964); Kanojo to Kare (1963); Kaseki (1974); Ran (1985); Rising Sun (1993); Seppuku (1962); Shinjo Ten No Amijima (1969); Shokutaku no nai ie (1985); Summer Soldiers (1971); Taiheiyo Hitoribotchi (1963).

RECORDINGS: Rising Sun. Fox 07822 11003–2.

TAUSKY, Vilem (1910–)

Czech-born conductor and composer who became a British citizen. Scored the Crown Film Unit's documentary 7 Years.

THEODORAKIS, Mikis (1925–)

Greek composer who has written orchestral music, oratorios, ballets, and theatre and film scores. Gained international recognition for his score for Zorba the Greek.

FILMS INCLUDE: The Barefoot Battalion (1953); Le Couteau dans la Plaie (1962); The Day the Fish Came Out (1967); Elektra (1961); Etat de Siège (1973); Ill Met By Moonlight (1956); Iphigenia (1976); Luna de Miel (1959); Phaedra (1961); Serpico (1973); The Shadow of the Cat (1961); They're a Weird Mob (1966); The Trojan Women (1971); Z (1968); Zorba the Greek (1964).

RECORDINGS: Phaedra. Sakkaris SR50060; Serpico. Sakkaris SR50061; Zorba The Greek. Silva Screen FILMCD180.

THIRIET, Maurice (1906–1972)

French composer who studied with Koechlin and Roland-Manuel. Devoted himself to writing film music after World War II.

FILMS INCLUDE: Les Amours Finissent a L'Aube (1953); Les Collants Noirs (1960); Crime et Châtiment (1956); Le Grand Jeu (1954); Les Grandes Familles (1958); Il Suffit d'Aimer (1960); Lucrece Borgia (1953); Retour de Manivelle (1957); Ronde des Eaux (1960); Thérèse Raquin (1953).

THOMPSON, Virgil (1896–1989)

American composer, critic and organist who partly studied with Nadia Boulanger in Paris. Wrote several successful film scores and much incidental music, especially for Shakespearean plays.

FILMS INCLUDE: *Feature*: The Goddess (1958); Louisiana Story (1948); *Documentary*: The Plow that Broke the Plains (US Government, 1936); Power Among Men (UN, 1959); The River (US Government, 1937); The Spanish Earth (1937, Contemporary Historians); Tuesday in November (US Government, 1945); Voyage to America (New York World's Fair, 1964).

RECORDINGS: Louisiana Story. Hyperion CDA66576; The Plow that Broke the Plains. Hyperion CDA66576; The River. Vanguard 08.8013.71

THORNE, Ken (1926–)

British composer and conductor.

FILMS INCLUDE: Arabian Adventure (1979); The Bed Sitting Room (1969); Dead Man's Evidence (1962); The Evil That Men Do (1983); Finders Keepers (1984); Fratello Sole, Sorella Luna (1972); Green Ice (1981); Hannie Caulder (1971); Head (1968); Help! (1965); How I Won the War (1967); Inspector Clouseau (1968); It's Trad, Dad! (1962); Juggernaut (1974); Lassiter (1983); The Magic Christian (1969); Master Spy (1963); Murphy's War (1971); Out of the Fog (1962); The Outsider (1979); Power Play (1978); The Protector (1985); The Ritz (1976); She Knows y' Know (1962); Sinful Davey (1968); Superman II (1980); Superman III (1983); They Might be Giants (1971); The Touchables (1968); The Trouble with Spies (1987); Welcome to the Club (1970); Wolf Lake (1979).

TIOMKIN, Dimitri (1894–1979)

Russian born composer and pianist, resident in America from 1929. Left Hollywood in 1968 after the death of his wife and settled in London. His first film assignments were writing ballet sequences in four MGM films in 1930 including *Devil-May-Care* and *The Rogue Story*.

FILMS INCLUDE: *Feature*: The Adventures of Hajji Baba (1954); The Alamo (1960); Alice in Wonderland (1933); Bugles in the Afternoon (1951); A Bullet is Waiting (1954); Champagne for Caesar (1950); Circus World (1964); The Command (1954); The Court Martial of Billy Mitchell (1955); D.O.A. (1949); Devil-May-Care (1929); Duel in the Sun (1946); The Fall of the Roman Empire (1964); Fifty-Five Days at Peking (1962); The Fourposter (1952); Friendly Persuasion (1956); Giant (1956); Great Catherine (1967); The Great Waltz (1938); Gunfight at the O.K. Coral (1956); The Guns of Navarone (1961); The High and the Mighty (1954 – Academy Award); High Noon (1952 – Academy Awards for the best score and the best theme song); I Confess (1953); It's a Wonderful Life (1947); Land of the Pharaohs (1955); Last Train from Gun Hill (1959); Lost Horizon (1937); Lucky Partners (1940);

McKenna's Gold (1968); Mad Love (1935); Night Passage (1957); The Old Man and the Sea (1958 – Academy Award); Red River (1947); Resurrection (1931); Rio Bravo (1958); Search for Paradise (1957); Shadow of Doubt (1943); So this is New York (1947); Spawn of the North (1947); Strange Lady in the Town (1955); Strangers on a Train (1951); The Sundowners (1960); Take the High Ground! (1953); Tarzan and the Mermaids (1948); Tchaikovsky (1970); Tension at Table Rock (1956); The Thing From Another World (1951 – introduced a wind machine and the ondes martinot into the score); Town Without Pity (1961); The Unforgiven (1959); The War Wagon (1967); The Westerner (1940); Wild is the Wind (1957); You Can't Take it With You (1938); The Young Land (1957). *Documentary*: Rhapsody of Steel (US Steel Co., 1959).
RECORDINGS: The Alamo. RCA 09026 62658–2; Fifty-Five Days at Peking. Cloud Nine CNS 5006; The Guns of Navarone. Silva Screen FILMCD151; High Noon. Unicorn UKCD 2011; Red River. Unicorn UKCD 2011.

TOCH, Ernst (1887–1964)
Austrian composer and pianist who went to Hollywood via Berlin (1929–32) and London (1933–34)
FILMS INCLUDE: Address Unknown (1944); The Cat and the Canary (1939); Catherine the Great (1934); Four Men and a Prayer (1938); The Ghost Breakers (1940); Ladies in Retirement (1941); Little Friend (1934); Peter Ibbetson (1935); The Unseen (1945).

TOWNS, Colin
British composer who has written for the cinema and television (e.g. *Cadfael*, 1996, *Ivanhoe*, 1997) besides music for the concert hall including a trumpet concerto.
FILMS INCLUDE: The Buccaneers (1995); Full Circle (1976); The Puppet Masters (1995); The Rocking Horse Winner (1982); Shadey (1985); Slayground (1983); The Wolves of Willoughby Chase (1988).
RECORDINGS: Full Circle. Koch International 38703–2; The Puppet Masters. Klavier STC77104.

TOYE, Geoffrey (1889–1942)
British composer and conductor who had great success with his ballet *The Haunted Ballroom* (1934).
FILMS INCLUDE: *Feature*: Men are not Gods (1936); Rembrandt (1936). *Documentary*: Music to accompany British Movietone's film about the Coronation of King George VI (1937).

TROTTER, John Scott (1908–1975)
American composer, conductor and arranger.
FILMS INCLUDE: Abie's Irish Rose (1946); A Boy Named Charlie Brown (1969); East Side of Heaven (1939); Rhythm on the River (1940).

TRZASKOWSKI, Andrzej (1933–   )
Polish composer.
FILMS INCLUDE: Baltic Express (1959); The Call (1971).

VANGELIS (1943–   )
Greek composer and keyboard player whose real name is Vangelis O. Papathanassiou.
FILMS INCLUDE: Bitter Moon (1992); Blade Runner (1982); The Bounty (1984); Chariots of Fire (1981 – Academy Award); 1492: Conquest of Paradise (Christopher Columbus) (1992); Francesco (1989); Missing (1981); Nosferatu a Venezia (1987).
RECORDINGS: Blade Runner. Wealdon 4509 96574–2; Chariots of Fire. Silva Screen FILMCD180.

VAN HEUSEN, James (1913–1990)
American songwriter, usually with lyrics by Johnny Burke.
FILMS INCLUDE: Anything Goes (1955); Career (1959); Come Blow Your Horn (1962); Duffy's Tavern (1945); High Time (1960); The Joker is Wild (1957); Journey Back to Oz (1971); Journey to the Centre of the Earth (1959); Little Boy Lost (1953); Love and Marriage (1969); Mr Music (1950); Ocean's Eleven (1960); Pardners (1956); Riding High (1950); Road to Bali (1952); Road to Morocco (1942); Road to Zanzibar (1941); Robin and the Seven Hoods (1964); Say One for Me (1959); Some Came Running (1958); Surprise Package (1960); The Tender Trap (1955); Wake Me When It's Over (1960); Who Was That Lady? (1959); The World of Suzie Wong (1960).

VARS, Henry (1902–1977)
American composer born in Warsaw.
FILMS INCLUDE: Battle at Bloody Beach (1961); Flipper (1963); Flipper's New Adventure (1964); Fools' Parade (1971); House of the Damned (1963); The Little Shepherd of Kingdom Come (1960); Man in the Vault (1956); The Phoenix City Story (1955); Seven Men from Now (1956); The Two Little Bears (1961); The Unearthly (1957); Womanhunt (1961).

VAUGHAN WILLIAMS, Ralph (1872–1958)
British composer who studied at the RCM with Hubert Parry and Charles Standford. Muir Mathieson asked him to write his first score in 1941 for *The*

49th Parallel. His music for the film *Scott of the Antarctic* (1947) later formed the basis of his Sinfonia Antarctica (1949–52).
FILMS INCLUDE: Bitter Springs (1950); Coastal Command (1942); Dim Little Island (1949); The England of Elizabeth (1955); The Flemish Farm (1943); 49th Parallel (1940–41); The Loves of Joanna Godden (1946); The People's Land (1941–42); Scott of the Antarctic (1947–48); Stricken Peninsula (1944); The Vision of William Blake (1957).
RECORDINGS: Coastal Command. Marco Polo 8.223665; The England of Elizabeth. Marco Polo 8.223665; Scott of the Antarctic. EMI CDGO2059.

VEALE, John
British composer.
FILMS INCLUDE: Clash by Night (1963); Emergency (1962); Freedom to Die (1962); High Tide at Noon (1957); The House in Marsh Road (1960); No Road Back (1956); Portrait of Alison (1955); The Spanish Gardener (1956).

VERESS, Sándor (1907–1992)
Swiss composer of Hungarian birth who studied with Bartók and Kodály. Taught in the USA and Australia.
FILMS INCLUDE: A Plot of Earth (1948).

VICKERS, Michael
British composer.
FILMS INCLUDE: At the Earth's Core (1976); Dracula AD 1972 (1972); My Lover, My Son (1969); Press for Time (1966); The Sandwich Man (1966); The Sex Thief (1973); The Stud (1974); Warlords of Atlantis (1978).

VILLA-LOBOS, Heitor (1887–1959)
Brazilian composer who wrote operas and twelve symphonies.
FILMS INCLUDE: The Discovery of Brazil (1937); Green Mansions (1958).
RECORDINGS: The Discovery of Brazil. EMI CZS7 67229–2.

VINTER, Gilbert (1909–1969)
British composer, arranger and conductor.
FILMS INCLUDE: *Documentary*: Story of Omolo (CFU).

VLAD, Roman (1919–   )
Italian composer of Romanian birth who wrote operas and ballets, together with incidental music.
FILMS INCLUDE: La Beauté du Diable (1949); Knave of Hearts (1954); The Law (1960); The Mighty Ursus (1962); Romeo and Juliet (1954); Sunday in August (1950); Three Steps North (1951).

WAKEMAN, Rick (1949–   )
British composer and keyboard player. Member of the rock band Yes.
FILMS: The Burning (1982); Creepshow II (1987); Crimes of Passion (1984); Lisztomania (1975); White Rock (1977).

WALLACE, Oliver (1887–1963)
American composer who worked for Disney.
FILMS INCLUDE: The Adventures of Ichabod and Mr Toad (1949); Alice in Wonderland (1951); The Best of Walt Disney's True-Life Adventures (1975); Big Red (1962); Cinderella (1949); Darby O'Gill and the Little People (1959); A Fire Called Jeremiah (1962); Geronimo's Revenge (1960); The Incredible Journey (1963); Jungle Cat (1959); The Lady and The Tramp (1955); The Legend of Lobo (1962); The Million Dollar Collar (1963); Nikki, Wild Dog of the North (1961); Old Yeller (1957); Peter Pan (1952); Sammy – The Way Out Seal (1962); Savage Sam (1963); Ten Who Dared (1960); Tonka (1958); White Wilderness (1958).

WALLER, 'Fats' (Thomas Wright) (1904–1943)
American composer and jazz pianist.
FILMS: Hooray for Love (1935); King of Burlesque (1936); Stormy Weather (1943).

WALSWORTH, Ivor (1909–   )
British composer who studied with William Alwyn.
FILMS INCLUDE: *Documentary*: American Hospitals; Papworth Village Settlement (1945); Star and the Sand; Unity of Strength.

WALTON, William (Sir William Walton) (1902–1983)
British composer who wrote two operas and two symphonies. Also had considerable fame with the entertainment *Façade*. Entered films in 1934 with *Escape Me Never*, directed by Paul Czinner. Walton was also offered such films as *The Amateur Gentleman* and music for a René Clair film in 1936, together with *Pygmalion* in 1938, but refused.
FILMS: As You Like It (1936); The Battle of Britain (1968 – this score was 'pulled' and the substitute score written by Ron Goodwin); Dreaming Lips (1937); Escape Me Never (1934); The First of the Few (1942); The Foreman Went to France (1942); Hamlet (1947); Henry V (1944); Major Barbara (1941); The Next of Kin (1942); Richard III (1955); A Stolen Life (1939); Three Sisters (1969); Went the Day Well (1942).
RECORDINGS: As You Like It. EMI CDM5 65585–2; The Battle of Britain. Chandos CHAN 8870; Escape Me Never. Chandos CHAN 8870; Hamlet. Chandos CHAN 8842; Henry V. Chandos CHAN 8892; Major Barbara.

Chandos CHAN 8871; Richard III. Chandos CHAN 8841; Three Sisters. Chandos CHAN 8870.

WANNBERG, Ken
American composer.
FILMS INCLUDE: The Amateur (1981); Blame It on Rio (1984); The Late Show (1977); Lepke (1974); The Philadelphia Experiment (1984).

WARD, Edward (1896–1971)
American composer.
FILMS INCLUDE: After the Thin Man (1936); Another Thin Man (1939); Bride of the Regiment (1930); Kismet (1931); The Mystery of Edwin Drood (1935); Nick Carter, Master Detective (1939); Young Tom Edison (1940).

WARK, Colin (1896–)
British composer of light music and director of music of Fox Films.
FILMS INCLUDE: The First Mrs Fraser (1932); The Mill on the Floss (1937).

WARRACK, Guy (1900–1986)
Scottish composer and conductor who studied with Vaughan Williams and Adrian Boult.
FILMS INCLUDE: *Documentary*: A Defeated People (CFU, 1945); The Last Shot (CFU, 1945); A Queen is Crowned (1953); Theirs is the Glory (CFU, 1946); Twenty-fourth Olympiad: The Glory of Sport (1948).

WARREN, Harry (1893–1981)
American songwriter who wrote many songs for Warner musicals of the 1930s.
FILMS INCLUDE: An Affair to Remember (1957); Artists and Models (1955); The Barkleys of Broadway (1948); The Belle of New York (1951); The Birds and the Bees (1956); The Blue Angel (1959); The Caddy (1953); Cinderfella (1960); Dames (1934); Down Argentine Way (1940); Footlight Parade (1933); The Gang's All Here (1943); Go Into Your Dance (1935); Gold Diggers in Paris (1938); Gold Diggers of 1933 (1933); The Great American Broadcast (1941); Iceland (1942); Just for You (1952); The Ladies' Man (1961); Moulin Rouge (1934); My Dream is Yours (1949); Pagan Love Song (1950); Rock-a-Bye Baby (1958); Separate Tables (1958); Skirts Ahoy! (1952); Summer Stock (1950); Tea for Two (1950); Texas Carnival (1951); Winterhawk (1975).
RECORDINGS: Dames. EMI CDODEON8; Gold Diggers of 1933. EMI CDC5 55189–2; Moulin Rouge. RCA 7321 38656–2.

WASHINGTON, Ned (1901–1976)

American composer.

FILMS INCLUDE: College Lovers (1930); Five Card Stud (1968); The Forward Pass (1929); The Greatest Show on Earth (1952); Gunfight at the O.K. Corral (1957); The Last Sunset (1961); Let's Do It Again (1953); The Man from Laramie (1957); Miss Sadie Thompson (1953); Night Passage (1957); Search for Paradise (1957); The Unforgiven (1960).

WAXMAN, Franz (1906–1967)

German composer and arranger who went to the USA in 1934. Wrote his first score for Fritz Lang's *Liliom* (1934) before moving to Paris and then on to America where he had success with his score for James Whale's *Bride of Frankenstein* (1935) which set a new standard for horror films. In 1940, David Selznick asked Steiner to add some of his own music to Waxman's score for Hitchcock's *Rebecca*; he thought it was not sufficiently romantic, yet Waxman regarded it as his best score.

FILMS INCLUDE: Back from Eternity (1956); Beloved Infidel (1959); The Bride of Frankenstein (1935); The Bride Wore Red (1937); Career (1959); Cimarron (1960); Count Your Blessings (1959); Crime in the Streets (1956); Demetrius and the Gladiators (1954); Destination Tokyo (1943); The Devil-Doll (1936); East of Java (1935); Ernest Hemingway's Adventures of a Young Man (1962); Fury (1936); Honky Tonk (1941); The Indian Fighter (1955); The Invisible Ray (1936); Johnny Holiday (1949); King of the Roaring 20s: The Story of Arnold Rothstein (1961); Lost Command (1966); Love Before Breakfast (1936); Love in the Afternoon (1956); Magnificent Obsession (1935); Man-Proof (1938); Miracle in the Rain (1955); Mister Roberts (1955); My Cousin Rachel (1952); My Geisha (1961); The Nun's Story (1958); Peyton Place (1957); The Philadelphia Story (1940); Phone Call from a Stranger (1952); Prince Valiant (1954); Rear Window (1954); Rebecca (1940); Return to Peyton Place (1961); Run Silent Run Deep (1958); Sayonara (1957); The Silver Chalice (1954); The Spirit of St Louis (1957); Stalag 17 (1952); The Story of Ruth (1960); Strange Cargo (1940); Sunrise at Campobello (1960); Sunset Boulevard (1950); Sutter's Gold (1936); Taras Bulba (1962); Task Force (1949); Test Pilot (1938); This Is My Love (1954); Three Comrades (1938); To Have and Have Not (1944); Too Hot to Handle (1938); The Unsuspected (1947); Untamed (1955); The Virgin Queen (1955); The Young in Heart (1938).

RECORDINGS: The Bride of Frankenstein. Silva Screen FILMCD180; Demetrius and the Gladiators. Varèse Sarabande VSD5242; The Nun's Story. STAN ST2114; Prince Valiant. Silva Screen FILMXCD 187; Rebecca. Marco Polo 8.223399; The Silver Chalice. Varèse Sarabande VSD5480; Taras Bulba. Silva Screen FILMXCD 187.

WAYNE, Bernie (1919–1993)

American composer and songwriter.

FILMS INCLUDE: Blues Busters (1950); Duffy's Tavern (1945); Out of this World (1945); Viva Las Vegas (1964).

WEBB, Roy (1888–1982)

American composer and arranger who later worked in television. Wrote over three hundred film scores.

FILMS INCLUDE: Alice Adams (1935); The Americano (1954); Another Face (1935); At Sword's Point (1952); Bachelor Mother (1939); Bedlam (1946); Bengazi (1955); Betrayal from the East (1945); The Big Street (1942); Blond Cheat (1938); Blood Alley (1955); Blood on the Moon (1948); The Body Snatcher (1945); Bringing up Baby (1938); Cat People (1943); Clash by Night (1952); The Curse of the Cat People (1944); Curtain Call (1940); The Devil and Miss Jones (1941); Dick Tracy (1945); Easy Living (1949); The Ex-Mrs Bradford (1936); The Falcon in Danger (1943); The Falcon's Brother (1942); The Fallen Sparrow (1943); Flight for Freedom (1943); Forty Naughty Girls (1937); The Ghost Ship (1943); A Girl, A Guy and A Gob (1941); The Girl He Left Behind (1956); The Great Man Votes (1939); Here We Go Again (1942); Higher and Higher (1943); Hips, Hips, Hooray! (1934); I Married a Witch (1942); I Remember Mama (1948); I Walked with a Zombie (1943); In Name Only (1939); The Iron Major (1943); Journey into Fear (1943); Kentucky Kernels (1934); Kitty Foyle (1940); The Last Days of Pompeii (1935); The Leopard Man (1943); The Life of the Party (1937); Look Who's Laughing (1941); The Mad Miss Manton (1938); Magic Town (1947); Marine Raiders (1944); Marty (1954); Mr Lucky (1943); Mummy's Boys (1936); Murder My Sweet (1944); The Navy Comes Through (1942); New Faces of 1937 (1937); Next Time I Marry (1938); Notorious (1946); Our Miss Brooks (1956); Passport to Destiny (1944); Playmates (1941); The Plough and the Stars (1936); Quality Street (1937); Riff-Raff (1947); The Saint in Palm Springs (1941); The Saint Strikes Back (1939); The Saint Takes Over (1940); The Saint's Double Trouble (1940); The Sea Chase (1955); Sea Devils (1937); The Seventh Victim (1943); Shoot-Out at Medicine Bend (1957); Stage Door (1937); Stranger on the Third Floor (1940); Sylvia Scarlett (1935); Teacher's Pet (1957); Those Endearing Young Charms (1945); Tom, Dick and Harry (1941); Top Secret Affair (1957); Track of the Cat (1954); The Tuttles of Tahiti (1942); Two O'Clock Courage (1945); Where Danger Lives (1950); Without Reservations (1946).

RECORDINGS: Bedlam. Cloud Nine CNS5008; Dick Tracy. Cloud Nine CNS5008; Notorious. Cloud Nine CNS5008.

WEIL, Kurt (1900–1950)
German-born composer who became an American citizen in 1945. Studied with Busoni and Humperdinck. Wrote many popular operas, some of which were filmed.
FILMS INCLUDE: A Salute to France (1944); You and Me (1938).

WELCH, Edward
British composer.
FILMS INCLUDE: The Boys in Blue (1983); Confessions from a Holiday Camp (1977); Confessions of a Driving Instructor (1976); Funny Money (1982); Out of the Darkness (1985); Rosie Dixon – Night Nurse (1978); Stand Up Virgin Soldiers (1977); The Thirty-Nine Steps (1978).

WHELAN, Christopher (1927–   )
British composer and conductor who has written many scores for the theatre, television and radio.
FILMS INCLUDE: Coast of Skeletons (1965); The Face of Fu Manchu (1965); The Valiant (1962).

WHETTAM, Graham (1927–   )
British composer who was virtually self-taught. Has written works in many genres including chamber music.
FILMS INCLUDE: Mystery on Bird Island (1954).

WHITAKER, David (1930–1980)
British composer.
FILMS INCLUDE: Charlie is My Darling (1965); Danny Jones (1971); The Desperados (1968); Dominique (1978); Don't Raise The Bridge, Lower The River (1967); Dr Jekyll and Sister Hyde (1971); Eyewitness (1970); Hammerhead (1968); Mistress Pamela (1973); Playbirds (1978); Psychomania (1972); Queen of the Blues (1979); Run Wild, Run Free (1969); Scream and Scream Again (1969); Sweet Hunters (1969); The Sword and the Sorcerer (1982); That's Your Funeral (1972); Threesome (1969); Vampira (1974); Vampire Circus (1971).
RECORDINGS: Vampire Circus. Silva Screen FILMCD127.

WHITEMAN, Paul (1890–1967)
American jazz band director and composer. Formerly a viola player in the Denver Symphony Orchestra and the San Francisco Symphony Orchestra. Formed the Paul Whiteman Orchestra in 1920. Commissioned Gershwin's *Rhapsody in Blue*.
FILMS INCLUDE: Broadway after Dark (1924); La Figlia di Frankenstein (1971); Rhapsody in Blue (1945).

WHITING, Richard (1891–1938)
American composer and songwriter who went to Hollywood in 1929 to write for Maurice Chevalier.
FILMS INCLUDE: Adorable (1933); Bright Eyes (1934); Coronado (1935); Cowboy from Brooklyn (1938); Hollywood Hotel (1938); Innocents of Paris (1929); Monte Carlo (1930); One Hour With You (1932); Playboy of Paris (1930); Ready Willing and Able (1937); Take a Chance (1933).

WHYTE, Ian (1903–1960)
Scottish composer and conductor. Musical director of the BBC in Scotland (1931–46). Formed the BBC Scottish Orchestra in 1935.
FILMS INCLUDE: *Documentary*: Highland Doctor (1943); Power in the Highlands (1943).

WIENER, Jean (1896–1982)
French composer.
FILMS INCLUDE: Au Hasard Balthazar (1966); Benjamin (1968); Le Crime de Monsieur Lange (1935); Les Demons de Minuit (1961); Drame à La Nanda Devi (1951); La Faute de L'Abbé Mouret (1970); Une Femme Douce (1969); La Femme et Le Pantin (1959); Futures Vedettes (1955); La Garçonne (1957); L'Homme du Jour (1936); Lady L (1965); Ni Vu Ni Connu (1958); Le Petit Théâtre de Jean Renoir (1969); Pot-Bouille (1957); Rendez-vous de Juillet (1949); Sois Belle et Tais-toi (1958); Sous le Ciel de Paris (1951); Touchez pas au Grisbi (1954); Voici Le Temps des Assassins (1956).

WILKINSON, Marc (1929–)
British composer and conductor.
FILMS INCLUDE: Blood on Satan's Claw (1970); The Darwin Adventure (1971); Eagle in a Cage (1970); Eagle's Wing (1978); Enigma (1982); Family Life (1971); The Fiendish Plot of Dr Fu Manchu (1980); The Hireling (1973); If . . . (1968); Looks and Smiles (1981); The Royal Hunt of the Sun (1969); Scenes and Songs from Boyd Webb (1984); Three Sisters (1970); The Triple Echo (1972).

WILLIAMS, Charles (1893–1978)
British composer and music director. Originally a violinist who led for such conductors as Landon Ronald, Thomas Beecham and Sir Edward Elgar. Accompanied silent films, and became conductor of the New Gallery Cinema in London's Regent Street. Worked on the first British all-sound film, Alfred Hitchcock's *Blackmail* (1929). Had great success with 'The Dream of Olwyn' for the film *While I Live* (1947).
FILMS INCLUDE: *Feature*: Candles at Nine (1944); Flesh and Blood (1951); It Happened One Sunday (1943); Kipps (1941); The Lady Vanishes (1938); The

Life and Death of Col Blimp (1943); Love on the Dole (1941); A Medal for the General (1944); My Wife's Family (1931); The Night Has Eyes (1942); The Noose (1946); Quiet Weekend (1946); The Thirty-Nine Steps (1935); Thursday's Child (1942); Tower of Terror (1941); Twilight Hour (1944); Warn That Man (1943); While I Live (1947); You Can't Escape (1955); The Young Mr Pitt (1942). *Documentary*: This is Britain (1945, BBC).
RECORDINGS: The Lady Vanishes. Silva Screen FILMCD159; The Night has Eyes. EMI CDGO 2059.

WILLIAMS, Christopher à Becket (1890–1956)
British composer.
FILMS INCLUDE: Kamet Conquered; A Night with Madame.

WILLIAMS, Edward
British composer.
FILMS INCLUDE: *Feature*: Doublecross (1955); Five have a Mystery to Solve (1964); Unearthly Stranger (1963). *Documentary*: Bridge of Song (1955); Down and Along (1965); Dylan Thomas (1961); Journey to the Sea (1952); London's Victorian Life (1969); The Rivers of Time (1957); Wild Highlands (1961).

WILLIAMS, Grace (1906–1977)
Welsh composer who was a pupil of Vaughan Williams and Gordon Jacob.
FILMS INCLUDE: Blue Scar (1949); David (1951); A Letter for Wales (1960).

WILLIAMS, John (1932–   )
American composer who trained to be a concert pianist. Has worked with Steven Spielberg, and received Oscars for *Jaws* (1975), *Star Wars* (1977), *E.T.* (1982), and *Schindler's List.* (1993).
FILMS INCLUDE: Always (1989); Bachelor Flat (1961); Because They're Young (1960); Black Sunday (1976); Born on the Fourth of July (1989); Close Encounters of the Third Kind (1977); Conrack (1974); The Cowboys (1971); Diamond Head (1963); Dracula (1979); E.T. The Extra-Terrestrial (1982); Earthquake (1974); Empire of the Sun (1987); The Empire Strikes Back (1980); Family Plot (1976); Fiddler on the Roof (1971); Fitzwilly (1967); The Fury (1978); Gidget Goes to Rome (1963); Goodbye Mr Chips (1969); A Guide for the Married Man (1967); Hook (1991); How to Steal a Million (1966); I Passed for White (1960); Images (1972); Indiana Jones and the Temple of Doom (1984); Jaws (1975); Jaws 2 (1975); Jaws 3-D (1983); J.F.K. (1991); John Goldfarb, Please Come Home! (1964); Jurassic Park (1993); The Killers (1964); The Long Goodbye (1973); The Man Who Loved Cat Dancing (1973); Midway (1976); The Missouri Breaks (1976); Monsignor (1982); A Murderous Affair: The Carolyn Warmus Story (1992); None But the Brave

(1965); Not With My Wife, You Don't! (1966); Penelope (1966); Pete 'n' Tillie (1972); The Plainsman (1966); The Poseidon Adventure (1972); Raiders of the Lost Ark (1981); The Rare Breed (1965); The Reivers (1969); Return of the Jedi (1983); The River (1984); Schindler's List (1993); The Secret Ways (1961); Sleepers (1996); Star Wars (1977); Storia di una Donna (1969); The Sugarland Express (1974); Superman (1978); Superman II (1980); Superman III (1983); Tom Sawyer (1973); The Towering Inferno (1974); Valley of the Dolls (1967); The Witches of Eastwick (1987).

RECORDINGS: Close Encounters of the Third Kind. RCA GD82696; E.T. MCA MCLD 19021; Empire of the Sun. Wealdon 7599–25668–2; The Empire Strikes Back. RCA Victor 09026 68773–2; Hook. Sony SK68419; Indiana Jones and the Temple of Doom. Silva Screen FILM CD160; Jaws. Varèse Sarabande VSD5207; Jurassic Park. Silva Screen FILM CD160; Raiders of the Lost Ark. Silva Screen FILM CD147; Return of the Jedi. RCA Victor 09026 68774–2; Schindler's List. Silva Screen FILM CD160; Star Wars. RCA Victor 09026 68772–2.

WILLIAMS, Patrick (1939–)
American composer.

FILMS INCLUDE: All of Me (1984); Best Defence (1984); The Best Little Whorehouse in Texas (1982); Breaking Away (1979); Butch and Sundance, The Early Days (1979); Casey's Shadow (1977); Charlie Chan and the Curse of the Dragon Queen (1980); The Cheap Detective (1978); Cuba (1979); Evel Knievel (1971); Framed (1974); Hot Stuff (1979); How Sweet It Is (1968); How to Beat the High Cost of Living (1980); It's My Turn (1980); Macho Callahan (1970); A Nice Girl Like Me (1969); The One and Only (1977); Shampoo (1975); The Sidelong Glances of a Pigeon Kicker (1970); Some Kind of Hero (1981); Ssssnake (1973); Swing Shift (1984); The Toy (1982); Two of a Kind (1983); Used Cars (1980); Wholly Moses! (1980).

WILLIAMSON, Lambert (1907–)
British composer.

FILMS INCLUDE: The Adding Machine (1969); Beat the Devil (1953); The Case of Express Delivery (1953); The Case of Gracie Budd (1953); The Case of Soho Red (1953); The Case of The Black Falcon (1953); The Case of The Bogus Count (1953); The Case of The Pearl Payroll (1954); The Case of The Studio Payroll (1953); A Countess From Hong Kong (1966); Cross Channel (1955); Good-Time Girl (1947); The Green Buddha (1954); Green Grow the Rushes (1951); The Innocents (1961); A Matter of Life and Death (1946); Romeo and Juliet (1954); Sons and Lovers (1960); The Spaniard's Curse (1957); Term of Trial (1962); This Other Eden (1959); To Dorothy a Son (1954); Track the Man Down (1955); The Whole Truth (1958).

WILLIAMSON, Malcolm (1931–)

Australian-born composer, pianist and organist. Later had lessons in London with Elisabeth Lutyens. Has written operas, ballets and orchestral music. Appointed Master of the Queen's Music in 1975, in succession to Sir Arthur Bliss.

FILMS INCLUDE: The Brides of Dracula (1960); Crescendo (1972); The Horror of Frankenstein (1970); Nothing but the Night (1975); Watership Down (1976 – part).

WILSON, Mortimer (1876–1927)

American composer and early pioneer in film music.

FILMS INCLUDE: The Black Pirate (1926); Don Quixote (1925); The Thief of Bagdad (1924).

WILSON, Stanley

American composer.

FILMS INCLUDE: Alias the Champ (1949); The Blonde Bandit (1950); Covered Wagon Raid (1950); Daughter of the Jungle (1949); Fort Dodge Stampede (1951); Frontier Investigator (1949); Hideout (1949); Night Raiders of Montana (1951); Pride of Maryland (1951); Rough Riders of Durango (1951); The Showdown (1950); Untamed Heiress (1954); Utah Wagon Train (1951); Wells Fargo Gunmaster (1951); Wild Horse Ambush (1952); The Woman They Almost Lynched (1953).

WINDT, Herbert (1894–1965)

German composer.

FILMS INCLUDE: Die Entlassung (1942); Hunde, Wollt ihr ewig leben (1959); Olympische Spiele; Fest der Schönheit (1938); Paracelsus (1943).

WISEMAN, Debbie (1963–)

British composer who has worked extensively in television e.g. *Children's Hospital, People's Century, The Upper Hand, A Week in Politics.*

FILMS INCLUDE: Haunted (1995); Tom and Viv (1994).

RECORDINGS: Tom and Viv. Sony SK64381.

WOOLCUTT, Charles

American composer.

FILMS INCLUDE: The Blackboard Jungle (1955); Key Witness (1960); Salvados, Amigos (1942); Sky Full of Moon (1952).

WOOLFENDEN, Guy (1937–)
British composer and conductor who has written much music for the theatre.
FILMS INCLUDE: Conquest of the South Pole (1989); A Midsummer Night's Dream (1968); Work is a Four Letter Word (1967).

WOOLRIDGE, John (1911–)
British composer.
FILMS INCLUDE: Angels One Five (1954); Conspirator (1959); Count Five and Die (1958); Edward my Son (1949); Fame is the Spur (1947); The Last Man to Hang (1956); RX Murder (1958); The Woman in Question (1950).

WRIGHT, Geoffrey
British composer and song writer for numerous stage revues and musical shows.
FILMS INCLUDE: Fiddlers Three (1944); Ships With Wings (1941).

WRUBEL, Allie (1905–1973)
American composer, bandleader and saxophonist. Went to Hollywood in the 1930s and joined Warner Brothers.
FILMS INCLUDE: Broadway Hostess (1935); Dames (1934); Flirtation Walk (1934); Housewife (1934); I Live for Love (1935); The Key (1934); Life of the Party (1937); Never Steal Anything Small (1958); Radio City Revels (1938); Sing Your Way Home (1945); Song of the South (1946 – Academy Award for the song 'Zip-a-Dee-Doo-Dah').
RECORDINGS: Song of the South. EMI CDCS 56177–2.

YARED, Gabriel (1949–)
French composer.
FILMS INCLUDE: Un Autre Homme une Autre Chance (1977); The English Patient (1996); Des Feux Mal Eteints (1994); La Diagonale du Fou (1983); Gandahar (1987); La Lune Dans le Caniveau (1983); Map of the Human Heart (1993); Les Mille et Une Nuits (1990); Miss O'Gynie et les Hommes Fleurs (1974); Profil Bas (1994); Sarah (1983); Sauve Qui Peut (La Vie) (1980); Tatie Danielle (1990); 37.2° Le Matin (Betty Blue) (1986).
RECORDINGS: The English Patient. Fantasy FCD 16001.

YOUMANS, Vincent (1898–1946)
American song composer of the 1920s shows.
FILMS INCLUDE: Hit the Deck (1930); Oh No No Nanette (1930).

YOUNG, Christopher (1958–   )
American composer.
FILMS INCLUDE: Copycat (1996); The Fly II (1989); Haunted Summer (1988); Hellraiser (1987); Hellraiser II (1987); Highpoint (1984); Invaders from Mars (1986); Jennifer 8 (1992); Judicial Consent (1995); Norma Jean as Marilyn (1996); Oasis (1984); The Vagrant (1992).
RECORDINGS: Copycat. Milan 74321 33742–2; Haunted Summer. Silva Screen FILM CD037; Norma Jean as Marilyn. Intrada MAF7070.

YOUNG, Victor (1900–1956)
American composer and arranger who wrote over 300 film scores. Moved to Hollywood in 1936 and joined Paramount Pictures. Nominated for an Academy Award 19 times, but only won posthumously for *Around the World in Eighty Days*.
FILMS INCLUDE: Around the World in Eighty Days (1956); Beyond Glory (1948); The Big Clock (1947); The Blue Dahlia (1945); The Brave One (1956); Buck Benny Rides Again (1940); The Buster Keaton Story (1956); Caught in the Draft (1941); Champagne Waltz (1937); China Gate (1957 – unfinished score, completed by Max Steiner); The Conqueror (1955); The Country Girl (1954); Dark Command (1940); Drum Beat (1954); Flight Nurse (1953); The Glass Key (1942); Golden Boy (1939); The Greatest Show on Earth (1952); Gun Crazy (1949); Hold Back the Dawn (1941); Jubilee Trail (1954); The Left Hand of God (1955); The Lemon Drop Kid (1951); Little Boy Lost (1953); Man About Town (1939); A Millionaire for Christy (1951); Ministry of Fear (1943); My Favorite Spy (1951); The Palm Beach Story (1942); The Proud and Profane (1955); The Quiet Man (1952); Raffles (1939); Reap the Wild Wind (1941); Rhythm on the River (1940); Rio Grande (1950); Road to Morocco (1942); Road to Singapore (1940); Road to Zanzibar (1941); Run of the Arrow (1957); Samson and Delilah (1949); Shane (1952); Son of Sinbad (1955); Strategic Air Command (1954); The Sun Shines Bright (1953); The Tall Men (1955); Three Coins in the Fountain (1954); Timberjack (1954); The Uninvited (1943); The Woman they Almost Lynched (1953).
RECORDINGS: Around the World in Eighty Days. MCA MCD3164; The Quiet Man. Scan'nan SFC1501; Shane. Chesky CD71.

ZAHLER, Lee
American composer.
FILMS INCLUDE: Boss of Rawhide (1945); Delinquent Daughters (1944); Ellery Queen, Master Detective (1940); Ellery Queen and the Murder Ring (1941); Ellery Queen and the Perfect Crime (1941); The Ghost and the Guest (1943); Gunsmoke Mesa (1944); The Lady Confesses (1945); Prairie Rustlers (1945); Symphony of Living (1935); Who's Guilty? (1945).

ZAPPA, Frank (1940–1993)
American composer and bandleader. Scored 'B' films in the 1960s.
FILMS INCLUDE: Baby Snakes (1979); Run Home Slow (1965); 200 Motels (1971); The World's Greatest Sinner (1962).

ZAZA, Paul
Canadian composer. Associated with the director Bob Clark.
FILMS INCLUDE: A Christmas Story (1983); Cold Sweat (1993); Curtains (1982); From the Hip (1987); Hog Wild (1980); It Runs in the Family (1994); Loose Cannons (1990); Meatballs III (1987); Murder by Decree (1978); My Bloody Valentine (1981); Popcorn (1991); Porky's (1981); Prom Night (1980); Prom Night IV: Deliver us from Evil (1991); Title Shot (1979); Turk 182! (1985); White Light (1991).

ZHUKOVSKY, German L. (1913–1976)
Soviet composer.
FILMS INCLUDE: Schedroye Leto (1950); Sredi Dobrykh Lyndei (1962); Sudba Mariny (1953).

ZIMMER, Hans (1958–   )
German composer who studied in Britain. Also worked as an assistant to film composer Stanley Myers. Lives and works in Los Angeles.
FILMS INCLUDE: Backdraft (1991); Beyond Rangoon (1994); Cool Runnings (1993); Crimson Tide (1995); Driving Miss Daisy (1989); House of the Spirits (1993); I'll do Anything (1994); Insignificance (1985); Lifepod (1993); The Lightship (1985); The Lion King (1994); Moonlighting (1982); My Beautiful Launderette (1985); Nine Months (1995); The Power of One (1992); Radie Flyer (1992); Rain Man (1985); Renaissance Man (1994); Success is the Best Revenge (1984); Thelma and Louise (1991); True Romance (1993); A World Apart (1987).
RECORDINGS: Backdraft. Milan 262 023; Driving Miss Daisy. Varése Sarabande VSD5246; The Power of One. Wealdon 7559–61335–2.

ZIMMER, Ján (1926–   )
Slovak composer and pianist who has written for the theatre and the cinema.

Select List of Feature and Documentary Films with Music Wholly or Partly by Classical Composers

Ace Ventura Pet Detective (1994)
Eine Kleine Nachtmusik, 2nd and 3rd movements   W.A. Mozart

Adventures of Priscilla, Queen of the Desert (1994)
La Traviata, Sempre libera   G. Verdi

The Age of Innocence (1993)
Piano Sonata No. 8, 2nd movement   L. van Beethoven
Radetsky March   J. Strauss (senior)
Blue Danube Waltz   J. Strauss (junior)

Akenfield (1974)
Fantasia Concertante on a theme by Corelli   M. Tippett

Amadeus (1984)
Piano Concerto No. 20, 2nd movement   W.A. Mozart
Requiem Mass   W.A. Mozart
Symphony No. 25, 1st movement   W.A. Mozart
Symphony No. 29, 1st movement   W.A. Mozart

American Gigolo (1980)
Clarinet Concerto, 2nd movement   W.A. Mozart

Another Woman (1988)
Cello Suite No. 6   J.S. Bach
Gymnopedie No. 3   E. Satie

Apocalypse Now (1979)
Die Walküre, Ride of the Valkyries   R. Wagner

Au Revoir les Enfants (1988)
Movement Musical No. 2   F. Schubert

Autumn Sonata (1978)
Cello Suite No. 4, Sarabande   J.S. Bach
Prelude (Op. 28, no. 2)   F. Chopin
Recorder Sonata (Op. 1, no. 11)   G.F. Handel
Aufschwung   R. Schumann

Babette's Feast (1987)
Don Giovanni, La ci darem la mano   W.A. Mozart

Badlands (1973)
Carmina Burana   C. Orff

Barry Lyndon (1975)
Harpsichord Suite No. 11, Sarabande
Piano Trio No. 2, 2nd movement   F. Schubert

Battle for Music (1943, Strand Films)
Symphony No. 5   L. van Beethoven
La Calinda   F. Delius
Piano Concerto in A minor   E. Grieg
Symphony No. 40   W.A. Mozart
Piano Concerto No. 2   S. Rachmaninov
Symphony No. 2   J. Sibelius
Romeo and Juliet Fantasy Overture   P. Tchaikovsky
Tristan and Isolde (excerpts)   R. Wagner

Beyond Bedlam (1994)
Libera Me, Requiem   G. Faure

Breaking Away (1979)
Symphony No. 4, Saltarello   F. Mendelssohn

Brief Encounter (1945)
Piano Concerto No. 2 in C minor   S. Rachmaninov

A Canterbury Tale (Archer Films, 1944)
Toccata and Fugue in D minor for organ   J.S. Bach

Carrington (1996)
String Quintet, 2nd movement   F. Schubert

C.E.M.A. (1947, Strand Films)
Piano Concerto No. 1   P. Tchaikovsky
Fantasia on 'Greensleeves'   R. Vaughan Williams

Chariots of Fire (1981)
Miserere   G. Allegri

A Child in a Million (1946)
Symphonic Variations   C. Franck

Children of a Lesser God (1986)
Concerto for 2 Violins, 2nd movement   J.S. Bach

Clear and Present Danger (1994)
Symphony No. 9, 2nd movement   A. Dvorak

A Clockwork Orange (1971)
Symphony No. 9, 4th movement   L. van Beethoven
Pomp and Circumstance March No. 1   E. Elgar
Funeral March for Queen Mary, March   H. Purcell
William Tell Overture   G. Rossini

Un Coeur en Hiver (1991)
Piano Trio, 1st movement   M. Ravel
Violin Sonata, 2nd movement   M. Ravel

The Common Touch (1941)
Piano Concerto No. 1   P. Tchaikovsky

Cries and Whispers (1972)
Cello Suite No. 5, Sarabande   J.S. Bach
Mazurka (Op. 17, no. 4)   F. Chopin

Crimes and Misdemeanours (1989)
English Suite No. 2   J.S. Bach

Dangerous Liaisons (1988)
Organ Concerto No. 13, Allegro   G.F. Handel
Largo, Serse   G.F. Handel

Dead Poets Society (1989)
Piano Concerto No. 5, 2nd movement   L. van Beethoven
Symphony No. 9, 4th movement   L. van Beethoven
Water Music, Allegro   G.F. Handel

Death and the Maiden (1995)
String Quartet No. 14, 1st movement   F. Schubert

Death in Venice (1971)
Symphony No. 5, Adagietto   G. Mahler

Die Hard (1988)
Brandenburg Concerto No. 3, 1st movement   J.S. Bach

Die Hard 2 (1990)
Finlandia   J. Sibelius

Dr Jekyll and Mr Hyde (1931)
Orgelbuchlein   J.S. Bach
Toccata and Fugue in D minor for organ   J.S. Bach
Aufschwung   R. Schumann

The Doors (1991)
Carmina Burana   C. Orff

Driving Miss Daisy (1989)
Rusalka, Sing to the Moon   A. Dvorak

E La Nave Va (1983)
The Force of Destiny, Overture   G. Verdi

The Elephant Man (1980)
Adagio for Strings   S. Barber

Elvira Madigan (1967)
Piano Concerto No. 21, 2nd movement   W.A. Mozart

Excalibur (1981)
Carmina Burana   C. Orff
Götterdämmerung, Siegfried's Funeral March   R. Wagner
Tristan and Isolde, Prelude   R. Wagner

Exposed (1983)
Partita No. 4, Courante   J.S. Bach
Violin Concerto, 3rd movement   P. Tchaikovsky

Fantasia (1940)
Toccata and Fugue in D minor for organ   J.S. Bach
Symphony No. 6 (The Pastoral)   L. van Beethoven
The Sorcerer's Apprentice   P. Dukas
Night on a Bare Mountain   M. Mussorgsky
La Gioconda, Dance of the Hours   A. Ponchielli
Ave Maria   F. Schubert
Rite of Spring   I. Stravinsky
The Nutcracker, Waltz of the Flowers   P. Tchaikovsky

Fatal Attraction (1987)
Madame Butterfly (extracts)   G. Puccini

Fearless (1993)
Für Elise   L. van Beethoven

Piano Concerto No. 5, 3rd movement   L. van Beethoven
Symphony No. 3, 3rd movement   H. Gorecki

Five Easy Pieces (1970)
Prelude (Op. 28, no. 4)   F. Chopin
Symphony No. 40, 1st movement   W.A. Mozart

Four Weddings and a Funeral (1994)
Arrival of the Queen of Sheba (Solomon)   G.F. Handel
Wedding March (Midsummer Night's Dream)   F. Mendelssohn

Frances (1982)
Symphony No. 7, 2nd movement   L. van Beethoven
Piano Sonata No. 11, 1st movement   W.A. Mozart

Frankie and Johnny (1991)
Clair de Lune   C. Debussy

The French Lieutenant's Woman (1981)
Piano Sonata No. 15, 2nd movement   W.A. Mozart

Gallipoli (1981)
Adagio   T. Albinoni
The Pearl Fishers, Duet   G. Bizet
Centone di Sonate No. 3   N. Paganini

Godfather III (1990)
Cavalleria Rusticana, Intermezzo   P. Mascagni

Goodbye Again (1961)
Symphony No. 3, 3rd movement   J. Brahms

The Great Mr Handel (1942)
Serse, Largo   G.F. Handel
Messiah (excerpts)   G.F. Handel

Green Card (1991)
Clarinet Concerto, 2nd movement   W.A. Mozart
Flute Concerto No. 1   W.A. Mozart
Flute and Harp Concerto   W.A. Mozart

The Grey Fox (1982)
Martha (excerpts)   F. von Flotow

Greystoke: The Legend of Tarzan, Lord of the Apes (1984)
Minuet   L. Boccherini
Pomp and Circumstance March No. 4   E. Elgar
Symphony No. 1, 1st movement   E. Elgar

Hannah and her Sisters (1986)
Manon Lescout, Sola perduta   G. Puccini

Hard Target (1993)
Piano Sonata No. 23, 3rd movement   L. van Beethoven

Heartburn (1986)
Arrival of the Queen of Sheba (Solomon)   G.F. Handel

Heat and Dust (1982)
Tales from the Vienna Woods   J. Strauss (junior)

Heavenly Creatures (1994)
Madame Butterfly, Humming Chorus   G. Puccini
Tosca, E lucevan le stelle   G. Puccini

Howard's End (1992)
Symphony No. 5, 3rd movement   L. van Beethoven

The Hunt for Red October (1990)
Finlandia   J. Sibelius

Immortal Beloved (1994)
Für Elise   L. van Beethoven
Piano Sonata No. 14, 1st movement   L. van Beethoven
Piano Sonata No. 8, 2nd movement   L. van Beethoven
Symphony No. 5, 1st movement   L. van Beethoven
Symphony No. 6, 4th movement   L. van Beethoven
Symphony No. 7, 2nd movement   L. van Beethoven
Symphony No. 9, 4th movement   L. van Beethoven
Violin Concerto, 1st movement   L. van Beethoven

I've Heard the Mermaids Singing (1987)
Lakmé, Flower Duet   L. Delibes

Jean de Florette (1986)
The Force of Destiny, Overture   G. Verdi

Jesus of Montreal (1989)
Stabat Mater, 1st movement   G.B. Pergolesi

J.F.K. (1991)
Horn Concerto No. 2, 3rd movement   W.A. Mozart

Kalifornia (1993)
Symphony No. 8, 2nd movement   L. van Beethoven

Kika (1993)
Spanish Dance (Op. 37, no. 5)   E. Granados

Kind Hearts and Coronets (1949)
Don Giovanni, Il mio tesoro   W.A. Mozart

The Ladykillers (1955)
Minuet   L. Boccherini

Larger than Life (1997)
Tales from the Vienna Woods   J. Strauss (junior)

Last Action Hero (1993)
Marriage of Figaro, Overture   W.A. Mozart

Law of Desire (1987)
Symphony No. 10, 2nd movement   D. Shostakovich

Listen to Britain (1941, CFU)
Piano Concerto in G (K453)   W.A. Mozart

The Living Daylights (1987)
String Quartet No. 2, 3rd movement   A. Borodin
Symphony No. 40, 1st movement   W.A. Mozart

Lorenzo's Oil (1992)
Adagio for Strings   S. Barber
Cello Concerto, 2nd movement   E. Elgar
Symphony No. 5, Adagietto   G. Mahler
Oboe Concerto, 2nd movement   A. Marcello
Ave Verum   W.A. Mozart

Love and Death (1975)
The Love for Three Oranges, March   S. Prokofiev
Lt. Kije Suite, Troika   S. Prokofiev

Madame Souzatska (1988)
Piano Sonata No. 23, 3rd movement   L. van Beethoven
Piano Concerto   R. Schumann

The Madness of King George (1994)
Zadok the Priest   G.F. Handel

Man Trouble (1992)
B Minor Mass, Et Resurrexit   J.S. Bach
Nocture in E flat (Op. 9, no. 2)   F. Chopin

Manhattan (1979)
Rhapsody in Blue   G. Gershwin

Maurice (1987)

Miserere   G. Allegri
Goldberg Variations   J.S. Bach
Symphony No. 6, 3rd movement   P. Tchaikovsky

Meeting Venus (1990)
Tanhaüser, Overture and Pilgrim's Chorus   R. Wagner

A Midsummer Night's Dream (1935)
A Midsummer Night's Dream   F. Mendelssohn, arr. Korngold

A Midsummer Night's Sex Comedy (1982)
A Midsummer Night's Dream, Intermezzo and Scherzo   F. Mendelssohn
Piano Concerto No. 2, 2nd movement   F. Mendelssohn

Misery (1990)
Piano Sonata No. 14, 1st movement   L. van Beethoven
Piano Concerto No. 1, 1st movement   P. Tchaikovsky

Mona Lisa (1986)
Madame Butterfly, Love Duet   G. Puccini

Mr Jones (1993)
Symphony No. 9   L. van Beethoven

A Month in the Country (1987)
Violin Concerto, 2nd movement   F. Mendelssohn

Moonlight Sonata (1937)
Moonlight Sonata   L. van Beethoven
Minuet   I. Paderewski

Moonraker (1979)
Prelude (Op. 28, no. 15)   F. Chopin
I Pagliacci, Vesti la giubba   R. Leoncavallo
Tritsch Tratsch Polka   J. Strauss (junior)

Moonstruck (1987)
La Boheme (excerpts)   G. Puccini

The Music Lovers (1970)
1812 Overture   P. Tchaikovsky

My Beautiful Launderette (1985)
The Skaters Waltz   E. Waldteufel

My Dinner with André (1981)
Gymnopedie No. 1   E. Satie

My Geisha (1962)
Madame Butterfly, Un bel di   G. Puccini

My Left Foot (1989)
Cosi fan tutte, Un'aura amorosa   W.A. Mozart
Quintet (The Trout), 4th movement   F. Schubert

New Wine (1941)
Various pieces by F. Schubert, arr. M. Rozsa

New York Stories (1989)
In a Persian Market   A. Ketelby

A Night at the Opera (1935)
Il Travatore, Anvil Chorus   G. Verdi

Nijinsky (1980)
Prelude a l'après-midi d'un faune   C. Debussy
Scheherazade   N. Rimsky-Korsakov
The Rite of Spring   I. Stravinsky

Nikita (1990)
Eine Kleine Nachtmusik, 1st movement   W.A. Mozart

Ordinary People (1980)
Canon   J. Pachelbel

Out of Africa (1985)
Clarinet Concerto, 2nd movement   W.A. Mozart

Peter's Friends (1992)
Orpheus in the Underworld, Can Can   J. Offenbach
Madame Butterfly, Un bel di   G. Puccini

Philadelphia (1993)
Andrea Chenier, La mamma morta   U. Giordano

Picnic at Hanging Rock (1975)
Piano Concerto No. 5, 2nd movement   L. van Beethoven

Pink String and Sealing Wax (1945)
Songs by Henry Bishop, James Cook, John Gay, and G.F. Handel

Platoon (1986)
Adagio for Strings   S. Barber

Pretty Woman (1990)
La Traviata, Duet   G. Verdi

The Prince of Tides (1991)
Symphony No. 104, 3rd movement   J. Haydn

Prizzi's Honor (1985)
The Barber of Seville, Overture   G. Rossini

The Proud Valley (1939)
Elijah (excerpts)   F. Mendelssohn

Raging Bull (1986)
Cavalleria Rusticana, Intermezzo   P. Mascagni

Richard III (1996)
Te Deum, Fanfare   M-A. Charpentier

Rollerball (1975)
Adagio   T. Albinoni
Toccata and Fugue in D minor for organ   J.S. Bach
Symphony No. 5, 4th movement   D. Shostakovitch

A Room with a View (1985)
Gianni Schicchi (excerpts)   G. Puccini
La Rondine, Doretta's Dream   G. Puccini

Rosemary's Baby (1968)
Für Elise   L. van Beethoven

Roxanne (1987)
The Blue Danube Waltz   J. Strauss (junior)

Schindler's List (1993)
English Suite No. 2, Bourée   J.S. Bach
Tango Jalousie   N. Gade

Serpico (1973)
Tosca (excerpts)   G. Puccini

The Seven Year Itch (1955)
Piano Concerto No. 2   S. Rachmaninov

The Seventh Veil (1945)
Pathétique Sonata   L. van Beethoven
Prelude No. 1   F. Chopin
Piano Concerto in A minor   E. Grieg
Sonata in C major   W.A. Mozart
The Merry Wives of Windsor, Overture   O. Nicolai
Piano Concerto No. 2   S. Rachmaninov

Shine (1996)
Includes: Gloria   A. Vivaldi
Piano Concerto No. 3   S. Rachmaninov

The Shining (1980)
Music for Strings, Percussion and Celesta   B. Bartok

Silence of the Lambs (1990)
Goldberg Variations

Slaughterhouse Five (1972)
Brandenburg Concerto No. 4, Presto   J.S. Bach

Sleeping with the Enemy (1990)
Symphonie Fantastique, 2nd movement   H. Berlioz

Sneakers (1992)
Waltz No. 14   F. Chopin
String Quartet No. 1 in E minor   B. Smetana

Someone to Watch Over Me (1987)
Lakmé, Flower Duet   F. Delibes

Somewhere in Time (1980)
Variations on a theme by Paganini, Var. 18   S. Rachmaninov

Song of Scheherazade (1947)
Scheherazade   N. Rimsky-Korsakov

A Song to Remember (1945)
Various pieces by F. Chopin, arr. M. Rozsa

Sophie's Choice (1982)
Kinderszenen   R. Schumann

The Spy who loved me (1977)
Suite No. 3, Air   J.S. Bach

Streetfighter (1975)
Carmen, Habanera   G. Bizet

Strictly Ballroom (1972)
The Blue Danube Waltz   J. Strauss (junior)

Sunday, Bloody Sunday (1971)
Cosi fan tutti, Soave sia il vento   W.A. Mozart

Swing Kids (1993)
Piano Trio (The Archduke), 1st movement   L. van Beethoven

10 (1979)
Bolero   M. Ravel

They Came to a City (1944)
The Divine Poem   A. Scriabin

Through a Glass Darkly (1961)
Cello Suite No. 2, Sarabande   J.S. Bach

To Be or Not to Be (1983)
Military Polonaise   F. Chopin

Torrents of Spring (1989)
Concerto for 2 violins in D minor, 2nd movement   J.S. Bach
Etude (Op. 10, no. 6)   F. Chopin
Don Giovanni, Overture   W.A. Mozart

Trading Places (1983)
The Marriage of Figaro, Overture   W.A. Mozart

True Lies (1994)
The Blue Danube Waltz   J. Strauss (junior)

True Romance (1993)
Lakmé, Flower Duet   L. Delibes

The Turning Point (1977)
Romeo and Juliet, The Balcony Scene   S. Prokofiev

20,000 leagues Under the Sea (1954)
Toccata and Fugue in D minor for organ   J.S. Bach

2001: A Space Odyssey (1968)
The Blue Danube Waltz   J. Strauss (junior)
Also sprach Zarathustra   R. Strauss

The Untouchables (1981)
I Pagliacci, Vesti la giubba   R. Leoncavello

Wall Street (1987)
Rigoletto, Questa, O quella   G. Verdi

Wayne's World (1992)
Romeo and Juliet   P. Tchaikovsky

Where Angels Fear to Tread (1968)
Lucia di Lammermoor, The Mad Scene   G. Donizetti

White Nights (1985)
Passacaglia in C minor   J.S. Bach

Who Framed Roger Rabbit? (1988)
Hungarian Rhapsody No. 2   F. Liszt

Whom the Gods Love (1936)
The Magic Flute and *The Marriage of Figaro* (excerpts)   W.A. Mozart

The Witches of Eastwick (1987)
Turandot, Nessun dorma   G. Puccini

Index of film titles listed